Kids & Grief

Also by Karen Petty

Deployment: Strategies for Working with Kids in Military Families

Developmental Milestones of Young Children

Kids & Grief

Talking with Children About Death & Dying

Strategies for Parents, Teachers, and Caregivers

Karen Petty, Ph.D.

Copyright © 2023 by Karen Petty
All rights reserved. Published 2023
Printed in the United States of America

No part of this publication may be reproduced, stored in a retrieval system, or transmitted in any form or by any means–electronic, mechanical, photocopying, recording, scanning, or otherwise–without the express written permission of the author. Failure to comply with these terms may expose you to legal action and damages for copyright infringement.

Petty, Karen L.
Kids & Grief: Talking with Children about Death and Dying
Strategies for Parents, Teachers, & Caregivers

Includes bibliographical references.
ISBN: 979-8-9866517-1-2

Note
The names, details, and circumstances may have been changed to protect the privacy of those mentioned in this book.
This book is not intended as a substitute for the advice of health care professionals.

To all children who have loved and lost!

For life and death are one, even as the river and the sea are one.
-Kahlil Gibran *The Prophet*

Contents

How to Read This Book   ix
My Story   xi

PART 1   GIVING YOURSELF GRACE!
1–Graced!   3
2–Finding Your North Star   13
3–UFO's (Unfinished Objects)   17
4–When We Are the First Responders   20

PART 2   LET'S TALK ABOUT DEATH AND DYING
5–What Kids Want to Know About Death & Dying   25
6–Death and Life–So Closely Related   29
7–Don't Dodge the Questions!   33
8–Looking for Signs Your Child Is Grieving   41
9–Why Death is Such a Taboo Topic   44
10–Children Will Grieve in Their Own Way   50
11–Grief–The Good and the Bad   55
12–Yes, Kids Can Anticipate Loss   59
13–Sheltering Trees and Secure Bases   65
14–When Pets Die   70
15–Children's Tears Are Sacred   79
16–Your Child's Grieving Style   85
17–When Grieving Children Act Out   89
18–How Culture Shapes the Way We Grieve   95
19–Talking About School Shootings   102
20–School Violence–Safety, Prevention, & Warning Signs   115

21–Talking About Death By Suicide   125

Part 3   Children, God, & Grief
22–Talking About God and Death   135
23–Faith Development & Children   147
24–Spirituality & Children   156

Part 4   Grief Through a Child Development Lens
25–Grief and Loss–Developing Stages of Children   167
26–Kids and Kübler-Ross' Stages of Grief   172
27–Denial–Stage One   177
28–Anger–Stage Two   181
29–Bargaining–Stage Three   190
30–Depression–Stage Four   193
31–Acceptance–Stage Five   198
32–Emotional Milestones, Children, and Grief   202
    Infants and Toddlers: Ages Birth to Three   204
    Preschool Children: Ages Three to Five   209
    School Age Children: Ages Six to Twelve   213

Part 5   Resilience & Grief
33–Growing Resilience in a Grieving Child   219
34– Staying Upright During Loss   224
35–Risk and Protective Factors   227
36–Bouncing Back, Moving Forward from Loss   233

PART 6 HeARTful Activities for Grieving Children

37–Bridging Home and School   239

38–Grief Play   244

39–Using Art to Heal a Broken Heart   248

40–Journaling Their Way Through Grief   256

41– Music as Therapy During Grief and Loss   259

42–Books to Help Grieving Children   262

PART 7   Saying Goodbye

43–When Kids Say Final Goodbyes   269

44–Funerals, Burial & Cremation   274

45–Don't Feel Bad, We'll Buy You a Puppy   282

46–Grief-How Long Does It Last?   285

47–Seeking Help for Your Child   289

48–Left Behind   297

49–It's Not Over Yet! Signs Down the Road   300

50–Continuing Bonds   306

Final Thoughts on Children & Grief   310

–Notes & References   313

–Bibliotherapy Books for Children   328

–Index 333

–About the Author   339

–Appreciation   340

–Thank You!   341

PRAYER OF FAITH

We trust that beyond absence there is a presence.
That beyond the pain there can be healing.
That beyond the brokenness there can be wholeness.
That beyond the anger there may be peace.
That beyond the hurting there may be forgiveness.
That beyond the silence there may be the word.
That beyond the word there may be understanding.
That through understanding there is love.

—Unknown

How to Read This Book

I don't know what I'm doing. I just know that not doing it feels worse.
—Unknown

The quote above just about says it all for (and of) me. Most things I try to accomplish come from just getting out there. My grandmother Evie would say, "Just strike out down the road!" Get going! So here we are. I had to write this book because not writing it felt worse. Writing it felt better. "I'm striking out!" I want this book to be one that is helpful, one to come back to again and again as you or someone you know struggles when talking about death and dying with children.

Choose to read your most needed or relevant topics first, navigating or sailing through the information and strategies that you need now, and reading others later.

This book provides strategies for all kids—from the ones who are casually curious about death and dying to the one who has experienced unimaginable loss.

The terms kids and children are used interchangeably throughout, but the book is written for children who begin to question or understand death and dying in early childhood through school age years. These children are often three to twelve years old.

I included "Strategies" at the end of each topic to use as you talk with children about death and dying. They provide the "blueprint" for content on each topic and each strategy has been constructed to break down the information into actions. You will often scaffold children as they work alongside you until they are ready to independently continue.

There are 7 clusters of topics. Part 1, *Graced* addresses the concept of giving ourselves grace and getting or keeping ourselves prepared before we approach talking with kids about death and dying. Our own wellbeing comes first.

Part 2, *Let's Talk About Death and Dying* includes information for talking with kids about school shootings, death by suicide, losing a pet, anticipating loss, and many more important topics.

In Part 3, *God, Children, Death, & Dying*, I draw from many studies that indicate children are "born believers."

Part 4, *Grief Through Children's Development* takes us through *Kübler-Ross' Stages of Grief and Children* as well as *Emotional Milestones* from Infants and Toddlers through School Agers.

In Part 5, *Resilience and Grief*, I describe the importance of risk and protective factors in grieving children and in Part 6, *School, Kids, & Grief*, strategies are provided for going back to school. There are "HeARTful Activities" that include the arts—music, art, literature, and journaling for teachers, parents, and caregivers to use with children.

Part 7, *Saying Goodbye* provides strategies for final acts such as attending funerals and talking about burial and cremation.

Finally, a "Notes" section that contains references to all cited material as well as other information about contributors to this book can be found at the end. A Bibliotherapy list of children's books for ages three to twelve that address death and dying topics such as losing parents, grandparents, and pets is also included.

There's no destination, no place you have to be on a grief journey with kids. So, let this book help as you just strike out down the road...go somewhere you've never been as you explore talking with kids about death and dying.

My Story

We often approach talking about death and dying with children with more silence than answers. But children's questions have been getting louder. The traditional stance on protecting children from death is no longer a practice that we can afford.

Just over the course of my life I have seen us go from including children in the death experience such as bringing loved ones home for us to mourn, to now shielding them from the pain of grief as much as possible. And, since families have often moved farther away from their larger, extended families this has caused children to become less familiar with the mourning rituals that their grandparents and even parents grew up with.

I began as a teacher of young children in Texas public school classrooms for almost 20 years. Then, I earned a doctorate from Texas A&M University where I was required to complete a residency, leaving our home in East Texas and moving to College Station with my two daughters in tow. I later spent over two decades as a university professor of early childhood development and education at Texas Woman's University.

These experiences shaped my journey as a sort of kid whisperer in that I look for ways in which to talk with children to meet their needs. My publications have mostly included curriculum for children, especially social/emotional development and resilience. I think this book is a continuation of what I'm best "at." Because heartbreak is universal, my goal in writing this book is ultimately three things: (1) comforting children, (2) bringing understanding and awareness to parents, teachers, and caregivers of children who have lost someone or something they love; and (3) providing strategies on how to talk with children about those experiences.

It's important to note that I am a child developmentalist, not a counselor or therapist. My toolbox of knowledge used to write this book comes from education and experience in child development and early childhood education. My viewpoint in teaching children about death and dying relies heavily upon the experiences I've had in studying children's ages and stages of development, teaching children directly in classrooms, teaching about children in university classrooms, and researching topics primarily in resilience and children. I've also worked closely with counselors and play therapists at Texas Woman's University, and throughout this book, I wholeheartedly encourage and support adults to seek additional help from health professionals for grieving children when appropriate and necessary.

I firmly believe that as parents, teachers, and caregivers we play a huge part in helping children grieve. Counseling and therapy may be needed, but in the meantime, or what I call the between times, they have us. Someone has to be available to foster a positive environment in which they can grieve well. As the adults in children's lives, it is our most sacred responsibility and privilege to capture moments to accompany them on this journey of grief.

One of the biggest surprises in writing this book was how much I didn't know, that I didn't know. Coming from an outsider/etic perspective is very familiar to me as a researcher, but the research for this topic as well as recent experiences took me to depths of emotion that changed the trajectory of my understanding of grief.

I hope that I paint verbal portraits of all the wonderful people who shared their grief journeys with me so that you can see them as I do. I also hope the time spent listening to so many stories from people who have lived with grief for short as well as long periods of time has brought more compassion and empathy to this book. Maybe it will benefit you, too, as you navigate through "grief storms" with your children.

The greatest challenge in writing this book was making sure that everything included speaks to the heart of the readers, that the hills and valleys of sadness and hope, despair and promise are hiked with a new perspective in talking with kids about death and dying. I'll leave My Story with this wonderful quote:

Never underestimate the power of hope.
Hope fuels us with the energy and courage to go forward.
—Adele Basheer

Part 1

GIVING YOURSELF GRACE!

Amanda C., Mom of Hannah

Am I doing something that would make her proud? Staying in bed all day...She would not be proud. I give myself grace by getting up to do what I need to do for my living children.

Erikah, Mom of Daylen

Giving myself grace is not easy...I often take the back seat...try to take care of my son—he deserves my best. But when I take time for me, to process, it gets me back to my baseline, fills me up so that when I get to a crisis, I can cope...I refill my cup...refuel my tank.

Rick, Grandfather

I find grace in knowing him, the kind of person he was at such a young age. I find blessings in my memories of him.

~1~

Graced!

*And grace is a circular blessing. The more grace
enters your life, the more grateful you are,
the more easily grace seems to enter.*
—Buddhist Teaching

It's sort of like if God had a refrigerator, your picture would be on it! You give yourself a hall pass, always cut yourself some slack, or get an infinite number of do-overs!

Grace. It is unmerited, there for the taking without having to do anything to earn it. You are loved and cherished just because you are you. The Apostle Paul pretty much summed it up when he wrote 2 Corinthians 9:8. *You can give yourself the gift of grace if you can give yourself sufficiency in all things at all times and open yourself to blessings.* SUFFICIENCY—an adequate or just the right amount!

But, most of us are absolutely terrible at giving ourselves grace, this thing called unconditional forgiveness, kindness and care. Self-condemnation, perfectionism, unrealistic expectations, and what I call *not-enoughness* are just a few *grace bombs*.

For years, you have been taking care of everyone, making sure that children are healthy and happy. Nothing has changed, and yet everything has changed as you endure unbearable loss. Stuart Scott gives us words to live gracefully by in his book, *Counseling the Hard Cases.* "Hope is not defined by the absence of hardship.

Rather, hope is found in God's grace in the midst of hardship."[1]

Giving yourself grace is mandatory. I refer to it as being "GRACED!" Taking care of you, or *putting on your oxygen mask first* may be the most important thing you do for you and grieving children. Healthy adults, both emotionally and physically, are poised to take on this task. But if the loss that you and your children have faced has taken its toll on your wellbeing, getting back your strength has to come first as you maintain, or even gain your position in your family as caregiver.

Now is not the time to give up on you. I have adopted this quote from Megan Devine in her book on grief, *It's Okay That You're Not Okay*.[2] "This is all just as crazy as you think it is!" She adds fuel to the notion that we/you are NOT crazy during this grief walk. "That some things cannot be fixed. They can only be carried."

There is no shame or guilt or blame in not knowing how to re-center or get back to your emotionally healthy home. Feeling uncomfortable when we don't have all the answers can perpetuate inadequacy and incompetence. But, we can see courage in the baby steps of progress we make each day past devastating loss. We see ourselves putting one foot in front of the other as painful as it may be. Look behind you. Your children are following in those footsteps.

A Lighted Path

Long before we realize it, a tiny path to feeling better lights up in front of us. We are carefully walking on this unknown ground toward hope and a version of what is normal. Even when we don't recognize the path, it is still there because we carve it out with each step we take using bravery and courage.

Listen to what Elizabeth Ann Seton wrote as a wife and mother who became the first born American to be canonized as a Saint. "We know that God gives us every abundant grace, and though we are so weak of ourselves, this grace is sufficient to carry us through every obstacle and difficulty."[3] There's that word again—sufficiency—enough!

Years ago I learned the word, tacit—when you just know that you know something. You accept grace as truth, even when you don't have evidence for it. Your compass is set to the lighted path. You can take side roads and shortcuts, or the long way around if you choose, but the path is there, like a runway in the night for a plane that's lost its way. We know that thanksgiving and gratitude make the path brighter. We choose to express feelings or emotions that bring good health and wellness rather than pain and doubt or sadness and disharmony.

How we recognize our feelings one by one, especially during times of grief is a *vade mecum* or guidebook for children—a sort of blueprint for them to follow us on a path to grief recovery. We learn to express them, and then move on.

Read what Paul the Apostle wrote that seems to be a paradox:

> *My grace is sufficient for you, for my*
> *power is made perfect in weakness.*
> —2 Corinthians 15:10

What if it takes a moment when we feel we have no power to accept that strength often comes from struggle, a dimly lit path? What if weakness is necessary to find our path? What if Paul was right?

Laughter

One way to find the lighted path is through laughter, lots of it. "Don't think death puts a ban on laughter," writes depression expert and psychologist Deborah Serani.[4] In future chapters in this book, I write how children switch between sadness and play/laughter during the most difficult moments of sadness. They inherently know that laughter and play are lifelines to managing grief.

But sometimes adults outgrow or forget about laughter as a natural painkiller and mood improver. And so, our best medicine is to spend time with those who always make us laugh. Or, we ask a child to tell their favorite knock-knock joke. We make a point to revisit places where we were happy, or favorite places of the deceased. We look at videos, photos and mementos to remind us of good times with our children and our loved one who died.

We "recreate." The root of the word *recreation* (activity done for enjoyment) is *re-create* or create again. When was the last time you recreated (had fun) or re-created? And, children can now be our best teachers as we allow ourselves to grieve, then laugh (or play).

Relinquishing Control aka Letting Go!

I've pretty much stopped setting deadlines, making plans, or even setting goals for myself in my "later life" as I try to create more, enjoy more, and just "be" more. I recently got to see Julia Cameron at a writer's retreat in Santa Fe. She is the national best-selling author of *The Artist's Way* in which she writes, "Creativity requires faith. Faith requires that we relinquish control."[5] Amen, Julia!

My definition of relinquishing is letting go. I'm letting go more as I often replace the word **goal** with the word **suggestion**. And whenever I feel anxious about not completing a project, or making a meeting on time or at all, or finishing everything on my To-Do List (and I make lots of those), I try to stop and give myself grace. I keep in mind that many of those to-do's (unfinished objects or UFO's) are just ideas, thought proposals, suggestions. They usually aren't mandatory, or life threatening, or altering. Instead, I cash in a "grace chip!"

When grieving, you deserve to take time out for you; reduce your plate; your calendar; and your commitments if only momentarily or in "little whiles." Be your best advocate—caregiver just as you do this for your children. And, allow others to pick up the slack and take care of you. There will be time to pick back up where you left off before an anticipated loss or death. But now may not be that time. Now may be the time to let go and activate "grace."

Grace "Bombs"

Check out the following grace bombs. Do any of them resonate with you? Do you feel them going off daily, exploding without warning? Here's how you know you may be running low on grace or mercy as you grieve:

- You feel tired, even after resting or vacationing, dread going to work, and are anxious or restless much of the time.
- You feel hopeless and can't let go.
- You have chronic stress and pain that wasn't there before the loss, practice self-care last and always putting others first.
- You feel hypersensitive to any talk of loss but keep your grief close by because you need it to keep your loved one present.
- You get constant "thought bombs" where you are chugging along, doing your daily tasks and then right out of the blue, you get the saddest thought of not only the one who died, but also of your other children or grandchildren, the fear that something may happen to them too.
- You go the extra mile for others but won't even go a hundred steps for yourself.

Give yourself grace by focusing on one "bomb" at a time. Counteract the effects of a lack of grace. Begin with one that affects you and children the most. They are your constant audience and are often affected the greatest. Let this book be your encouragement to take the first step toward that next step and then the next; know how important you are, how worthy, how "graced."

Fellow East Texan and author Melissa Radke says "You are one of God's personal favorites...As in, if He was having a huge get-together with loud music and friends and family, He would make sure you were invited."[6]

Linda and Laura's Story

Linda is one of my camping buddies and a fellow "Airstreamer." She introduced me to a group of ladies who tow or drive RVs to camping events in Texas and surrounding states. We are the "Get Away Gals." I was able to sit down with Linda while camping to hear her story about how grief can steal your bliss, your "self."

Linda's fifteen-year-old daughter Laura was out walking when she was killed by a drunk driver almost forty years ago. The raw emotion that Linda still feels after all this time shows how losing a child is a kind of grief that never goes away, but changes over time. "It's like a butcher knife stabbing your heart every time you think about your dead child, lying in that cold grave. It happens all over again when you remember them."

This led me to ask about the in-between times, and those triggers that bring grief back to the surface. "You don't go around feeling bad all the time," she said. "But certain things bring it up, like when you hear of the death of other people's children, and holidays—especially Thanksgiving and Christmas, and birthdays. Her death becomes real all over again. I keep myself very busy; I work in my church, go camping, and lots of other things. I have to go on...other people depend on me."

I wanted to know how she talks about Laura's death with others, including her other daughter. "We never talk about it...not then and not now. I guess it's our way of coping with it."

My final question to Linda was, "How do you give yourself grace?" In the most sincere voice she said, "I don't feel that I did. I prayed, worked, drank, wanted to kill the driver and when I finally found him, I couldn't do it. I felt relief after that." I asked her later if she was okay sharing this last part with my readers. She said, "Absolutely. It's the truth."

Linda's story, like so many others, is very much a verbal portrait of the rawness of grief, how it never leaves, but in time, you find a way to exist alongside it. But, as Linda said, grief never ends.[7]

A Grandfather's Grief

Let me begin by saying that I understand this interview could not have been easy. I am so grateful for Rick's willingness to talk about and share with us his grief and grace journey over the past two years since his 10-year-old grandson was killed tragically on a horse.

I began by asking him to tell his story. "It's a day-to-day thing. Not one goes by that I don't still think about him. I get up every morning and it's the first thought that goes across my mind—but then I think I've just gotta make it through the day."[8]

After a breath of silence—that tiny pause that comes after you've just expelled the most heart-wrenching words you will ever say, we talked about triggers. "Oh, the triggers don't stop. It might be...you might see something, most anything. Or it can be nothing."

I then asked Rick, "How have you given yourself grace or have you?" His kind of grace was the blessings he received by knowing what kind of child his grandson was. "That's what keeps me going." He continued, "And, he was already a strong Christian. Even at his age, he loved people and cared about everyone he met. He was always concerned for their welfare and not his own. You don't see that in many kids that age. Everybody loved him and he loved everybody."

My final question was what he would want you (my readers) to know. "I'd say it's gonna' be hard to move on, but it's necessary." And then I asked a question that I immediately felt guilty for asking. "Why is that?" His response was quick and better than perfect, if there is such a thing. "There's really no other way to go. But having said that, you never really move on without him. He's always with you." His final words were, "I would also say, I've asked myself, why not me, instead of him? Especially when they're that young."

Ride high little Cowboy!

Grace and Children

Dr. Justin Barrett researches children's ability to believe in something else! Regarding grace, he writes, "But maybe children do not have the same problems with grace and gratitude that many adults have. They are able to accept grace without a need to earn it." He wonders if children may be better able than adults to accept grace from God, not needing to earn it or do good deeds for it.[9]

Kids readily accept presents and other kind acts from us without even thinking about having to do something in return. We can take a page from their playbook. So, take a look at the following strategies as you practice "being graced." Begin with one and then add others to expand your "grace pool!"

❧Strategies❦

1. Practice not being perfect. Let your life get messy; fire your mental housekeeper!
2. Tell others your story! Dr. Maria Kefalas, the mother of a child

with a terminal illness wrote about discovering the "superpower of grief."[10] "Once I realized that you can tame grief, not conquer it, by telling your story, I was able to get outside of my pain and harness it to do good things."

3. Don't try to go it alone or be afraid to seek professional help. Talk to someone. How intense are your feelings and how long have you had them? Length of time and intensity of grief are two strong indicators of wellbeing, both physical and emotional. Again, there's no shame in getting help.

4. Consider your grief in this way as you give yourself grace. Dr. Joanne Cacciatore says "...grief isn't a medical issue...it is a human issue and a spiritual issue." She calls it "bearing the unbearable. Our love is worth all the pain I feel. It's all I have left," she says. "Remember that you are allowed to be unhappy, feel numb; you don't have to feel better—just feel."[11]

5. I've had children draw an imaginary patience button on their hand to "push" when they were stressed because of impatience, or having to wait. What if we as adults draw an imaginary "grief button" on ours so that when we get overwhelmed, pushing our grief button can keep us going, just one more step, and then eventually one more mile?

6. Move! If you don't already have a movement/exercise routine, start one. Begin slowly. Count your steps around the house. Increase your distance daily and then take it outside. Dance as you clean. Work in the yard. There are emotional and physical benefits to moving our bodies during grief. And remember, there's sacredness in doing the mundane or the unexciting. Just do it! You will love it when you don't hate it!

7. Find others who are working on their grief. And find those who are not. Seek balance between grappling with the past and being in the now. Find grief groups to share and receive grief stories, but also seek non-grief groups such as painting, sewing, quilting, writing, camping, cooking, and groups who serve others. Add yours here: _____. And, if you can't find one, start one!

8. Journal your grief; spend 20 quiet minutes every morning to release those emotional toxins. In the book, *The Artist's Way*, Julia Cameron tells us to write what she calls, "morning pages." (Maybe these can be our "mourning pages.") Julia says, "Three pages of whatever crosses your mind; that's all there is to it. If you can't think of anything to write, then write, *I can't think of anything to write*... and do this until you have filled three pages." I did this even before I saw her in Santa Fe. It was very hard at first, but within a few days, I was filling more than three pages. Julia calls this "writing to get to the other side."[12]

9. Sing; play the piano or another instrument; listen to your favorite music.

10. This part of your life is your "Second Act," the one where you continue on with the important parts from your "Act One." Give yourself a graceful second chance to continue on to the next act and the next. Your play won't be over until you say it is!

11. Access your spiritual side more, especially the gratitude part! Read M. J. Ryan's book, *Attitudes of Gratitude*.[13] Every day, find the ordinary as well as something out of the ordinary to be grateful for.

12. Be glad! Find something pleasing, that makes you happy or joyful, something you look forward to.

-2-
Finding Your North Star

Give thanks to the Lord, for he is good.
Who made the moon and stars to rule by night.
—Psalm 136:9

Stella Polaris, the bright, unwavering "North Star" at the outermost handle of the Little Dipper, is also called the polar star. This "fixed star" has been used over centuries as a guide for navigation on land and sea, and even the moon. But what does our north star have to do with grace?

Grace comes from the word grâtia and means "favor" or "blessing." Martha Beck, in her book, *Find Your Own North Star* tells us, "When troubled or tangled, ask yourself: How could my North Star guide me with this?" She says it's okay for it to change over time and we may have more than one in our lifetime, "but whatever it is right now, let it guide you."[1]

Next question. But why is this important to those who grieve? Grief throws us off course and moves us off center like nothing else. We need constants just as our children do, things that we can depend on to remain unchanged. We need to know that no matter what happens, we can find our way. We need the light from our North Star—favor, blessing.

Your Stella Polaris can be your faith as you emotionally and physically trudge on. It can be a personal mission or an unwavering plan to see you and your children through grief. To get to the "other side" is knowing that the other side simply means keeping on, not letting up, even when the shore remains distant, or even hidden.

As you follow your North Star aka Stella Polaris, you stay the course, even if you don't know where you will land. In this quest to keep your North Star in sight, you make discoveries about your strength that you didn't know you had. You keep moving toward the home of your soul and all things that bring you peace. Your direction can change, taking you back and forth, or left to right. This is your Light. Grace. Sufficiency. Self-blessings.

Martha Beck also writes that using your North Star to realize your true life's calling becomes your purpose.[2] But I'm wondering, maybe walking with grief IS one of our true life's callings. It IS what we are compelled or meant to do when called upon. Now, I don't believe we have just one purpose in life, or just one calling. But it may be possible that at a time when grief is overwhelming, we label our grief journey with the words *priority purpose*.

Blue Zones & Ikigai (ee-key-guy)

Years ago I visited Okinawa, Japan to work with youth staff on a US military installation. Little did I know I was right smack dab in the middle of one of the world's five "Blue Zones," places where people live longer and have fewer diseases than anywhere else in the world. According to journalist and health activist, Dan Buettner, there are certain things that are associated with longevity, and having a life purpose is one of them.[3]

Okinawans are known to live about 7 years longer than other people, attributed to having this sense of purpose, or *Ikigai* (ee-key-guy).[4] It is the thing to get up for each day and a reason for being. It is a guiding force and the way to find balance in daily routines. As you continue to find your North Star and follow it, you will show children possibilities of their own Stella Polaris, and their *Ikigai*, while on their personal quest to find answers to questions about life, death, and dying.

☙Strategies❧

For You

1. Begin exploring or increasing one of these:
   - What do I love to do, my passion?
   - Where can I help myself, my child, my family, my community, and the world?
   - What do I want my legacy to be?
   - What are my talents/my strengths?

2. Read the book *Ikigai: The Japanese Secret to a Long and Happy Life*. Authors Garcia & Miralles ask, "What do you get up for each day? What are your reasons for being, finding your bliss? How do you find balance in daily routines?"[5] If you answered, "I don't know" to any of these questions, get a special journal and start writing. Sit quietly and just "be." Some call this meditating or mindfulness.

3. Identify your inner circle, those people who reinforce your best self and add to, rather than take away from your wellbeing. Who are your stress reducers? Gravitate to them.

4. Decide if following your North Star requires goal setting or just being open to stops on your journey.

5. Nap! Dan Buettner, in *Blue Zones*, says people who nap regularly have up to 35 percent lower chances of dying from heart disease. Let's use this statistic for "broken heart disease" too! "Napping lowers stress hormones and rests the heart."[6]

For Children

1. Talk to children about a life's purpose. Model your own Stella Polaris or unwavering guide for them. Many consider their faith to be the fixed star in their lives. Teach children steps to work toward their own life compass by helping others, focusing on their strengths and identifying their challenges as opportunities for improvement.

2. Allow children to see you use your own North Star to bring you out of a grief wilderness. Share how your North Star teaches us to listen to an inner voice, to follow our instincts.

3. Have kids who are grieving create drawings of a big star that can be their North Star. Talk about how it guides us when we are lost. Have them put other landmarks beneath it that are important to them such as their house, school, baseball field, Grandma and Grandpa's house, or a favorite restaurant. No matter where they are, it stays above them, always constant.

4. Use a compass to show children how the North Star is always in the same place, no matter how we turn. Take kids camping to give them a chance to practice finding their way with a real compass. Use a telescope or a dark night sky away from the city to locate other stars and constellations in relation to the North Star. Although young children find metaphors hard to understand, using them can make the world more relatable, especially when we use tangible objects and experiences.

~3~
UFOs (Unfinished Objects)

Keep going!
—Austin Kleon

I like to quilt, and in a quilter's world, the term UFOs is very common. These are the unfinished objects/projects that patiently wait for attention or to be completed. But it's also a term that describes an unfinished slew of sewing, painting, crafting, DIYs, landscaping and writing projects. The purchases were made with such good intention but then another idea for a different project came along, and the class we signed up for lapsed without fruition.

The career goal we had may be a distant memory and now additional goals have come and gone. And dealing with children's needs can now preempt our own. Grief, the biggest thief of time, has taken the front seat and flung those projects into a distant backseat if not right out the window. Now we have a real excuse.

I once journaled about my hesitancy in accomplishment—bringing things to fruition and how that's a stumbling block for me at times. Well, maybe all the time! It stems from what Pauline Clance and Suzanne Imes[1] found to be *impostor syndrome*, or not being good enough; not being perfect; or not wanting to put it out there for fear of criticism, etc.

But then I journaled, *Maybe fruition is merely the creation of thought, the birth of an idea.* If that's so, then the act of coming up with ideas of things to do is *fruitful*; that is the first step. What if planting the fruit (or project) is as important as harvesting?

What if we embrace it and hang on to the idea, even if doesn't come to life yet? This will bring new light to creating. You can provide a safe harbor for those creative gems with no shame and no regret during grief.

Dictionaries define fruition as *to enjoy*; "the point at which a plan or project is realized." What if fruition is in the eye of the creator only? That's okay. What if we hold dear the first part of the definition...to enjoy and let go of the second part... realized? Won't that free us to give ourselves grace and create to our heart's desire? What if we never mind the outcome, or forget about the realization of the "thing" and just enjoy the thinking of it?

This speaks to me so loudly! And it parallels the early childhood mantra that many of us have used routinely with children, "process over product!" So do just one thing. Make a plan to complete one project. What would be the first step you would take? And give yourself grace, knowing that it does not have to be perfect or even come to life at this time. Grieving is hard enough.

Think about how this impacts our children when grief moves in. Just seeing us in a creative state can provide hope for them. And think about this, too. Is it possible to include them in our quest to finish our UFOs? Any movement can be considered progress. Any path forward helps to take a side trip from grief, for us and for our children.

❧Strategies☙

1. Austin Kleon, New York Times best-selling author, tells us to "Keep going" in his book of that same title. He offers ways to stay creative in good times and bad, and writes, "I wrote this

book because I needed to read it!"[2] Austin found a way to keep going even when things did not get easier. He writes that things may never get easier, but we have to keep going anyway. I highly recommend his book, mostly because I used it to finish this book!

2. Create a "10 Day Challenge." Make a list of things or just one thing you want to finish or begin working on for the next 10 days. It may be a simple project that can be completed quickly and grief has stolen the time or energy to complete it. Attend to that one thing first.

3. Have your older children help you prioritize, giving you the child's perspective of what's important.

4. Determine if a UFO even needs finishing. Can it be discarded as if it had an expiration date? Cull these from your list first.

5. Set a timer to make those unpleasant UFOs more palatable or to prevent you from being compulsive about them now that you are giving them attention again. I use the Pomodoro© technique where a timer helps me break up my tasks into 25 minutes, followed by a short break, and then 25 more. During those breaks I make the bed, clean one thing, walk for 5 minutes, or just sit on the patio and watch the birds. (Note: Professor and author Cal Newport's book *Deep Work* is another great book on time management and productivity that I've used and can highly recommend.)

6. Adopt a rule of "Finish one, start one."

7. "Do you like it or do you love it?" My friend Emma shared this with me as it helps her daughter Liz decide which projects are worthy of her and her children's time (and I'll add money).

-4-

When We Are the First Responders

It is the process of grieving that's important and necessary, not the understanding of it.
—Unknown

When death comes, we are the first responders to a child. You may be the first one that a child sees, or are called upon to break the news of someone's death. You want to protect them, shelter them, keep them innocent and out of emotional harm's way. But they need to know. And they need to hear it from someone they know and trust. In reality, you can't hide it from them for very long.

Begin by preparing yourself, giving yourself a heaping cup of grace. What you will say will be based upon the truest version of what has happened that you can get.

Get your thoughts in order so that when you tell a child something devastating, you won't blurt it out with so much emotion that your feelings speak louder than your words! Talk it over, or rehearse with someone else first if there is time.

We know that younger children and even teens grieve differently from adults because of their emotional maturity and ages and stages of development. Their knowledge of what is real and unreal or fact and fantasy can vary. Take this into account when you prepare your words to break the news to them. Children as young as two or three years will be able to comprehend in a much different way than school agers. If you have more than one child, you will need to decide if you want to tell them together or individually. More grace needed now!

After the News

When was the last time you communicated through feelings and not words; through hugs and not talk? Be ready for this possibility as you prepare the words to say to children. Words may not be enough or even needed after you bring the news of the death of someone.

Just listen. Try to concentrate on the child's response without judging. Can you hear what she is saying without interrupting? I have to practice this one as my brain is always racing toward my next thought, my next task, my next interjection (or interruption). Pushing our "pause button" is harder than we think, especially when we are bringing news about death of a loved one.

Listen more. This may not be the time to tell the child how we feel unless they ask. You are just giving them the opportunity to "percolate" or talk through their grief without expectations from you. By doing this, you will ensure children know that we value them and that they are not responsible for our feelings. This is hard. I know.

Meeting children where they are and giving them the space to feel what they are feeling is possibly the best way to show love and compassion. Kids don't need to change their thoughts or feelings for us. They can truly grieve in their own way by taking time to figure out what's best for them, with a little help from their first responders.

❧Strategies☙

1. Be ready to be their first responder, the first on the scene. Sometimes you are more prepared than at other times. However, it's okay if you can't do it, can't get to them right away. Can you find someone else who is close to your children, someone they trust and can break the news in your absence? Or, do you need someone to be with you?

2. Be with them as much as you can or at least close by. Kids need consistency at this time, especially if you are dealing with your own grief. You are their anchor or at least their tether. The younger they are, the more tied to you they will be.

3. Give older school agers, and teens especially, personal space after giving them news of someone dying or news of the anticipated loss of someone.

4. Prepare a place or space to tell them or a place in the home that brings them comfort. Or, outside of home; at a park? This simple space of privacy can convey to them a sense that you value their grief.

5. For younger kids, bring a stuffed animal or something they use for comfort to have on hand just in case it's needed.

6. Use statements such as, "I hear you. This is really tough on you," "I'm going to answer your questions with my truest words," and, "I'm sad too." Those phrases can go a long way in assuring our children that we are the ones to be their "first responders."

Part 2

Talking About Death and Dying

-5-
What Kids Want to Know About Death and Dying

The best way out is always through.
—Robert Frost

It may just be one of the most difficult things in life—talking to children about death and dying. Losing at least one person they love during their childhood can profoundly affect them for the rest of their lives. But listen to the words of Elizabeth Kubler-Ross and her colleague David Kessler: "Children are old enough to grieve if they are old enough to love; they are the forgotten grievers."[1]

Recently, we've been faced with a global pandemic where death in our nation has risen to unseen heights as we surpass 1 million losses. Everyone knows someone who died because of COVID complications. But the pandemic is not the only thief of love. Other diseases, accidents, war, and tragedy such as death by suicide and gun violence steal our loved ones every day. Children are often front and center enduring these tragic losses.

We hear the words *gone too soon* and *"Why her,"* or, *"Why him"* over and over. Maria Shriver calls us a "grief illiterate nation" and we lack the how to when we deal with tragedy and loss. She says we often move through our grief without the tools that we need to go forward. And guess what? There is no timetable for it. Maria writes this about grief: "We don't make space for it. We don't feel safe talking about it."[2]

We are often taught to turn away from our thoughts and feelings, so we avoid letting death and dying take their rightful place. Death appears as an impostor, the unwelcome guest. "We want it to follow predictable steps and then everything to get back to normal." But everyone who has ever lost someone knows that there is no "normal," says Maria.[3] There is no comparison, nothing to liken it to.

This challenge to cope with loss filters down. We perpetuate the inability to help our children improve their "grief literacy," generation after generation. Think back to your own childhood and how you acquired coping skills during death and dying. How was death explained to you? Did you have a go-to person willing to answer when you asked questions or did you "figure it out"? Was there someone providing a safe haven to you during a time of grief and loss? Were you able to get any kind of understanding how life and death surround us, in equal parts? If you answered "yes" to these questions, you are one of the fortunate ones who does not remain emotionally adrift when talking about death and dying.

Erikah and Daylen

This mother and son lost several close family members and a friend to complications from COVID-19. Even though Daylen has sickle cell disease, Erikah shared with me that Daylen never talked about death before losing loved ones to "COVID. But now, he has questions. "Are you going to die?" he asked her.

"I can't talk about death very well," she said. Then she thanked me for writing a book to help her and others with strategies to talk about death and dying with children as it is such a prevalent and necessary topic.

Erikah puts action above words and models love in its best sense, while volunteering at a local children's hospital to help other parents take care of themselves with children like Daylen. I think her strength and willingness to help others supersedes her self-reflection. And, she does all of this when not teaching kindergarten![4]

Grief is an Expression of Love

Through life and death, we have the responsibility and opportunity to make closer connections with our children. We can model good grieving or grieving well—what they will need for their children, and their children's children as the circle of life and death continues. Tim VanDerKamp writes, "Grief is an expression of love," or more simply stated, "We grieve because we love."[5]

If grief is an expression of love, it seems only fair children are given the opportunity to grieve; to express love for the one who died. But how we talk with children about loss—death and dying is a critical component of our response to the needs of children.

Someone close may have died today. Lamenting the death of that loved one is appropriate, just as teaching our children to look forward (or what my younger daughter Kassidy labeled as a young girl as "seeing next") is germane to their emotional wellbeing.

If we believe what Kahlil Gibran wrote in 1923, that "Life and death are one, even as the river and the sea are one,"[6] then we are closer to giving kids what they want to know about death and dying, and learning to "seeing next!"

❧Strategies❧

1. Be willing to go to their "emotional well" with them, to go deep, and to share your own sadness, but at the same time, allow their sadness to present itself in all kinds of ways.

2. Increase "grief literacy" by reading books such as this one and others suggested throughout this book as well as in bookstores,

on-line and bricks and mortar. Use the references as well as the children's Bibliotherapy list at the end of this book.

3. Find or develop your own pearls of wisdom to hold on to so that they are the first thing you think of when you have to talk about death and dying. Make them your go-to's, your scripts, prayers, or mantras. There are also many quotes in this book that you can use or adopt as you talk with kids about death and dying.

~6~
Death and Life–So Closely Related

*You can't steer from the pain. If you do you'll
rob yourself of every last memory.
The pain is the only way to
keep them with you.*

—UNKNOWN

In a more perfect world, we would see how closely death and life are related. Everything lives and then dies. We would include it in our casual conversations, thoughts, and everyday activities. And most importantly, we would make it part of reality for our children. But for many reasons, we shy away from the topic and consider it just too painful for them to experience.

In many local cultures, it is a common belief that we shouldn't talk about death or dying; we shouldn't hold it in the same regard as life. We think that talking with children about death too early can rob them of their innocence, or exposing them to death and dying will frighten them. We fear they may have nightmares or distressing thoughts that are beyond their control.

It is anything but simple in most societies in America to respect death as the end result of living, or as the passing of one thing, making room or allowing for the next. It's hard for us to hold talking about death on the same plane as talking about life as they do in many other global cultures.

If we look at this from the child's view, we know that open, honest communication can facilitate the grieving process. Children want and need us to be open about all topics of conversation, but especially about death and dying.

For many of us, it may be the hardest thing ever to provide them with a sense of safety, calm, and control amid our own grief. An eventual acceptance of loss coupled with hope for the future is a real possibility when we prepare ourselves and our children for loss. Then we can we begin to look at death as a natural part of life.

Tammie and Elizabeth

I want to share a story about Tammie and her grief journey. Over the years, three of her five children have died. She has endured what no parent should. And yet her understanding of how death and life are closely related is remarkable. I've told her that she is my "she-roe."

If you were to look up the word, extraordinary in the dictionary, you would find Tammie. I struggled to take notes and process what she had to say about her experiences at the same time. I've known Tammie for quite a while and had heard her heartfelt stories of how each child died, but that didn't make this any easier. It was if I was sitting at the feet of someone who knew more about life and death than most of us could know in several lifetimes.

Tammie talked about her third and most recent loss, her 15-year-old daughter Elizabeth who died from an illness. "Parents have so much guilt. We look forward to growth and change in our children and death is the end." She continued, "Once I accepted death as part of life, I lost fear of my other children dying. We <u>all</u> die." "It's almost a relief to accept it," she explained. "Our days are numbered. We have to know that." Then she shared, "It gets easier to tell their stories. But, it doesn't make it easier; nothing is easy about this."

My Heart is Full

I'm trained. As a long time qualitative researcher, I was schooled on how to take notes without including too much emotion or bias. I'm not sure I succeeded with Tammie or in any of the stories from the people in this book. I could see my hand moving, the pen writing, but this is different. Emotional hijacking was coming on fast...not for Tammie, but for me. Up until now I considered these authentic stories as research. Not anymore. This is "in the weeds"—overwhelming!

I'm a retired professor so I'm old enough that I've experienced lots of death in my lifetime. I know about death and dying first-hand. But every story is different. Every story must be honored and accepted as unique, that person's journey and then that other person's journey. You are real people with unique wisdom and understanding, struggles and over-comings. Grief cannot be painted with a broad brush or lumped into categories and book chapters. I know that better now.

I am honoring the stories that you have to tell, the ones that I will never get to hear, and those you are not ready to share. But they are so important in connecting the dots of life and death, especially for children. And not just any stories, but stories from those whom kids love and with whom they are connected. It's your stories that will bring them connections between life and death.

...

In 1992, an American poet named Mary Oliver won a Pulitzer Prize for her poem, *When Death Comes*. She labeled death "an uplifting reminder of the joy and importance of a life well-lived."[1] Mary told us not to dwell on death, but to be open to the big questions of life and possible answers. She encouraged each one of us to look back on life and all that it offers us, rather than what death takes away.

❧Strategies☙

1. Share your own stories with children about LIFE and DEATH. Talk with grandparents and great-grandparents while they are still alive to get the most authentic stories to pass on to your kids.

2. "The struggle is real," as my daughter Lyndsay reminds me when things get challenging! It's a way of taking another step forward, recognizing suffering but trying not to let it overcome us or drag it with us.

3. Talk about the circle of life. "Everyone and everything has a season and a time to die." Approaching death in a natural, kid-friendly sort of way rather than staging a talking session about death and dying often allows us to share experiences with children without sounding morbid and gruesome. Let them lead the conversations by asking questions about death and dying, long before they face the loss of loved ones.

4. Use movies to refer back to when kids encounter loss, such as, "Remember when Bambi lost his mother?" or, "I'm remembering that Old Yeller died and the boy was so sad." Hint: Preview any movie first in order to decide if it is appropriate for your child and aligns with your beliefs about death and dying.

    For younger children, watch G-rated movies with them such as *Lion King*; *Bambi*; *Land Before Time*; *Old Yeller*; *Finding Nemo*; *Charlotte's Web*; *The Fox and the Hound*; *The Princess Frog*; and *All Dogs Go to Heaven*. For older kids, PG movies that include scenes of death and dying are *Coco*; *The Book of Life*; *Big Hero 6*; *Onward*; *The Never Ending Story*; *Nanny McPhee*; *Up*; and *My Dog Skip*.

-7-

Don't Dodge the Questions!

*No rule book. No judgment. Grief is as individual as
a fingerprint. Do what is right for your soul.*
—UNKNOWN

Most children in the US don't get formal or informal education on topics like loss and death. Why is that? In my experience, most schools want parents to take the reins on these topics; there isn't room in the school day or curriculum to add more content. Or, schools feel it is not their responsibility and teachers feel they are ill-equipped to teach about these topics. And, parents feel kids are just too young to learn about death and dying. We want to protect them from unnecessary pain, or at least from the pain that we may have some control over. But take prekindergarten teacher Emily as an example of what we "can" do.

Many years ago, Emily was a student in my first-grade class in a small town in east Texas, and now she teaches prekindergarten in another small east Texas town. Time flies! When I asked her to tell me about her experience talking with kids about death and dying, she told a story about a little girl in her class whose mom died tragically. "I just allowed her to talk to me at her own pace and gave her lots of love." Emily described the four-year-old as being "matter of fact" with her mother's death, as she relayed to Emily her preschooler's version of what happened. The decision to just listen and provide nurturing was a perfect response from Emily, as many of us don't feel comfortable enough to allow children to talk about dying. Emily didn't have to "educate" her prekindergartener on all the concepts of death and she wasn't alarmed or disturbed by the details. She just listened.[1] Her response reminded me of author, Tim Elmore, who wisely wrote, "Do not mistake the role of comforter as being one who removes all discomfort."[2]

We already know life is hard and keeping children from failing or being uncomfortable doesn't make it any easier for them or us in the long run. I, like everyone else, want my kids and grandkids to be happy, but their happiness should not override their need to experience life's lessons. We are not called to constantly fix things, to mask or take away our children's struggles. But it can be so hard. Right? Again, "The struggle is real."

You Know Your Child Best

Children get mixed messages from us when we tend to avoid those hard conversations about death and dying. They overhear us talking with other adults or older kids, so why won't we talk with them?

As uncomfortable as it may be, they need a safe, comfortable place to learn, to ask questions and get honest answers about sensitive topics. It's possible we've sent them messages in the past that say, "Don't ask me, ask your ____." Or, "That's something we don't talk about in this family." And, "You're too young to know about things like that."

I get it. Talking about a topic like death can be overwhelming if done all at once. So, spoonfuls or bites of information may better suit your child and easier for you. Keep the conversation brief by talking about only one or two things at a time, or avoid big words and long explanations. This improves conversations on not only death and dying but pretty much all topics with children.

But, even though children are naturally inquisitive, they receive information at different rates and in different quantities, and with varying amounts of emotion. You know how much he or she can receive without overload. Watch for verbal and physical cues to know when you've said enough. Notice how they lose eye contact or increase their distance between us. Maybe they even walk away. Again, share the information in small doses or sips.

Younger children often think that death is temporary and reversible. They can't understand its permanence, that we don't come back. Typically, around 8 years they begin to understand the finality of death. But sometimes, even younger kids will surprise us.

A friend shared with me a story about a 6-year-old whose father died suddenly last year. After the funeral, Grandmother placed a photo on the mantel of her son (his dad) and the child demanded it be taken down. "He's dead so why do we have that up there?" he asked. I'm not sure how Grandmother responded, but these possible responses come to mind: "He is still alive in our hearts." "We will always keep him with us." And, "Just like I have photos of you and everyone else in our family, he is still part of our family."

Not Dodging Kids' Questions!

Questions and statements from children about death may come all at once, or continue ongoing for days, weeks, months, or even years. You will answer on an "as needed" basis with kids, using their questions as a guide to how much information to share. And just as a reminder, we don't need to over-explain, ever, and I'm guilty of this. Just ask my daughters. They have taught me to try to listen without advising, which often appears as mom- or teacher-splaining!

Sample questions and answers about death and dying:

Q: Can I talk to Dad even though he isn't alive?
A: "I believe that he still hears us." (If this is your belief, state it honestly and matter-of-factly.) "Yes, I think he can." Or, give children the choice to believe their loved one can hear them. "If you think he hears you, of course you can talk to him." If your beliefs are counter to this, state them honestly. "I'm not sure, but it makes me feel closer to him when I talk to him." Children form their own beliefs, depending on age and stage of development, their culture and the ability to understand the finality of death.

Q: Where do we go when we die?
A. *State your belief.* I looked to two people with opposing views to answer this question. Karla Jac, grandmother to six grandchildren who fondly call her "Maw Jac," shared with me a common belief and how she uses her faith. When talking about the sudden and traumatic death of their young cousin, she told the young grandchildren who lived with her at the time, "*I believe we go to a place called heaven when we die. Sometimes God needs the best little ones to come and help him. Your cousin had been a warrior for Christ and enjoyed helping to further Heaven down here.*"[3]

By contrast, Leslie G. is a family therapist who does not believe in God. She shared her best response to children for this question: *"Our bodies may die but we (our spirits) continue to live on, here on earth in the minds and hearts of those touched by the deceased. So in essence, we don't die; we don't "go" anywhere."*

Q: Why did he die?
A: *"He died because he was in an accident that made his body stop working."* Or, *"He had a disease that his body could not control."* And, *"Her body couldn't breathe anymore."* This is how Elke from Germany

explained it, as we shared a ride to the airport in Santa Fe. She said they often use the phrase, *"Grandpa was too tired to live anymore so he died."*

Q: *What does it mean to be dead?*
A: *"You know how our pet died? He just wasn't alive anymore."* Relate someone's death to other things that live and then die, such as plants and animals and even TV cartoon characters. Use factual statements as much as possible. Stay true to your beliefs, remembering the developmental side of children regarding their thinking and emotions in the younger years. Their understandings are very limited initially, but expand as they grow older.

Q: *Was it my fault?*
A: *"He got really sick and couldn't get better."* Or, *"It was an accident. She was driving and someone in another car hit her and she died."* Assure them it wasn't their fault and that sometimes death happens and we can't do anything to stop it.

Use the actual event as truthfully as you can. In the event that someone takes his own life, your responses will vary by the age of the child. But, when death by suicide stems from mental illness, an honest response to a child would be related to how sick a person was when they took their life. "He decided he didn't want to live on earth anymore. " Or, "She chose to die because she was so sick." Note: I address this more fully in Chapter 21, talking with kids about death by suicide.

It is important to let children guide the conversations with their questions. Again, assure them they are not responsible for another's death.

Q: *Will I die, too?*
A: *"We all die and we don't know when, but that's why we want to stay safe and healthy as long as we can."* This is a tough one. Someone once

said (and I love this), *"For this question, I take a breath and breathe into my heart before I answer."*

Q: *"When are you going to die?"*
A: *"When my body doesn't work anymore. But I'm going to take very good care of myself so that I may live a long time."* Or, *"We don't know when we will die. We just know that all people die. Just like everything that is born will eventually die."*

...

Note: Kids around 4 years have an insatiable curiosity about everything, and death is no exception. They are in the "why" and "when" stage. They ask questions about death even before they experience human loss and this brings us to honesty.

Honesty Pie

I'm sure you've heard the old saying, "Honesty is the best policy," and it certainly is when talking about death and dying with children. If we find this topic difficult, it may be time to revisit or take a truthful look at our own feelings. Does it make us uncomfortable, do our facial expressions change, or do we change the subject?

Even saying the word death can be hard. Maybe it's easier to use a euphemism in place of something that could be considered harsh or hurtful. It's easier to say, "passed" or "passed away," "lost her life," "We lost her today," or "He's not with us anymore," rather than, "Grandpa died today."

Truthfully, I think it's more about our comfort level in talking about death than what we call it. Kids are forgiving, even if it confuses them. The tone of your voice may be more important than the delivery. I know; I'm way out on a limb on this one because I know what the research says about not using the substitute terms for death with children. But keep reading anyway!

Let's revisit this idea. Younger children will have a hard time with euphemisms, alternative words for death because of the concrete nature of their thinking. Maribeth Ditmars writes, "One of the hardest conversations I have ever had was when my husband Rob and I had to tell our 7-year-old son that his older brother Chris was dying." She says that children deserve the truth to avoid using phrases that are confusing and vague like "going away" or "going to a better place."[4] Again, I'm in total agreement, but like grandmother Karla, we say what we know, what is most comforting. And, if said in love and kindness, there is no room for shame or blame.

Sometimes it takes being able to talk about and accept the concept of our own death as a natural part of life. If we hide from or avoid hard conversations on most/or a lot of sensitive topics or subjects, not just death and dying, it can be difficult for children to trust that we will always give them our most honest information.

Look at the following strategies, but don't get overwhelmed. Tackle one or two, for starters.

❧Strategies❧

1. When you're ready, try to use the term "died," even if it sounds harsh or is uncomfortable, instead of substituting words that mask what really happened. We often use euphemisms such as, "met her maker," "resting in peace," "asleep in Jesus," "went to a better place," or "walking with Jesus now," but these can be difficult for children to understand. "He is in a better place," "God needed another angel in Heaven," or "Papa has gone to sleep" are used to soften the blow, or take away the emotional pain. But, developmentally, concrete phrases are easier for children to comprehend. Some phrases that dodge the questions may even be hard to believe. "Your Grandma went on a long trip,"

instead of "Grandma died when her body stopped working," may bring up additional and certainly future questions about, "When is she coming back?"

2. Speak to the reality of death in simple terms such as, "Your friend Jonah was killed today," or, "Once someone dies, they can't come back because they don't think or breathe anymore."

3. Kids must "feel the feelings," even the biggest ones, no matter how unpleasant or difficult the topic is to understand in order to move through the grief process. They grow stronger and more resilient each time they face those big feelings.

...

Before moving on to the next topic, I want to share something from Dr. Bob Deits' book *Life After Loss*. He writes that adults play an important role in the future after children have experienced tremendous loss. We can help them work through their grief (just as we will work through ours) and prevent them from having long-lasting scars. But, he warns, "When adults cannot respond in helpful ways, the effects may be seen for the rest of the child's life."[5] I think he is trying to tell us, "Don't dodge the questions!"

~8~
Looking for Signs Your Child is Grieving

Grief is like glitter. You can throw a handful of it in the air,
but when you try to clean it up, you will never get it all.
Even long after the event, you will find glitter tucked
in the corners. It will always be there...somewhere.
—UNKNOWN

As I write this chapter, the sun is shining on a warm, winter Texas day. I'm reminding myself that grief has no timeline or end time. It's not uncommon to see lots of resilience or what appears to be courage in children during times of grief and loss. But there is a darker, less resilient side of grief.

Some kids grieve out loud and some grieve in silence. Either is normal or typical if we can say that anything is normal or typical during this time. When we can let go of our own preconceptions and misconceptions of what grief is supposed to look like, we can see it as a very raw emotion that chooses its own path.

But how do we know if children are grieving? How does that appear in our mirrors of grief? One day a child is fine and the next day she becomes a different child altogether. Yesterday, he seemed to cope well, but today he cries at nothing. Absolutely nothing. Or shows emotions that are SO. NOT. HIM! This is grief.

There are other signs that your child may be grieving, too. Let's dig deeper. Do you recognize any of the signs below? If yes, then take a look at some strategies for coping during loss.

Signs of Grief

- Change—Watch for big and small changes in typical behaviors
- Anger—There's lots of it, for what seems like no reason
- Preferring to be alone (more than usual)
- Difficulty concentrating at school and at home
- Physical ailments—stomachaches and headaches
- Sleeplessness
- Withdrawing from family and peers
- Unwillingness to talk about the loss
- Feelings of guilt for someone's death
- Clinging to you or someone else
- Anxious behavior/stress
- Regressing to a former developmental age or stage
- Fear of abandonment or fear of a next loss; being left alone
- Loss of interest in normal routines and daily activities
- Not wanting to go to school
- Loss of interest in activities with friends
- Seeming unaffected by the loss

These are good litmus tests or signs your child is grieving. Use them when deciding to intentionally provide more assistance on a daily basis or when deciding to seek professional help.

⊱Strategies⊰

1. Choose the most challenging signs of grief to focus on just for today. Prioritize the behaviors so that little by little, you attend to that one biggest thing and then the others.

2. Look at the severity of the signs of grief that you choose to address. Are they so severe that professional help is needed immediately? Or are they slight enough that you can go into action with your own strategies from this book or other resources before seeking help?

3. Make three categories: (1) Biggest signs that need addressing at this moment, now; (2) Medium sized signs that need addressing but others supersede or override them—they can wait a while longer; and (3) Smaller signs or challenges to place on the back burner until other, biggest issues are addressed.

4. Consider endurance or how long a behavior is lasting. Is it extreme or is it a slight behavior? Has it been going on for a while or has it just begun? Use your "gut." What does it tell you? Older kids can let you know if they want to have a professional to help them. Younger kids need you to make the decision for them. And, you can always go with them to a counselor or therapist and let the professional help you decide. Keep to what works best for you.

~9~
Why Death is Such a Taboo Topic

*The subject of death is taboo. We feel...to be in contact with
death in any way, even indirectly, somehow confronts us
with the prospect of our own deaths, draws our
own deaths closer and makes them
more real and thinkable.*
—Raymond Moody

I don't know about you, but as I was growing up, talking about death was pretty much a taboo topic. We were exposed to death, but we didn't talk about it. We felt its enormity as we watched our parents, other adults, and friends become sad. But, as children, we lacked the tools needed to get through the process of grief because our adults didn't want to, or couldn't "go there" for fear of making us sad or not knowing what to say. Instead, they grieved in silence, or we saw them grieving but knew it was a taboo topic of discussion. Can you identify?

Dr. Allana Canty says just the opposite is true. "It is a common mis-belief that we shouldn't talk about death or dying, that such conversations change a child's innocence, and that children cannot cope with this information."[1] As a grief specialist, she reminds that children can grieve in a healthy way and learn to accept loss if we provide them with honest and open communication.

Remember my friend Tammie? She knows. She calls it the

"unspoken elephant in the room that nobody wants to talk about." When her daughter Elizabeth was dying, Tammie's 12-year-old niece came to the hospital, and sort of half-asking, half-stating said, "She's gonna' be okay?" Tammie explained, "No. Her brain is very damaged. It didn't have oxygen for a while." Not giving up, Tammie's niece said, "But her hands are moving." It was important to Tammie that she used words that honored her daughter but also provided understanding for her niece. "Yes. That's because her organs are shutting down. That sometimes happens. But she is dying."[2]

What's So Taboo About Death?

Think about it for a moment. Death (and sex) are the most important topics that most adults shy away from when talking with children. There's fear in saying the wrong thing, or sounding insensitive due to being uncomfortable with these topics. Or maybe, when we were children, we weren't informed early or directly. We haven't embraced these topics as important growth milestones for our own children.

As a professor for many years, I taught basic child development, a subject that covers from "womb to tomb" as my friend and colleague Ron would say. But, of the many child development textbooks that I consulted when writing this book, not one of them addressed children and grief or children and death in depth and only a handful mentioned death at all. I think that speaks volumes about the United States mainstream culture and how we approach these topics as taboo.

I'll say it again. Sometimes, we shy away from the unpopular, the uncomfortable conversations, and we hope that someone else will address them. Or, children will somehow learn through osmosis! Children do learn from siblings and peers or get bits of information stolen from adult conversations. But that information is often incomplete, or incorrect, much like the telephone gossip game!

Breaking the Taboo Topic of Death

Let's take a closer look at why death is a taboo topic for adults as they prepare for discussions with children. What is it about our society and its norms and traditions that foster this difficulty in talking about death and dying with kids? For many people, there is fear of the unknown. Not knowing for sure what happens when we die can make us doubt that what we tell our children is actually true. We may have our beliefs, but to provide evidence is another thing.

And, we think parents are supposed to know the answers to all our children's questions. The fear of not knowing what to say or saying the wrong thing drives us to silence, and through that silence, we avoid children's questions.

Some of us feel that discussing this topic may scare our children beyond their existing fears. We are afraid that just talking about it can cause unnecessary feelings and emotions, AND, bring on questions that we aren't ready for, or even willing to answer. There's just too much uncertainty surrounding death and dying that anything we say may be considered speculation. And for many, when death is so tragic and happens so close, it's just too painful to talk about.

For some of us, because of our own upbringing, death is a morbid, dark and disturbing conversation that we just don't want to have. We hand down this notion from generation to generation, blocking or at least hiding information that could enlighten children about the death and dying experience.

Sarah

Sarah was the oldest of four, big sister to my cousins Barbara (whom we fondly call Bob), Travis, and Debbie. I remember from an early age my parents talking about my cousin Sarah that I never knew; a little girl who died tragically in a driveway accident that my family and small town would remember for years to come.

When I told Bob I was writing a book about talking with children about death and dying, she immediately brought up Sarah. "You know, that's something we just didn't grow up talking about." Bob said she never heard her parents talk about Sarah and that she and her siblings, Travis and Debbie didn't discuss the accident with their parents, either.[3] "Mother and Daddy never mentioned her death again and we knew not to ask. It was their way of handling her death." I found my family's cultural perspective on death and dying so familiar and common, even today. Can you identify?

A "Good" Death

Professor Katherine Sleeman is a Palliative Medicine Registrar at the Cicely Saunders Institute in London. She would like for everyone to have a "good death," and she believes that ending the silence about death will diminish its terrors and lead to a new focus on improving the quality of life. Dr. Sleeman says we prepare for a new birth by planning and celebrating it. "It is part of our daily life. Why not prepare for death in the same way?"[4]

In their work at the Institute, much progress is being made with adults who are dying and have a hard time accepting death or talking about it. I think there's room for us to become more open, to follow their lead when we talk with children. The more open we are in talking about death and dying—ending the silence, the less taboo it becomes.

Hannah and Amanda

I want to end this chapter with a story from one mother who has kept the memory of her child alive; a mother who does not believe that talking about a loved one who died is taboo. Amanda, mom of Hannah, shared with me how the whole family has kept Hannah with them since her death at age five. She began by saying, *Tomorrow is my daughter's birthday. She would be 18. Grief is something you can visit but you can't stay there. I think about her every day, but I know that we've killed them all if we die when our other child dies. We have to keep going for our kids. They are a part of us just as our dead child is a part.*

Amanda and her two boys continue to talk about Hannah openly and each year on her birthday, Amanda and her husband, along with the boys always eat Hannah's favorites such as cheese pizza and Chinese food. Amanda said even after thirteen years, it's still too hard to sing, "Happy Birthday," but just gathering together as a family is important to safeguard Hannah's memory.

They have "Hannah days" where they cry and then continue on. She states that she knows children grieve in their own way. One son was two and knew Hannah but doesn't talk about her much, but the other son is very talkative, even though he wasn't born yet. He talks a lot about heaven and Hannah being there.[5]

...

It's stories like Amanda's that can begin to erase death as a taboo topic with children. She continues to speak at different events about grief in order to help others "bear the unbearable," sharing her faith and how God met her at her angriest time and filled the void. Incredibly, Amanda believes that, "All things work for good."

❦Strategies❦

1. Let's use a "taboo topic eraser," where children see that life goes on after loss, even when it doesn't feel like it should.

2. Use conversations about death to calm the fears of children, and begin talking about the importance of life and death.

3. Help children to feel more included, part of a family where secrets are kept at a minimum, and kids aren't excluded from tough conversations.

4. Assure children that no topic about death and loss is off limits as we openly allow them to share memories of the one who died. "Remember when's" are great conversation and story starters that allow us to ease in to memory talk. Or, "I was thinking about Hannah the other day when I saw the new pizza place. She would want to try their cheese pizza."

5. Gently step away from the idea that children are too immature or sensitive to experience talk about death and dying, even though it may be hard. We may have been taught that shielding our children from hurt and pain is what's best for them. But, look at children from a developmental perspective; we know their resilience, their bounce back ability is strong if we give them opportunities.

~10~
Children Will Grieve in their Own Way

Death ends a life, not a relationship
—Mitch Albom[1]

I know, we want to turn the world right side up when it has been turned upside down. But, just as Amanda says, allowing children to grieve in their own way is the kindest, most loving thing we can do. Because, I repeat, there is no right way to grieve. I've been with many children who have lost loved ones—people and pets. I've talked with so many parents whose children have suffered a loss, and the one thing that became clear is that grief becomes an individual experience for all children. Yes, there are similarities in patterns of grief, but each child grieves in his or her own way.

In my book *Deployment: Strategies for Working with Kids in Military Families*, I tell a story about a little girl I observed in before-school care. She appeared heartbroken. I was consulting with school age care providers at a US military installation stateside. A staff member shared with me the child's dad was part of a large deployment that occurred early that morning. The grief and uncertainty that she felt from his departure was apparent. She sat in silence until time to go to school.[2] Her reaction to "losing him" was honored by all those around her, children and adults.

We forget that, depending upon the ages of our children, they will not grieve the same way as adults, but we also want to believe that there is a right way to grieve. We try to equate our way of grieving to our children's and it just doesn't work.

Grieving / Playing

Here's the dilemma. We all need emotional releases, but children may actually be better at giving themselves permission get those releases as they grieve and play, grieve and play if we allow them to. Emotions are released in times of loss through mental breakaways or self-created intermissions and pauses from the youngest to the oldest kids.

We often see children playing outside during a wake or visitation, or finding distractions during a funeral, as they are getting the release and recharging needed to emotionally handle grief. Their ability to distract themselves from grief, as well as practice avoidance are ways they "grieve well." Although this can be misinterpreted as not having "enough" grief for the loved one, they are remaining emotionally healthy by the grief/play pattern. Many adults experience similar patterns of grief and play, but they do it in different ways. They may offer a smile to break the emotional tension of grieving, or they tell a funny story or remembrance about the deceased. But it should be comforting to know wherever kids are, that is the place that they need to be… their "starting point" according to Mia Roldan, author of a grief journal for kids.[3]

I don't want to make it appear that all children handle grief well. Some children hear the news of the death of a loved one, and they have many of the same emotions and fears, pain and sadness as adults. They are less equipped to handle the news due to a lack of resilience/emotional wellbeing or experience with death. Even the best parenting may not prepare children for what's coming. Emma Lee's story recounts how her two youngest adopted daughters responded when told the news about the death of an older brother.

Emma Lee's Story

My long-time friend Emma Lee grieves for the loss of two of her seven children. We talked about how losing eighteen-year-old Benjamin more than 30 years ago when taken off life support after a tragic auto accident still affects her. "You just go on," she said. "I had other children to think about and used my faith to get through it. It's still hard to believe, even after all these years later. I lose track of how many years it's been. That's terrible."

I asked her if she could recall the reactions of her younger girls. She responded, "You know, they were different personalities and grieved in their own way. One had been accustomed to taking care of other siblings when we adopted her as she was the oldest, but the other was so sensitive. She cried and cried, even though she had not been around him much."[4]

Emma is a true testament to how one uses faith to get through the death of loved ones, in the beginning and beyond. Using faith, I watched her pick up her other children and put them on her back to walk the long grief journey. "I didn't have a choice," she said.

This was a common theme I heard again and again from parents who lost loved ones, but remained committed to "keeping on" for their surviving children.

No One Can Say How Your Child Should Grieve

Good intentions from friends and family will be plentiful, but knowledge of your own child is power. You are your child's best nurturer and provider, teacher, and mentor. You are essential to their wellbeing, and no one knows them better than you!

Even as adults, many of us do not know how to prepare for grief, as we may use old sayings and adages called "grief myths" to get us through, or tales we accept as facts, even though there is no conceivable evidence they are true.

Here are my 7 all time <u>worst</u> grief myths:

1. "You recover from grief like you recover from a cold; it gets a little better every day until it completely goes away."
2. "Kids don't know anything about grief."
3. "Time heals all wounds."
4. "If you are still holding on to your loved one's things after __ years, you aren't OK."
5. "If you aren't crying, you aren't grieving."
6. "The goal of grief is to just get over it."
7. "Children should not attend funerals."
8. "Once you get through the firsts (Christmas, birthdays, etc.), it will get easier."

…

There are lots more grief myths to "bust." So, dust off the old "learn by doing" teaching technique as you play and interact with your children. Model and/or participate in the strategies below to set aside "grief time!"

⇜Strategies⇝

1. Tell funny stories or jokes and ask your child to tell you one.
2. Have your child read a book, a chapter, or even a page and tell you or someone else about it in two minutes. Yes, only two! Set the timer.
3. Have kids dance or listen to music. Try different genres and find out which ones they prefer. Add rhythm band instruments for fun such as bells and maracas.
4. Go "dollar store" shopping with a small budget.
5. Kids need to play, play, play. With you. By themselves. With others.

6. Have children visit a friend or have friends over.
7. Encourage your child to do a kindness for someone else.
8. Bake some favorite cookies with your child.
9. Play games with your child that requires imagination such as:
    - *I'm Thinking of an Animal*—"that runs fast and lives on an African plain."
    - *Make Something from a box (or boxes).*
    - *"What Happens Next" Story Game*—Read or tell a story and stop before the end. Ask, "What happens next?" Or, "Can you finish the story with your own ending?"
    - *I'm Going on a Trip to* ___ *and I'm Packing* ___ (tell 5 things to pack).
    - *Play Fortunately, Unfortunately Game*—"Fortunately, I have my baseball but unfortunately, I forgot my glove."
    - *Opposite Day*—Wear something inside out or backwards; eat dinner first, breakfast last; say "yes" for "no" and "no" for "yes"; eat dessert first; write or do tasks with the opposite hand; read a short book, starting at the end.

~11~
Grief—The Good and the Bad

*Grief is a natural cycle you can trust—how life
and the heart renews itself. Like the spring
after winter, it always does.*
—JACK KORNFIELD[1]

Children will experience good grief and bad grief. Authors Bill and Kristie Gaultiere write how good grief happens when we accept that every time we experience loss an "unwanted path of emotional healing growth opens up."[2] When we are emotionally available or we intentionally show up for our children every time they experience any kind of loss, not just death, we are laying the good grief groundwork. This prepares them to react in "good grief" kinds of ways, especially when they experience the ultimate loss of a close loved one.

Their needs are met; they feel empathy from us when it counts; and they feel that sort of "enoughness" that will carry them through the darkest times. Good grief keeps our loved ones near us in healthy ways and allows us to think of events such as funerals and memorial services as a time to be sad, but also celebrations of life. It serves as continuations rather than ends. Good grief allows us to cry when we need to and laugh when we can.

Bad grief happens when the hole of grief is too deep. The gap between mental wellness and despair is too wide and we think we will never escape. Hope is gone. All is lost. Bad grief overcomes us. It "emotionally hijacks" us, to borrow a term from Daniel Goleman's emotional intelligence theory.[3] This happens when our emotions cloud our thinking, and when we need to activate any type of mindful calming that we can.

My then 12-year-old daughter Kassidy heard me talk about "emotional hijacking" more than once. I picked her up from school one day and asked the proverbial mom question, "How was your day?" She answered, "Mom, my day was so emotionally jacked up!"[4] Did she nail it unintentionally? Out of the mouths of babes (middle-schoolers)!

Bad grief prevents us from making those small steps toward mental sobriety, able to sensibly feel our feelings. It blocks our mental acuity where the walkway forward is well lit, calling us into balance between loss and life. But, keep reading because grief is usually like a tide of good and bad, constantly moving in and out.

Grief May Come and Go

When we can let go of *shoulds* and *should nots*, we can foster a more realistic grieving period for our children, helping them find good grief. We realize that grief has a presence and an absence. Some children may feel a little better/less despair after a few days or weeks, and then have periodic episodes of triggered extreme grief.

And some will have something that seems chronic, always with them or persisting for a long time without relief in sight. It is always there to be quickly accessed, to be picked up and put down. These chronic, intense emotions may cause children to continue to feel sad for a long time as their grief is constantly triggered by places, events and occasions they experienced with their deceased love one.

With heart-rending loss, some children will experience a more *acute* grief, where it is sharp and painful at first, but doesn't last for a long time. Or their grief dissipates and then returns without welcome after being triggered.

Acute grief looks like this. Just when we think they are doing better, grief can overwhelm them by a song on the radio their dad always sang; finding something their mom wore; or seeing their brother's favorite food or restaurant. It just may be that grief is the crying of the heart, an outward painting of our soul in times of loss. In many instances, grief is a love language for our loss.

Good Grief or Bad Grief?

But how do we know if a child is experiencing good or bad grief? We look for signs of intensity and length of time or how long the grief has lasted. What do I mean by that? First, trust your gut. There's lots of research regarding the gut and intuition. Activate yours. You will know if you child's grief is so intense she cannot function. Are they sad most of the time? They won't eat, can't sleep? Has the grieving gone on too long? Again, trust your "gut" as you answer these questions.

There's no "grief by proxy" here. We can't stand in for them, but if we practice many of the strategies that follow, either with children or in their presence, we are showing them the way forward, one tiny step at a time.

In contrast, has everyone else found more good grief than bad? Have they developed problem solving and coping skills? And then there's this particular child who may experience bad grief that warrants professional assistance—someone who is skilled in grief counseling. We do all that we can do, but sometimes it isn't enough. There is no shame in getting the help that your child needs. You are human. If you've tried the strategies here with your child, and your little voice/intuition tells you he now needs more—it maybe in the form of grief therapy or counseling.

Start by locating and contacting a grief support center such as *The Warm Place* in Ft. Worth, Texas. Places like these provide grief support for children ages 3 and a half to 18 years who have experienced the death of a loved one. If you don't have a grief support center or grief counselors in your area, try to find virtual support such as *The Warm Place*[5] and others offer.

❧Strategies☙

1. There will be periods of good grief and bad. Ask children how you can help. Can they give you signs when they need your assistance and when they want to be left alone? Sometimes it's just too "peopley" out there. When we need alone time in my family, we use the English translation of the German phrase, *Ich fühle mich genug besucht*: "I'm feeling visited enough!"

2. Encourage more play with pets; visit a pet store or someone with pets if you don't have any. Older kids may offer to dog sit and/or dog walk. There are many psychological benefits for children when interacting with pets or other animals such as providing help with depression and anxiety, or increasing a child's self-esteem and self-confidence.

3. Talk to your child's school about getting a therapy dog for children who are grieving or going through loss of any kind.

4. Find out if there are possibilities to get your child his or her own therapy or emotional support dog. There are lots of websites with information for your area. Sometimes the dogs are free to children who qualify.

5. Go to a zoo (in person or a virtual zoo on-line). Connecting your child with animals is the key.

-12-

Yes, Kids Can Anticipate Loss

*They shall mount up with wings as eagles;
they shall run and not be weary...*
—Isaiah 40:31

Anticipatory grief. Sometimes when death is not sudden, children have to prepare for the death of someone they love. This anticipation can be stressful as they fear sadness and heartbreak that will continue for days, months, or even years as they prepare for the death of a loved one. This is a time for their "whole village" to come together to get ready for the combo of mixed emotions kids will feel during this time.

Dr. Elizabeth Kübler-Ross' work on death and dying relates so well to this. She wrote about anticipated loss and how we can understand it from a child development perspective. "In childhood we realize at some point that we will die, and not only will we die, but those around us will die someday too."[1]

Anticipating death develops earlier for some children and later for others. It is quite different from traumatic or sudden loss but both can be challenging for children. According to Dr. Kübler-Ross, "That is our beginning of anticipatory grief: fear of the unknown, the pain we will someday experience. It is present in most of our childhood stories and movies as if they were archetypally [typically] preparing us."[2]

Liminality — Betwixt and Between

Many children have loved ones who are terminally ill over weeks, months, or even years. They know someone who has gone to war, or has an extremely dangerous job. In both instances, anticipating the loss of a family member or friend (or pet) can be extremely hard as kids find themselves in a state of limbo or transition.

This is what cultural anthropologist Victor Turner called "liminality,"not quite in and not quite out.[3] While preparing for loss, children can live in two different realities; they are not able to move to a next stage of grief, but are challenged to continue with daily life. They are liminal, betwixt and between.

For example, I was moved by a fellow church member who told the story of a father who talked about the worst thing for his children when their mother was dying of cancer at home. His kids were in constant states of limbo and stress, always wondering if today, or this hour, would be their last moment with her. It was torture, waking up every morning and wondering if she was still alive, or dreading coming home from school to find that she had died. His children watched her become sicker and sicker. "I loved my wife," he said. "But I felt like we were all held hostage every day by her illness." This is an example of classic anticipatory grief and loss.

Getting Back to "Normal"

When children sense or even know the death of someone is imminent, it is very natural for them to feel distressed, especially if the end of life is near. They seek normality or homeostasis where everything stays the same or gets back to its center, and where they can find refuge.

Don't be alarmed if their thoughts and words turn to wishing their loved one was already gone. This is common as the stress of living with impending death may be all too much for them. We are the place they retreat to, their respite and shelter. When everything is disrupted, it can all become too much for children.

Author Keith Smith calls it "mourning sickness," and it comes in the time period leading up to death.[4] Children often cannot do the things they did before with the dying loved one. The relationship may deteriorate, even causing the adult/child role to become reversed. It is not uncommon for children to become caregivers of the dying.

The children's keen awareness of surroundings helps them interpret the slightest change in moods or the environment. They can "read our pages" so to speak, and their feelings can often mirror our feelings.

Even when children don't live in the home with the loved one who is dying or see them often, they can become distressed in absentia by thinking about the loved one. The absence of the one dying does not keep children from feeling anticipated loss.

As you prepare children for the death of a loved one, know that your efforts will be rewarded. Crossing the threshold from the old and familiar way to the new and unknown way brings hope. Be as honest as you can, but reassuring with your child. Telling them a loved one is going to get better when it is untrue may avoid having to face the truth in the short term, but confuse them or cause bitterness in the long term, after the loved one dies.

Managing Grief

Normal. Is there such thing now? Hope for things to get back to normal can supersede the need to be sad. Anger, guilt, confusion, and frustration set in. These thoughts and feelings are typical as well. They don't want their loved one to die, but they need to re-center, feel that everything is okay once again.

We don't have to be the one dying in order for children to feel the need to become our caregiver or caretaker. You may struggle with managing your own grief in the anticipation of loss. Children watch you go through your own anticipatory loss. They overhear your stressful conversations and reports of sadness to others, and feel a sense of loss as things have changed with you. You may be on double duty—the caretaker of the dying loved one and of your children, trying your best to balance love and care between all. Again, we cannot underestimate how much children sense, feel and know things are changing, moving toward a loss.

Chris' Story

Maribeth Ditmar's son was a very wise 13-year-old who anticipated his own loss during his four-year battle with cancer. As a Christian speaker and author, Maribeth has told her story to so many, giving them hope, and has given me permission to share Chris' story:

Chris and I used to talk about heaven a lot, especially in his last year of life, when he knew his chances of survival were slim. Even though he was only 13 at the time (he died a few weeks after his 14th birthday) his insight and optimism were remarkable. At the time, I wasn't a Bible reader, and we didn't read Bible passages about heaven, but I'll never forget what he said. It went something like this, "Mom, clouds and harps would be way too boring. I'll be able to snowboard without ever getting cold, and we can drink soda flavors that haven't been invented on earth." I think the Holy Spirit was shining through our precious son, who had become wise beyond his years. As a matter of fact, Chris is the reason I am a Bible reader today.[5]

Maribeth encourages us with her own authentic and wise words regarding anticipated loss. "If you have a terminally ill child, or someone they love is dying, be a safe person for them to talk to. Let their questions be your guide." I could not have said it better. Much thanks to her for sharing this story about Chris.

...

The strategies below are designed to use with children as you go through this uncharted territory of anticipated grief and loss.

❦Strategies❧

1. Saying goodbye, or making preparations is essential during anticipatory loss. Give prompts which lead to direct answers, and cues that are more indirect and serve as a hint, as you truthfully prepare them for loss. *Prompt*: "I need to give you an update on Grandma," and, *Cue*: "The doctor says her body is getting weaker and we may have to say goodbye to her soon."

2. Use phrases such as these when your child asks if someone who is ill is going to die, "Yes, but we can't know when." Or, "The doctor says ____." You can also respond with, "I don't know. But, we can always pray that Mommy is going to get better," or, "There is always hope. Sometimes miracles happen (if that is your belief)." Phrases such as "Mommy is not going to die. She is going to be okay," can be challenging, as we avoid making promises that we cannot keep.

3. "Why does my father have to die? Responses such as, "All living things die," or, "All living things are born and then have a time to die," are words that are as truthful as you can get with your child. Or, "The doctor has tried really hard but there is not a cure for ____." And lastly, if you just don't have the answers they need, it's okay to say, "We don't always know why things

happen," or simply, "I just don't know."

4. Keep children apprised of the health of the dying when they ask, and as much as you are able to share. This helps them to prepare much better than not knowing or being surprised.

5. Some children may want to visit the dying more than others, especially if the loved one isn't living with the child. Getting more comfortable with death is an important milestone in the life of anyone, especially children. Of course, you will want to respect the privacy of the dying, and in the event they are unable to have visitors, there are other alternatives.

6. Make a recording (video or audio) of your child if he can't visit and the dying loved one would like to have it when your child is not there.

7. Tell your child briefly what to expect when they live with a dying loved one. Or, they may visit them in a hospital, nursing facility, or hospice care. Then ask, "Do you have any questions for me about ___?"

8. During anticipated loss, watch for signs of prolonged/consistent despair in children as those are red alerts that counseling or therapy is needed. Don't be shy; make an appointment with your child's school counselor and ask for help during this period of anticipated loss. School counselors often take a grief course in their graduate counseling program. Or, they may be able to refer you to a play therapist who is skilled in grief play and therapy.

~13~

Sheltering Trees and Secure Bases

Friendship is a sheltering tree.
— Samuel Taylor Coleridge

Sheltering trees have spiritual and emotional meaning. Bible stories feature trees that were used over and over in stories and parables to provide protection from life's storms, unwanted events, as well as shade for weary travelers. For example, John writes how Jesus was refreshed beneath sheltering branches" (John 11:5). The prophet Ezekiel wrote, "All kinds of birds will find shelter under the tree, and they will rest in the shade of its branches" (Eph. 17:23). And, in Genesis 18:4, we are told to "rest yourselves under the tree."

As adults, we are sheltering trees protecting children during grief and loss. Other writers have used trees to convey significant meanings and symbols. Shortly before his death, author Samuel Taylor Coleridge wrote, "Friendship is a sheltering tree,"[1] to remind us that relationships with others can stand in/protect us from the harsh elements of life. Evangelical minister Charles Swindoll followed with, "Let's be busy about the business of watering and pruning and cultivating our trees."[2]

Sheltering trees are recognized by the way in which they provide comfort, respite from grief storms, connections, and support. Who are the trees in your life? Who has provided a barrier between you and life's hardships? Maybe they are standing now to shelter you as you grieve, and as you stand over your children to shelter them in their grief.

Secure Bases

I liken the concept of parents as sheltering trees to what pioneers in attachment theory, authors Mary Ainsworth and John Bowlby described as providing a "secure base." Our youngest children venture out, spread their developmental wings, and then return back to their base (or tree) often, especially when "the parent is known to be accessible and responsive..."Bowlby wrote, "These patterns of interaction between child and parent are known as exploration from a secure base. In order to become a protective barrier for children, we must be present, responsive!"[3, 4]

Wait! There are Two Sides of a Sheltering Tree

On one side, caring adults are children's sheltering trees and a secure base for them to return to again and again in times of loss. This speaks to adopting a parenting style where your child can explore, emotionally and physically, while staying in close proximity to you. You've watched babies when they begin to crawl, looking back to make sure you're still there. Children too need a secure base/a sheltering tree, someone to look back or return to after venturing out, especially during times of loss.

But on the flip side, using sheltering trees to keep them from knowing about and understanding death may work to their detriment. By this, I mean our cultures often promote protecting children from grief as we try to prevent them from experiencing the feelings that accompany death. In reality, as I've said before, we won't succeed in protecting them from death and loss as it is a natural part of living. Death is all around them. Children have heard the word "dies" in many contexts from their very earliest understandings and experiences. They see death in every living thing that is born, grows, and then dies. Or, when a pet, grandparents or other close family members die. They see death in inanimate objects too. Even the lawnmower or the car battery "dies."

Consider this. Don't let your "fathering" or "mothering" tree become a "smothering tree." It's important to let children feel the feelings rather than keep them in the dark or "in the shade" in this instance. Our children know us like no one else. If we try to shelter them from grief, they will sense there is more; they will continue to seek answers from us.

Don't Park a Helicopter Under Your Sheltering Tree

Sometimes, we hover over our children in order to protect them from pain and disappointment. It was Dr. Haim Ginott who coined the term "helicopter parent" back in 1969 in his book *Between Parent and Teenager,* to describe overly protective parents who hover closely, rarely out of reach.[5]

But there's a difference between sheltering and hovering. If you can answer "yes" to most of the following questions, you may be a "hoverer!"

Do I:

- make decisions for them, even when they can make them for themselves?
- have a need to protect them, even when they don't need it?
- try to keep them from being unhappy, disappointed, or struggling to find their own solutions?
- over plan free time, play dates, sports, music and dance lessons, etc.
- always choose my child's teachers and coaches, friends and activities?

- get overly involved in homework and school projects?

In contrast, if you are providing a shelter for them, but allowing them to stretch and grow through their own grief, you are sheltering rather than hovering. Parents who hover tend to rescue children and preclude them from being able to problem solve. And grieving certainly involves problem solving.

Finally, we as adults need our own sheltering trees to settle underneath when grief is so hard to bear, and we need a place to just "sit." Maybe we also need a secure base to run back to, one that provides a retreat to emotional safety, or one that provides a re-charging station! Seek out your own sheltering trees and secure bases in order to be prepared to provide them for children.

❧Strategies❧

1. Think of ways that you "helicopter" or hover over children in normal times and in times of grief. What is one tiny change that you can make today to ground your parenting helicopter? Make a list of the ways you "hover" and remove one at a time. Or, make the decision to become less controlling (or dare I say interfering) in order to increase their ability to problem solve. How can you decrease planning, or rescuing?

2. Are children letting you know they need their space (physical and emotional)? Think of some ways or spaces that you can create to help them feel secure but at the same time feel freedom to gain confidence, to grieve, and to work things out.

3. Are you shadow parenting? Are you always in the background, swooping in at the first sign of a problem? Can you move back just a tinch as we say in the south? Just a smidgen? How can you allow them to wander just outside your parental area as they

deal with grief? Stew over these questions as you thoughtfully make a plan.

4. Use walk-bys to check in with them. The idea is to not leave a child alone for too much time in their room or any other space when they are grieving. You may want to impose a no-closed doors rule if you have concerns, or have them leave a small opening so that you can continue to monitor without hovering.

5. Plan more time for them to venture out from you to play, knowing you are there. It reminds me of kids leaving the shore just far enough to enjoy the water, but not too far that they can't continue to see us, or retreat back to us.

~14~

When Pets Die

What we have once enjoyed we can never lose; all that we have loved deeply, becomes a part of us.
—Helen Keller

Your child's first experience with death may be losing a pet. They begin to think about or even verbalize their first questions such as, "What happens when something dies?"

Grief is grief and loss is loss and there is only one type of deep sadness children feel when they lose someone or something they love. They can grieve as hard for their beloved pets as they do for their human loved ones. This goes for adults as well! And the loss they feel for a pet seems unbearable, especially if they had a close relationship. Dr. Bob Deits writes, "Their sense of loss and grief needs to be taken seriously by parents and other adults."[1]

Children make such close bonds with pets that experiencing loss, especially for the first time, will seem harder than they can endure. It's a deep natural need to love and be loved that brings children and pets together. This need for companionship and unconditional love attracts children to pets and pets to children!

Sometimes They Pick Us

Our pets seem to attach to humans just as humans attach to other humans. Pure and unconditional love best describes how our pets respond to us, totally accepting and never judging. Sometimes our pets choose us rather than the other way around.

I picked up my then 10-year-old Kassidy from her friend's house one afternoon and this happened:

"Mom, Mom can we please, please go next door and see John's puppies."

"Why would we do that? We already have a puppy." That was my reasonable response when one dog for us was surely enough.

"But they already gave Amanda one and they said I could have one too. And Andy needs a friend." Note: Andy was our adorable male Brittany that was Kassidy's birthday present the year before. A breeder and his pilot friend had flown up from Houston to Lufkin, Texas for fun in the friend's plane to deliver Andy. He should be enough, right?

I responded in my most logical, parent-ly voice, "But our house is small and so is our backyard. I don't think we need another dog. And they are so expensive."

"But Mom, it's free." Uh-huh, I thought. Nothing about a pet is ever free. There's food, and vet bills and grooming and boarding. (We are definitely _not_ getting another dog).

"Mom, please! Can we just look?"

"Okay, we can just look." At this point I hadn't even asked what kind of dog. We will walk over, take a look, and then go home. But there they were—eight of the cutest golden retriever puppies you've ever seen. The tiniest one ran up to her and that was the instant we became lovers (and owners) of two dogs, Andy and Mase.

Years later, we would experience their deaths with excruciating sadness. They were both euthanized and even though I was never truly a pet person to the extent that so many of you are, I was a Mase and Andy person. They had become part of the family.

Whether it's rescue pets from the street, adopted from a shelter or breeder, born into your house by an older pet, or given to you by a neighbor, it doesn't matter. When the bonds are strong, the loss of a pet is devastating to children (and us)!

The devotion of pets brings a sense of well-being that is unmatched and when that is lost, children may feel their lives are changed forever. The loss of this two-way bond cannot be replaced. Children, like us, must somehow move in zigzag fashion toward the pain first, then through it, then to the other side of it (but not ever completely away from it) and then back again. Heartbreak is heartbreak and we have to honor it when pets, just as humans, die.

This period of active mourning where children show outward signs of grief after pet loss is what it is to be human. They often continue a relationship with the deceased pet in the same way that I've talked about in this book about their relationships with their people who die.

Getting Another Pet After Loss

A common question is how soon should we get another pet? Can there be such a thing as a replacement pet? This may sound like a good idea initially and even be a distraction in the short-run, but listen to your heart and your children. Do they need additional time to grieve before getting another pet? We don't want to send the message that any life is replaceable.

How will you know when it's time? Children's ages and maturity level, as well as their stage of development can all play a part in deciding when it will be time to bring another pet into their lives.

For example, because older kids are in a more advanced stage of development, they may have a harder time accepting the loss, just as they do when a person dies, and resist getting another pet. But, younger children may be much more open as they miss the companionship, love, and devotion so much that they feel a new pet will help them get back to their "normal." A lot can depend upon how long the pet has been a part of the child's life.

Do Pets Go to Heaven?

Many people believe they do and I think it really comes down to your belief system, and how you approach life after death, or life after life as some say. When my grandchildren recently lost a pet that was older than them, it was one of the first questions they asked. But that led to another discussion of, "Do all animals go to heaven when they die?" Even worms?" That's a bit trickier!

There's a debate about whether animals have souls and the beliefs range from an emphatic "no" for non-believers to a resounding "yes" to believers since the Bible refers to all living things as souls. Consider the words of Pope John Paul II. In 1990, he said, "Animals do have souls and are as near to God as men." You decide!

Belief in a life beyond, one where we will see our pets again can be comforting, especially if we have been taught to believe we will see all loved ones again. You will have to rely on your personal beliefs to address this question with children. If you believe that life ends with death or you just don't know, responses such as "Pets don't feel pain anymore when they die," or "He will live on in us and our thoughts about him," may be sufficient.

One parent told me now is not the time to address his non-belief in the afterlife. When his five-year-old grow s older, he will have the discussion then. But for now, whatever his young child wants to believe is just fine. Another parent who is a believer, made the distinction between pets and people. "I believe we go to heaven when we die, but I can't tell my children that about our pets. I just don't know." I am of the mindset that we can also let our kids (and grandkids) decide what to believe by asking, "Where do you think they go when they die?"

Explaining Euthanasia to Children

Making a decision to end your pet's life may be one of the hardest you will ever make; it has been for my daughters and me. There is nothing easy about it. Not one bit.

While visiting with friend Liz W. about her own children's loss and grief, she talked about pet loss being so hard—maybe as hard on kids. This is how they said goodbye to Cooper, an 11-year-old golden retriever who died after having cancer for two years. "We saw a slow decline but knew we would have to say goodbye. At the end, we had a vet come to our house so the kids could see how peaceful he was when he died."

We call it "putting pets to sleep" here in the South but in my experience, rarely do we explain the process of euthanasia to children. Maybe we should. If they experience anticipatory loss of pets, there can be questions such as, "What will the vet do to him?, "Will it hurt?, and Will he die?"

Some children will want to be present. Pet grief expert Marty Tously writes, "Some veterinarians are firmly against it; others say it depends on the child's age and maturity."[2] Some vets are willing to answer children's questions beforehand, but may not want them to be present at death.

But we can answer questions, too. "The doctor will give him a shot and his body will stop working." And, "She couldn't live a good life anymore because she was too sick." These answers are honest and not misleading, realistic but not morbid. We are allowed to show our own feelings too, as pets are often as much ours as our children's. "This was really hard for me to make this decision but I don't want Brooks to suffer any more," was how my daughter Lyndsay showed compassion and grief, feelings that she wanted to model for her children after having their 17-year-old Shih Tzu euthanized.

Sometimes it's just not possible to be present, but the experts tell us it's important to let your children be a part of this process and to know when euthanizing will happen; to make the decision to be there or not, even if it's in the waiting room or outside. It is important that they have a chance to say a final goodbye, to have closure if at possible.

If you decide to be with a pet when she dies, but your child cannot, have someone familiar to sit with your child in the waiting room or at home. If you have your pet cremated, your child will want to know what happened. If you and your child want remembrances such as hair clippings, paw prints, or a cast of a paw, decide beforehand. If you want your pet's cremains returned, ask for an individual cremation. There are decisions to make here as well. Will you want an urn with your pet's cremains? Will you bury the cremains or keep them close by?

I found that if you don't want the cremains, there are sometimes options to have your pet cremated with other animals and the ashes will be mixed and spread on the crematorium grounds rather than being returned to you.

After euthanasia, another option may be to bring your deceased pet home to bury. This is a decision that you will not make lightly as the hole must be very deep to prevent other animals from disturbing the grave or from the soil washing away and exposing the bones. I recently bought a house where a small dog's skeletal remains suddenly surfaced in the back yard. I found out from the prior owner that it was in fact theirs and had been many years since burial.

And, lastly, what if you decide to move? Will you want to leave your pet's remains behind? There are lots of considerations and decisions to make, but keeping your children's wellbeing in mind should come first.

Reaching Out

You are not alone. There are support groups and information sites to help you in making decisions as well as grieving pet loss well with children. There are other compassionate grievers ready to help and many of them will vary by state. I've provided a few below:

- The Pet Compassion Careline, 855-245-8214, which provides 24/7 grief support with trained pet grief counselors.[3]
- Laps of Love, which provides grief courses and 50-minute one-on-one support sessions with a grief counselor. https://www.lapoflove.com/our-services/pet-loss-support.[4]
- Everlife Support Groups[5] by state.
- Association for Pet Loss and Bereavement support groups, available at specific times throughout the week. These can be found at: https://www.aplb.org/.[6]

When it's Time: Saying Goodbye

Saying goodbye when something we love dies is a necessary "good" in order to continue the transformation process of moving from one feeling/emotion to the next, one life change to the other. Children relish opportunities to say goodbye to their pets in ritualistic ways that show how important the pet was (and is). how important it is to carve final memories; and to honor how much the pet meant to them.

Think about providing goodbye events and services in instances where pets were stolen, ran away, or tragically killed. These events are often without closure and children will want to say goodbye to these pets, as well. There are many ways for children to say goodbye in the following strategies.

❧Strategies❧

1. Honor children's strong attachments to their pets by providing validity to their feelings. Words like, "It's only a dog," and, "You can always get another one," disenfranchise their loss. Again, the level of grief experienced when losing a pet has been found to be equal to the grief of human loss for children. Their feelings may not distinguish loss for one over the other, depending on the relationship or connection with the deceased pet.

2. Provide a memorial service (and burial if possible). Children can plan or assist with planning and carrying out the service. Think of funerals you have attended for human loved ones with flowers, a eulogy, some remembrances, prayer, etc., and use those to make plans. Invite family and friends.

3. Create a memento with or for your child such as a plaster of the pet's paw, a painting, or a photograph.

4. Keep photos visible or close-by of the deceased pet to talk about with children. "Remember when Maxie dug a hole under the fence and ran away? She loved to go exploring!" And, "We're gonna' miss her waking us up every morning to go for a walk."

5. Will you keep the pet's cremains visible to your children? My grand-dog "Brooks'" cremains sat on the coffee table in a little box with a cross on top where he was always in sight until Lyndsay decided it was time to move him to a safer place. It was agreed to keep him visible in a glass cabinet and bring him out on special occasions. She allowed her children to make the decision but you have to decide how practical it will be to keep your pet's cremains.

6. Give children (and you, too) time to mourn before getting an-

other pet. "Sit" with these feelings of loss for a while before bringing a new pet home.

7. Include your children. Author Bob Deits tells us, "When a new pet is acquired, let the child be part of the process."[7]

8. For pets who are in severe decline, you may find it difficult to decide when it is time to say goodbye. Try using a scale such as Dr. Alice Villalobos', *Assess Your Pet: Is it time to Say Goodbye?*[8] The link can be found in the Notes section at the end of this book.

-15-
Children's Tears Are Sacred

*There is sacredness in tears. They are not the mark
of weakness but of power. They speak more
eloquently than ten thousand tongues.*
—WASHINGTON IRVING

Sometimes words just aren't enough. When children face extreme loss, tears may be the only thing that can help express grief. Crying may be their superpower! Tears can be the closest thing to connecting and communicating during unspeakable loss. Crying may be the best way for children to call attention to their pain when grieving, and to give themselves comfort.

Tears also announce that children need us, a way to let us know they are suffering, and can serve as a verbal alarm or a 911 to alert us to come now. Kids need us to allow and to encourage them to grieve with tears, and to know that crying is OK. They need to know that we understand why they need to cry, and that their tears are sacred.

Why Crying is Good For Children

There's goodness in crying. For example, the following Psalm written by King David tells us, "Those who sow with tears will reap with songs of joy. Those who go out weeping, carrying seed to sow, will return with songs of joy, carrying sheaves with them" (Psalm

126:5-6).

There's also a physical and emotional aspect to the goodness of crying. Think of emotions as little bits of steam that must "get out" and the more kids stuff them down, the worse it becomes. It is well established that tears are normal and they are one of the healthiest ways to express emotions. But our society doesn't always agree.

We may hear the "old tapes" that keep playing from growing up in cultures where crying is showing weakness, or being out of control. We fall back on the old adage, "Big boys (and girls) don't cry," or, we use idioms like, "There's no room for those crocodile tears," and, "Crying the blues won't change anything." And what about, "There's no use crying over spilt milk." And my all-time least favorite —"Stop crying like a baby." My background in child development often causes me to find that one challenging. There's nothing like calling a kid a baby to lower their self-esteem even more, especially in a vulnerable state of grief.

But seriously, if crying helps kids regulate emotions, then it just makes sense anything that can help them self-soothe or initiate calm should be welcomed during times of grief. Right? Then why is crying so often taboo in our society?

The Taboo of Crying

Crying may be just the right emotion to move kids off center, or even forward in grief. An "outburst" of emotion is really a "burst" of pent-up feelings that needs to be expelled, or even exploded. But when children cry, it can bring an added layer to our own grief, especially when we are barely hanging on.

So, if crying is such a natural part us, why is it still taboo in many cultures or societies to cry when grieving? Here a few more sayings from my southern US culture: "Be brave." "Don't let them see you cry." "You have to be strong for the other kids (or your mom, or your sister)." "Don't be a Sissie." "Be a man." And, "Cowboy up." Do any of these sound familiar? Some parents feel that when children cry over loss, it is a reflection of their parenting as in, "Why can't you control your children?"

Fear of what others will think drives us to be less tolerant of crying as it can make children appear to be less than "grown up." Where did this come from? Has this been continued from the Middle Ages where kids were portrayed as miniature adults and expected to behave like adults? It seems the more stoic children are, the higher regard they have in the court of public approval. And it's not just boys. Even Fergie and Frankie Valli and The Four Seasons wrote songs like, "Big Girls Don't Cry!"

So why do we cling to the "taboo" ways our parents and our parent's parents (and so on) dealt with crying? It seems these parenting imperfections, "Achilles heels" or weaknesses, filter down through lifetimes and generations of parenting. Crying is often seen as distasteful, disruptive, and interruptive to our "busyness" or our own grieving. After all, we don't want others to see us cry.

What to Do?

What if it's just a matter of not knowing what to do when children cry? We hurt when they hurt; we feel helpless and hopeless when we don't know how to protect them from loss. Or, as I mentioned above, we don't want to look like "bad parents." Death and dying bring a whole host of defenseless options. They literally bring us to our "knees tears," you know, those deepest emotions that require prayer beyond measure. The ones that overwhelm us and make us feel completely defeated.

Exposure as an incompetent or weak parent is scary and an imminent threat to our "parent of the year" nomination. I'm saying it again. Parenting is just so darned hard, even in the best of times.

If I haven't convinced you by now that crying should not be taboo for grieving children, maybe there can be a special grace given during a time of grief that would lift the taboo and allow them to cry without reproach. And not just for kids!

Loving Without Conditions

But what we cannot do, especially when children are grieving, is to send a message that, *It's great to be with you when you're happy, but not when you cry. Not when you are sad.* Instead, we encourage children to let the tears flow in a natural, ordinary way.

I'm sure you already know that another really hard part of parenting is to love unconditionally, the kind of love where there are no strings attached, no "If you do it my way, then I can love you." Loving without conditions is loving without judgment, without fear. It's allowing our children to unfold into who they are and embracing their tears while they are grieving.

Unconditional love is also called compassionate or agape love. It is love that you offer freely without expectations. Think about this. In his book *Love Without Conditions*, Paul Ferrini shares that loving others unconditionally begins with loving ourselves unconditionally.[1]

Physical Benefits of Emotional Tears

There's also a science to crying. Along with emotional benefits there are also physical benefits of tears. A "good cry," and we all know what that is, releases oxytocin endorphins that act as mood-enhancers and make us feel better. Emotional tension and then release gives a sense of calm after crying. And we all need a mood lift during a time that sees us at our lowest—literally in anguish and, figuratively in emotional pain.

But tears do something else. They contain stress hormones, giving the body a way to push out the stress as it builds up unwanted chemicals, washing away our pain and sorrow. This phenom alone should send us straight to our "cry rooms." One would think this discovery could pave the way for crying to be not only accepted but expected.

However, not all tears are created equal. Dr. Juan Murube, researcher and ophthalmologist, has helped unravel the mystery of tears. He found different experiences bring different kinds of tears. For example, *reflex* or eye irritant tears are very different than tears that flow out of sadness. Irritant tears don't contain all the "magic" released from crying *psycho-emotional* tears. When children get anything foreign such as dirt or an eyelash in an eye, these tears are more of a reflex action to protect the eyes, often called "onion tears."

However, as beneficial as reflex tears are, they don't provide the same emotional protection as grief tears. Dr. Murube claims from personal research studies that weeping tears "help eliminate chemical substances in the blood that are produced during states of unhappiness."[2]

Tear ducts operate as sort of a drain valve for the poisonous toxins created during stress, and times when emotional tensions are high such as during periods of grief. When children suppress those tears, they close a gateway to wellbeing.

Of course there's a limit to how much your child should cry. Let's return to our litmus test of normal, typical grief vs. the red flags that tell us a child may need professional assistance. The intensity of emotion (in this instance crying), and length of time a behavior has occurred are our best gauges for bringing attention to a crying child.

As challenging as it will be to let our grieving children's tears make them feel better, sometimes nothing or no one else can. We will have to trust the sacredness of those tears.

❧Strategies☙

1. Crying may be a child's superpower when grieving. Asking them to "be strong and brave" rather than allowing them to be vulnerable can be harmful as it requires them to wall back their tears until finally the dam breaks.

2. Offer a space for kids to cry, to unbottle these feelings and talk about the loss, now and later. It is a place that is off limits to criticism or shaming from others.

3. Offer to sit with a child when crying. "Do you need some company?" Set a time limit if your time is limited. "I can sit with you for a little while, but you can take all the time you need after that."

4. Check out the picture book *Crying Is Like the Rain: A Story of Mindfulness and Feelings* by Heather Hawk Feinberg and Chamisa Kellogg.[3] This is a wonderful book comparing tears to rain, and how our emotions come and go like weather but should never be ignored.

5. Redirect children to help them re-center. After they have a good cry, offer to do something they like to do; take a walk, bake some cookies, play a game, kick a ball, or paint a picture with them.

~16~

Your Child's Grieving Style

*We as parents must be as wise as Solomon,
stronger than Samson, and as patient as Job.*
—Unknown

Since there is no right or wrong way to grieve, how can we provide direction to a child's grieving while creating an accepting environment that supports them? We can't protect them from the pain of losing a loved one, but we can provide a place where the healing process can begin. And if we know their grieving style, we may understand what they are going through a little better.

Understanding <u>how</u> children grieve is the first step in providing them with a positive surrounding in which to grieve. A lot of things may influence children's grief, including the relationships to the deceased or with the people around them.

If you're thinking, *Great, I just need to be a perfect parent to help my child through grief*—not to worry. Although there isn't a road map to get children from one point in the grieving process to another, or, a guidebook on loss with a one–size fits all approach, there's you. You are the one to recognize that each child is unique and individual, and requires different emotional tools to sail across the waters of grief and despair.

All people have three grieving styles says Martha (Marty) Tousley in her book, *Finding Your Way Through Grief*.[1] Some people are *intuitive* grievers, some are *dissonant* grievers, and some are *instrumental* grievers. Let's use these as an overlay to describe children's grief. But, we'll use them for information, not as labels or pigeonholes to put our children in, keeping a child's cognitive and emotional development in mind.

Intuitive Grief in Children

Does your child do everything out loud? Every emotion is visible, every feeling is known to us, every response requires big tears or loud laughter. And, is she hyper-sensitive to what seems like everything? If this sounds familiar, then your child may be an *Intuitive Griever*.

They feel very strong emotions that can be characterized as an open book, and their thoughts and actions often mirror one another in one word—extreme! We can see their grief as well as hear it. And, sharing is the key word that comes to mind for intuitive grief in children. They may share every feeling and emotion with anyone who will listen, or is in close proximity. Don't say you don't know any children who are intuitive grievers!

There's no disagreement that some of the outward behaviors of children expressing their grief may be more acceptable when done in private. But the key is to let them grieve out loud if needed— let them process the pain verbally in order to heal.

Dissonant Grief in Children

Let's talk about dissonant grief—the absence of harmony. I love this quote from Kenneth Doka and Terry Martin in their book, *Grieving Beyond Gender*. They write, "...dissonant grief emerges when someone's grief is naturally experienced and exposed, clashes with what they think is expected and what is acceptable."[2]

Children are *Dissonant Grievers* when they want to be someone else in the way they present themselves to others, although they feel totally opposite on the inside. This dissonance causes them to be out of harmony with the rest of us. These are the children who feel very strong emotions but for one reason or another such as family traditions and social or cultural habits, feel they aren't at liberty to act their true selves. They are in conflict. The more accepting we are of a child's dissonant grieving style, the more the child can overcome the struggle to hide it.

Instrumental Grief in Children

Then there's the *Instrumental Griever.* Your child may be an instrumental griever if she expresses her intellect over her heart and explains loss with accurate information and facts. If she appears uncaring or distant, don't misread the behavior as unconcerned or unemotional. We can't pretend to understand how she interprets loss; she has to figure this grief thing out without expectations from us. She takes the lead and manages it reasonably and responsibly with help, but not interference. This is how she approaches everything in life—with reason, facts, and truths, so why would grief be any different?

This is the child who will have so many questions about death, and what happens after we're gone. This is the child who searches for sensible and realistic answers. There's nothing instinctive or intuitive about the "Instrumental Griever." She wants to do things in response to her grief, such as making a memory journal or helping plan the funeral rather than "feeling" something. Our job is to be honest and answer her questions as best as we can and include her in as much decision making and planning as possible.

...

Without exception, those of us who are determined to accept the grieving styles of our children will be closer to acting in ways that safeguard their hearts and our own. We may find ourselves represented in the descriptions of grieving styles. We may find solace in knowing and understanding that children's grief comes in lots of different colors and shapes and sizes.

❧Strategies☙

1. Reflect on *intuitive, dissonant, and instrumental* grieving. Can you identify the characteristics of one or more in your child? Use these types of grieving as guideposts to help grieving children, knowing that everyone goes through lots of different emotions on their grief journey, depending upon their age and stage of cognitive and emotional development. Let's recap:

    Intuitive: Displays big emotions verbally and with crying.

    Dissonant: Feels one way but acts another.

    Instrumental: Is thoughtful, asks questions, attempts to "figure things out" rather than respond emotionally. May even appear distant, uncaring.

2. Embrace (not judge) a child's style of grief. What's the first step you can take to become more accepting? For example, allow him to embrace his feelings, as well as encourage others to give him space and time to cry, if necessary. Or, allow him to ask as many questions as needed.

3. How does your child's grief compare to yours or those around her? Sometimes, recognizing or acknowledging grief is the first step in accepting it or learning to work with it.

-17-
When Grieving Children Act Out

*Whereas adults internalize their feelings,
children act them out.*

—UNKNOWN

Wouldn't it be great if children didn't need our attention when we need to give it to ourselves the most? It's hard to understand why they act out during the toughest moments, during grief so painful that we don't even know if we can survive until tomorrow. But they have emotions such as anxiety, sadness, anger, worry, and fear without exception, just like we do.

Someone once wrote that behind every behavior is a feeling and we know that behind every feeling is a need for expression. These may be in ways that are contrary or opposite of what we need in moments of despair. But did you know kids will act out to cover up their emotional pain?

The acting out behavior is just the "visible" feeling of the disguised or invisible emotion, displayed in acting-out behaviors such as losing control, using loud voices, constant anger over big and small things, regressive behaviors where they act like younger children, and using physical and verbal aggression without provocation.

Remember, children can become angriest, take the most risk or practice the riskiest behavior with the ones they love the most. It appears they take the most emotional risks with those whom they feel the most attached and connected. And that's us!

Acting Out as Typical Behavior

It's an error on our part to think that acting out is always a negative behavior when it's typical for children experiencing the death and/or dying of a loved one. If we know how children develop, expecting them to know how to feel and act in these unhappy times can be unrealistic. But with understanding and gentle guidance, there's hope.

Anxiety can fuel behaviors that are out of the ordinary, and worry causes children to act in unfamiliar ways. They get sidetracked with their grief and often approach the death of a loved one by worrying about their own death or the deaths of others.

While we can't guarantee the future for our kids, we are mindful as we respond to their anxiety openly and honestly, such as, "I will do everything that I can to keep you safe (or someone else)."

Let this simmer for a moment. Even infants may have behavior changes after a loss as they can't completely process it and certainly can't verbalize their emotions. They experience death as separation and abandonment, so their moods and wellbeing will be compromised, depending on how close they were to the deceased. Marked changes in behavior may be considered a kind of acting out, or deviating from their typical behavior. Toddlers are no exception.

Early preschoolers have language but may not have specific words to tell us how they feel, so they use behavior as expression. They may regress back to earlier behaviors that accompanied their development, either a few months or a few years ago. I'll repeat. Responses like, "Stop acting like a baby," and "Show us what a big girl you can be," are challenging in the throes of regressive behavior, as children often need our help to stop acting like a baby.

Try not to take it personally or let it "stick." Apply more Teflon coating to your heart so your child's "acting out" grief can slide off and leave you with a clean slate heart, ready for the next challenge. I think we can all agree with author Dr. Bob Deits—"Whereas adults internalize their feelings, children act them out."[1] Without exception, those of us who are determined to accept the grieving styles of our children will be closer to acting in ways that safeguard their hearts and our own.

Grief and Pretend Play

Children will often engage in pretend play that involves death and dying. They draw from their understanding of death and may even replay or "pretend play" the actual death of their loved ones. This is all part of appropriate child development, based on their ages and stages of cognitive, language, social, and emotional development. As a matter of fact, we know that those who learn healthy ways to act out those feelings are less likely to display behavioral problems and get through these tough times of loss.

But those who haven't learned to manage or cope with what I call big feelings that come with big sadness, can act out in ways that shout, "Help us!" Their need for help to manage their emotions is as necessary as needing food when they are hungry or medicine when they are sick. If you see that they are "stuck" in the death play of a loved one, or even an event they heard about such as a school shooting, pay close attention. Again, how long it occurs, how intense their play becomes, and how often they recreate the death scenario may be prompts to intervene and seek help.

...

What else can we do when they act out during this most difficult time? Take a look at the strategies below and try more than one.

❧Strategies☙

1. Acknowledge children's emotions rather than trying to squelch their feelings or rid them altogether. Give children your intentional, individual, and uninterrupted attention when needed. Just becoming aware can be the first step.

2. Use an imaginary feelings thermometer. "Show me how big (or hot) your feelings are right now." "How can you make them get smaller or cool down?"

3. Blow bubbles from a bottle to release pent up feelings. Also, blowing pretend bubbles with younger children can release stress induced anxiety. "Let's blow a really big bubble and watch it float away." "Now let's blow a middle-sized bubble."

4. Use phrases like these to show that you understand and embrace their feelings of grief. "I can see you are using your loudest voice." "What's a different way to show how angry you are your Papa died?" "I'm feeling angry too, so let's write our angry words down on paper." And, "I feel angry too, but I can't let you hit your sister" (or curse etc.).

5. Have children take a break, or time away, if just for a moment to allow them to calm down alone, or with just you or another significant person. This can replace the need for "time out." You are with them on this grief journey. Sometimes going on an errand with you is all it takes to stop the acting out behavior and allow them to re-frame or re-center with a more positive one.

6. Go for a drive in the car. I have found children are great at talking when there is silence—just the two of you. Prepare the ride without any other noises or interference such as phones or radios. "Let's not turn on the music today. What can we talk

about?"

7. Be proactive! Before you break the news of loss, say, "I'm going to tell you something that will cause you to have some pretty big feelings. If you feel out of control, I'm here to help."

8. Look for patterns for when grieving children act out the most. Is it when they feel you are not available to them because of so many details and arrangements to be made? Is it when you are most grieved or when you try to talk to them or get them to talk about grief? Is it a certain time of day such as getting up in the morning or bedtime? Maybe that's the time they miss their loved one the most. Are there triggers? Once you identify a trigger, you can be better prepared and take action.

9. Start by drawing a feeling that you are having, using any symbol or stick figure that comes to mind. Then have the child add to your drawing. Some kids may want to skip this step and make their own drawing. For example, one child drew a tornado to show how his feelings were so explosive. Another child drew a portrait of his family and then colored over it with a black crayon. Save any drawings that cause alarm and seek professional help as soon as possible.

10. Using a feelings chart, teach children to name any feeling, especially anger, and not just the ones related to grief. Identifying feelings is the first step in managing them.

11. Check in with children, even older ones. They want you to, even if they act like they don't, and even if they refuse to talk. Use a timer and tell them a number of minutes that you can spare. Don't make the conversation about death and dying unless they bring it up. All feelings are the same for them. They don't parcel out the grief feelings and circumvent their feel-

ings about everything else. Attention spans are much shorter in younger children, so prepare for brief check-ins unless they keep the conversation going.

12. It's hard I know, but schedule time to be with children when they are grief angry! Play a game. Go outside and look for flowers, or butterflies, or anything else. Take a walk around the block or down the road. This can provide enough space and time for them to regain their calm. Walks provide great opportunities for discussion when we let children take the lead in the conversation. It's hard to be quiet and just listen, but it does wonders for kids to know that the "talking stick" is theirs to use.

13. Find a church or community grief group for your children as it can work both ways; they can help others, too. Many children experience some of the same feelings and will share with one another things they won't share with us.

14. Get help from their teachers. Find a school grief support group, or, professional help in a play therapist or grief counselor who specializes in children's grief and behavior. Work with the professional. Again, you are the first responder and even if you seek outside professional help, what you do daily will be as important as professional advice.

...

Note: There's more about children acting out as well as how to know when it is time to refer them to a play therapist or children's counselor in Chapter 47, "Seeking Help for Your Child."

~18~

How Culture Shapes the Way We Grieve

The soul takes nothing with her to the next world but her education and her culture.
—PLATO

I can know everything about talking with children about death and dying, but if I don't consider their own individual cultures, there's something missing. I've missed the mark. All cultures have variations in their customs surrounding death, along with their own distinct practices and patterns. And, children are a huge part of this. Depending on habits, lifestyle, and social mores, there are many different approaches to death and dying where we help children with mourning and grief.

I find such insight in what James Gire from the Virginia Military Institute wrote: "Regardless of how or where we are born, what unites people of all cultures is the fact everyone eventually dies."[1] This very matter of fact, this is what happens way of looking at death is a blueprint for the rest of us as we guide our children.

But then, James provides a major distinction between cultures. He writes, "However, cultures vary in how they conceptualize death and what happens when a person dies." With this in mind, let's take a closer look at how culture shapes the way we grieve.

Death, Children and Culture

During the mourning process, children play different roles. Sometimes they are spectators, sometimes participants, and sometimes they are both, depending on the customs and beliefs of their unique culture. While some cultures focus on simple mourning rituals and customs to process and express grief, others practice elaborate customary celebrations where children are front and center.

How the dead are treated, as in family get-togethers, funeral planning, and additional cultural variations may change over time. But many cultures continue the same practices for generations, even centuries.

Take researcher Juanita Jacob for example. She visited with Maori parents in New Zealand regarding their views on talking about death and dying with children. Dr. Jacob found this indigenous tribe does not hide death from their children; in fact, they include them in *"tangi"* or death rituals by talking with them in very "open and age relevant ways."[2] And, this may be the catch. They have lots of kinship networks and support—lots of their "village" helping!

Another example of a cultural phenomenon regarding children and death is the "Day of the Dead" or *Dia de Los Muertos*.[3] In Mexico and the US as well as other places, children along with families, friends, schoolmates, and communities celebrate this important cultural ritual. It is blended with *All Soul's Day*, a Catholic holiday each November 1st and 2nd, but never to be confused with Halloween. It's just a coincidence these are celebrated around the same time each year.

Day of the Dead practices include the deceased being remembered by their loved ones who gather to give support to what they believe—transitioning to the afterlife. It is a time to celebrate and commemorate loved ones, helping adults and children remember the dead with candlelit altars allowing spirits to find their way back to relatives. Children play a large role as they engage in activities such as parades, making special treats, and crafting brightly painted Papier-mâché (pap-yay mash-ay) or as we say in Texas, "paper mashay," skeletons.

One thing to remember about children and culture is they often adapt and change more readily than adults. They embrace rituals and routines that ultimately make up our cultures.

Children are often surrounded by popular culture known as urban or "street culture" in their day-to-day lives such as block parties and street dances, free styling and marketplaces. Children participate in street sports such as jumping rope, hopscotch, skateboarding and streetball where playing outside for long periods of time is common.

They may also be a part of "high culture" which is the opposite of street culture and includes the arts of any given culture accepted and valued by the elites. These were once considered a subculture of the higher class.

I think all of us can appreciate the arts, even if in limited amounts, if given the exposure or experiences that value the arts. But it seems children are exposed to these in varying degrees as some have more interactions with street culture than high culture/the arts (literature, classical music, etc.). Just as some are exposed to more elaborate death celebrations such as "Day of the Dead" with hundreds if not thousands of people, many children experience very simple burials or funerals with only close family and friends. But neither type of culture is more valuable than the other. Both bring a richness to the lives of children.

Culture as Legacy

The Day of the Dead is just one culture highlighted here, due to its popularity. But there are so many others that are rooted in small towns and big cities, posing as cultures and subcultures. The variations are vast and equally important. But there are too many to write about in this book, and I apologize if I do not recognize yours. So, take a moment to reflect on children and your particular culture and celebrations or commemorations of death.

Add this ingredient to the cultural stew. Author Sandra Smidt talks about how the passing on of values and beliefs is seen as a way of handing a legacy to children in her book *The Developing Child in the 21st Century*. "It may help children make sense of life and death and develop relationships with one another."[4]

I interpret this as no matter how same or different our cultures are, children are enriched by being allowed, if not encouraged to participate in their own, as well as other cultures. We have been called a "melting pot" in this country because we have lots of cross cultures, mixed cultures, mono-cultures and multi-cultures which include death and dying experiences. And within each culture, children figure out their places, their roles and their responsibilities by watching us and engaging in customs and rituals. Take pride in participating with your children in those that are not only your legacies, but will also continue on as legacies of your children.

Cheryl's Story

Dr. Cheryl Mixon is a long-time acquaintance, early childhood educator and specialist from Louisiana with an extensive background in teaching about young children. She shared her thoughts and experiences on Black children and the southern Black culture in the US regarding death and dying. "Black children are most often included and welcomed at death events, but play less of a role in planning the rituals and making presentations."[5]

For example, she continued, "Black children often accompany

their parents to attend the wake, or get together with family in the days leading up to the funeral. In addition, they often attend funerals and the "repast" afterwards, usually back at the church where the funeral was held." I am embarrassed that I was unfamiliar with the word *repast*, and I found that it has Latin roots and simply means "to eat." But you probably knew that already!

Cheryl talked about the huge family gatherings when a loved one dies, and the time from death to burial can last one to two weeks. When her dad died, her mom bought him a new suit and a matching dress for herself. "The days before the funeral were filled with making arrangements, family coming, making a program for the funeral, lots of visiting where stories were shared about Dad, and lots of laughter and tears," says Cheryl.

She also shared that traditionally, in addition to the minister, about five people typically speak at the funeral which include family and friends. "The funeral can last from an hour and a half to two hours where the preacher provides the eulogy and sermon."

I thought about Cheryl's description of typical funerals in her culture, and was particularly struck by a statement that her mom made: "Everyone becomes comfortable with the loss."

As a child grieves, he may have questions about things he is experiencing. I asked Cheryl for an example of how children process death in her culture and she did not disappoint. In describing how her very spiritual family talks with children about the deceased, Cheryl shared, "The loved one is in Heaven always looking down, checking on us. He stays in our hearts. He's in a better place with Jesus." After Cheryl's dad died, her three-year-old niece Melanie asked, "Is Papaw in Heaven?" "Why didn't he take his truck?" Exactly! This integration of death with life in Cheryl's culture that includes children is a model for all of us.

"A Tree Without Roots"

Children should never feel their culture should grieve exactly the same as others, or that one type of grieving is better than another. As long as they are closely knitted within a family, a community, a village, or a tribe, children will have much more opportunity to grieve well. I am moved by what the late Marcus Garvey famously wrote: "A people without the knowledge of their past history, origin, and culture is like a tree without roots."[6]

Being different is what makes us unique and strong, even in grief. According to James Gire, "In whatever form they may take within a given culture, funeral and burial rituals are ways that each society tries to help the bereaved with the death of a loved one."[7]

You can help develop a sense of belongingness in children, using culture as the foundation, by teaching and celebrating your own culture. If children come from blended cultures, find ways for them to experience both (or all) cultures. They can't be "overexposed" if love and sincerity are at the core of the experiences. In truth, exposing children to their cultures provides the roots / the knowledge that Garvey refers to.

Your child discovers their cultural connections to not only the deceased, but also to the living. Connecting with their ethnic roots brings kids closer to family, and brings understanding of customs such as why the deceased wear certain clothing when buried, why the funeral service was filled with hymns and singing or prayers and chants, or why the family gathered after the funeral to share a meal in the memory of their loved one.

When I visited with my friend Dr. Tamara Banks, a child development specialist who is Black, about culture and funerals, she shared with laughter, "We aren't afraid to order color-coded matching T-shirts for everyone to wear at the funeral, or even wait a week until everyone can come, or even fly in for the funeral. We want everyone there!"[8]

When attending funerals or other activities for people outside your child's culture, consider how embracing diversity in others is a catalyst to accepting others, and building community. We have to guard against anything that will prevent our children from grieving well, within their own cultural values and provide experiences that help them understand the grief of others.

❧Strategies☙

1. Encourage children to embrace traditions that exist around their own cultures regarding death and dying. Also, discover different cultures of friends and family members. These will differ from culture to culture.

2. Help children replace words about other cultures such as "odd" or "weird" with words such as "unfamiliar" or "new." These cultural differences give children a sense of how we are all alike in some ways and different in other ways.

3. Create a sense of cultural belongingness for your child as you explain ways to connect to his family's culture and how it defines us as human beings. For example, tell stories about the deceased, cook a favorite recipe, read favorite poems and books about their culture, and travel to places that were important to them. These are ways to shepherd your child's heritage or cultural connections into the present as well as the future.

-19-
Talking About School Shootings

School should be their happy place, a place where children feel safe. But, every time we have a school tragedy involving guns, children feel less safe. There's a new tear in their safety net. The news rockets through our communities as well as the nation, and every person touched by these horrific acts of gun violence is left with sadness and differing levels of grief. Those closest to the event experience trauma they've never known before while those of us who are onlookers struggle to understand how it could happen again.

Did you know that in America, children are more likely to die by guns than anything else? But when it happens at their own school, additional suffering and heartbreak is eminent. And even if they weren't directly impacted, in other words the shooter did not enter their classroom, they can be traumatized by the sounds of gunshots and screaming peers and teachers. Stay put drills, lock-down practices and fear producing conversations can keep children on high alert, especially those who are the most sensitive to trauma and stress.

But, before we begin conversations about death related to gun violence in schools, we self-check our own wellness of the heart. Gun violence is not an easy topic to talk about, so we often find challenges to keep the message from getting hijacked by emotions.

Be the Guardian of Your Heart!

School shootings impact our own mental health as well as our children's. Turning down our emotional volume to protect ourselves when our stress reactions are high is one key to helping children survive tragedy. But, could it be that unless kids are directly impacted, adults tend to worry more about school shootings than most children? Or, that our children's responses could be directly tied to our own? Dr. Jamie Howard of the Child Mind Institute thinks so.[1] He tells us it is partially due to the egocentric nature of children and that their reactions are related to their ages and stage of development. Rachel Ehmke in that same article calls it, "developmental selfishness, a quality that often protects younger children from the kind of anxiety that the adults around them are experiencing."[2] We can take that as our cue.

You become the guardian of your heart as you weave a sense of calm, "enoughness" into your conversations with others and then with children, directly or indirectly. Intentionally take care of you first, as you focus on your own reactions to the news before talking with children. By giving yourself grace, you ease into processing this horrible event; you are taking care of you in order to take care of your children.

But, I get it! In most instances, we all have a need to discuss the shooting with others, or consume all the news we can to get a sense of why and how this could be happening (again). And that's okay. Answers to this kind of tragedy may come later, if they come at all. Unfortunately, over the years solutions have been slow to surface.

In being your own guardian, it's important to beware of "doom-scrolling," or spending lots of time binging on the news of the school shooting. We live in a time where we think the more we know, the more we feel in control, but that is often not the case. Regardless the reason, over consumption of news can not only emotionally and sometimes physically harm us, it can also harm our children. Think about it like this. If our hearts were a scale, when we consume unpleasant or even stressful information, we continue to tip the negative side (unwellness) of the scale, getting it out of balance.

When we consume positive information, our heart scales will remain steady, balanced. For example, making our next move, developing a plan to keep children safe, and contributing to the area where a school shooting occurred are ways in which we tip our scale to the positive side. And, of course we have survived as a species because we worry; we act on our concerns. But, we have also survived because we have the ability to love, care about one another, activate empathy, and put compassion into action in keeping ourselves and especially our children safe.

Waymakers and Light Bearers!

If you don't get the answers that you seek about school shootings, seek them anyway. Seek uprightness; get back to your emotional equilibrium that showcases your most resilient self. Children will turn to you as their source of strength. Remember, you are their first responders, their way makers and light bearers and they look to you for guidance. Enduring the unthinkable makes you the bellwether, the one who takes control and shows the way to others who are grieving.

I love what Brene´ Brown says about surviving trauma in her book, *The Gifts of Imperfection*: "...having a sense of purpose, meaning, and perspective in our lives allows us to develop understanding and move forward. Without it is easy to lose hope, numb our emotions, or become overwhelmed by our circumstances."[3] In a sense she is reminding us to return to our North Star—our Stella Polaris, to go back to our purpose or create a new one which includes providing children with a new set of grief tools. The old tools for talking about death and dying may not work to explain school massacres. So how do we talk to children?

Talking With Kids About School Shootings

Talking with children will be much different for those who were actually present versus those who heard about the school shooting. And, each child's emotional hardiness aka resilience will be a key factor in how well they bounce back after such tragedy.

With at least one patient, kind, and caring adult alongside them, each child should experience a "new normal" after a school shooting. If we can't be that adult, then we must find someone who can. That new normal is not a broken, chipped or cracked normal. It is reconciling the trauma with the need to move forward when they are ready. To me, new normal means remembering the traumatic event, but recasting or shaping it into our now—finding a place for it to "be" but not overtaking the whole of us.

We want children to hear news about school shootings from us (parents), or someone else they trust (teachers and caregivers). Having that safe place to talk, a sort of drop everything and talk (DEAT) space, or taking an immediate timeout to intentionally address their remembrances as well as fears is essential. It will be the cornerstone of taking action and moving on to the next phase—the next step toward emotional wellbeing.

Depending on how involved children were, talking about it with them will come from different perspectives—different outlooks. Taking their point of view to heart is a key component of fostering "good grief." Let's take a look at the ways children can be affected by school shootings.

Survivors

The survivors—these are the children who were there. They were possibly injured and/or witnessed the shootings. They tell stories of hiding and covering their ears from gunshots and their eyes from seeing teachers and classmates covered in blood (or worse). Because they survived, Doctors Schonfeld and Demaria caution us, "Children often feel guilt or shame associated with a school shooting, even when they have no objective reason to feel responsible."[4] They may feel guilt that they could not save their friends and teachers. But there's also a sort of relief/guilt that is felt when something happened to others but didn't happen to us.

The surviving children are the most impacted and need the most caring adults giving personal and professional help. Having classmates and teachers injured or killed by a school shooter can have everlasting effects and the recovery can be long and painful, both physically and mentally. There will be hills and valleys in the recovery, spikes in pain and depression and fear. It will take the whole village and, in this instance, the whole country to help them along this grief journey. They must not be forgotten!

The Fringe Survivors

Fringe survivors are the children who were there but did not directly witness the shooting. They have a liminal exposure to the violence, not quite in and not quite out. They heard gunshots down the hall or across the playground and then were put on lock down /shelter in place. The trauma of not knowing if they would be next has been well documented and is severe and long-lasting.

Children who survived the attack in Uvalde, Texas at Robb Elementary talked about continuing nightmares and the possibility of the shooter returning, bursting into their own classrooms once they returned to school. Fear often grips fringe survivors after surviving such traumatic events.

Children on the Outskirts

There are children who are on the outskirts, who live in the community and beyond and know someone who survived. They may have connections through others who go to that school or know someone who knows someone. These are the siblings, cousins, peers, and friends. Or maybe they have a connection to the school. They were at that very school last year or in years past and can visualize where it happened, the very hallway and classroom.

Children Who are Curious

And finally, there are children who have that etic, outsider perspective. They weren't directly impacted in any way, but are curious as they hear about the shooting from the news, social media, parents, and others. These children may internalize the shooting, imagining if it happened to them, or try to perspective take—feeling as those directly impacted may feel. Younger or less egocentric children may not experience emotion but will take their cues from the adults who care for them.

Children who are sensitive but curious/interested may have more empathy for those who were there and even try to understand what others are feeling, within their own frame of reference, or try to place themselves there. And, there are children who are curious, wanting to hear about the shootings but then activate their "developmental selfishness" to protect their own wellbeing—to guard their hearts. Curiosity can be fickle.

No matter how they were affected by a school shooting, children's mental health can be impacted, immediately after the shooting and in the years to come. Let's keep talking with them!

Different Ages, Different Talks with Children

Young school age children will most likely do more talking than listening and that's a perfect way for them to express their feelings, while letting us know how they are feeling. Older school age children will very often talk to their peers, use social media to get their information, and check in with you to verify or validate what they've heard. By simply asking, "What have you heard?" you can start the conversation to get a sense of their knowledge and perspective. Go from there.

Children who witnessed the shooting will require different conversations. As parents, teachers, and care providers, use open-ended questions and statements such as "What happened was really scary." "Do you want to talk about it?" Or, "What do you want us to know about what happened to you?" Know that sometimes talk isn't necessary. Connections don't always have to be verbal with children. Hugs or just being with them will often suffice.

Middle Ground

We can read any story of a child who witnessed a school shooting and our hearts become full. We do our best from the outside looking in to begin to understand their fear and their pain. And yet I struggle to write about this topic without sounding like I am minimizing how traumatic any school shooting can be, especially to the children, teachers, and parents who were there.

I feel compelled to share information that moves forward the conversation about school safety, and at the same time, it is not my intent in any way to appear indifferent to the heartbreak of school shooting survivors. Of course we will talk with kids about school shootings, but at the same time, we have to find ways to lessen the fear of going to school in America's classrooms. Again, we have to find "middle ground," continuing (if not beginning) the conversation.

As children hear conversations, it must be confusing and challenging all at the same time, getting different versions of what to do next. Some kids hear adults blame school shootings on mental health issues of the shooters and how school active shooter drills, locked classroom doors, armed guards patrolling schools, and more guns are the answer, even to the extent of arming their classroom teachers.

Other children hear adults who believe that removing mass shooters' guns of choice, automatic and semi-automatic weapons, from access are necessary to ensure school safety, with the argument made for stricter background checks and higher ages to purchase guns legally.

Children may also hear talk of taking our 2nd Amendment rights as a driving force behind keeping automatic and semi-automatic weapons available to those as young as teenagers (18 and 19-year-olds). I frequently hear, "Guns don't kill people; people kill people with guns." On the flip side, there are claims that the 2nd Amendment was written at a time when the right to bear arms was about forming militias to protect Americans, not for personal use with rifles meant for war. Imagine how confusing these conversations can be for kids. We have to find middle ground!

Kimberly Mata-Rubio's ten-year-old daughter Lexi was one of 19 children and two teachers killed at Robb Elementary in Uvalde, Texas, in May of 2022. A lone gunman with a legally purchased AR-15-style rifle committed the massacre. He turned 18 just days before the shooting. Kimberly never thought she would become an activist for gun law revision. But she found herself doing just that. On the steps of the US Capitol, she said, "What if that Uvalde teenager had never been able to get his hands on an AR-15-style rifle in the first place."[5] One can make the argument that yes, it takes people to kill people with guns, but if the guns aren't readily available, killings can't occur in that manner. It's a debate that we will continue to have again and again. Someone wrote recently, "I'm a gun owner my whole life. I'm not advocating to take away guns, just that gun." Middle ground.

For sure, this is a very volatile and prolific topic of discussion in the US and people argue their beliefs (on both sides) passionately. But here's where these discussions should not be party-line, religious, or constitutionally driven. <u>No child should be afraid to be at school</u>.

We have to keep conversations with kids about school shootings in perspective. James Alan Fox is a criminologist at Northeastern University and he reminds us that hundreds of children die every year in so many other acts of gun violence outside of schools, as well as drownings and vehicle accidents. These contribute to many more deaths than there are in school shootings. James writes that due to the number of child drownings versus the number of children killed in school shootings, "We need lifeguards at pools more than armed guards at schools."[6]

Whatever you believe, no matter which side you take on school shootings and gun violence, it is necessary that we become aware of children's developmental needs and understandings. It is critical that we consider their ages and stages of development when we have conversations either with children or in their presence. Creating a veil of safety where children can focus on play and learning must be our focus in tandem with keeping them safe. That's also "middle ground!"

How School Shootings Impact a Child's Mental Health

Children respond to trauma they have witnessed in all kinds of ways. So, let's take a look at kids' stress related issues of school shootings from a child development perspective. I've already mentioned how some children live out loud, where every feeling and emotion is known, but we know children who may not have any observable signs of distress or trauma that may go undetected. It is their way of coping. Both kinds of reactions to stress have to be on our radars. In fact, if you parent more than one child, it is highly possible you are witness to both types of reactions.

But what about children who are the outside listeners, especially the younger ones, who are the unconcerned? They are the ones who would not know about school shootings were it not for parents discussing them, and seeing it on TV over and over.

There is no reason to cause undue stress to children. The American Academy of Pediatrics' position is that there is no need to share the news of school shootings with children if it did not directly affect them and they are not at risk of hearing it from others on social media or TV. I think the key words here are "at risk." And, younger children will be less tuned in to the news than older ones. You know—if it didn't happen to them, it didn't happen!

When people like David Osher talk, I try to listen. He is a school safety expert with the American Institutes for Research and says we must make the distinction between security and safety. Security is the state of feeling protected against <u>intentional</u> threats, and safety is protection against <u>unintentional</u> hazards. He writes, "Things I might do to make a school very, very physically safe may make students feel less safe, such as having active shooter drills, arming teachers, and keeping all doors locked, etc." On the extreme side of the discussion, Osher gives a compelling argument that, "We could create the equivalent of a fallout shelter for students to attend, but would we want to?" He adds, "School shootings are still very rare, and shouldn't be our only concern."[7] This too, is all part of finding that middle ground!

Listening to Play Therapists and School Counselors

I turned to my friend and colleague/play therapist Dr. Pedro Blanco for his perspective on school shootings. He is a respected researcher, professor, and licensed professional counselor. I've known Dr. Blanco (P. J.) for a long time and have been in awe of his research with school aged children. When we talked about school shootings, he shared with me his concerns about the mental well-being of children and school insecurity.

With his permission, I am including part of that conversation below. He is offering one possible solution to the problem.

Most recently in our work in the school setting, we have noticed some dramatic shifts in the schools. There is an increased hyper-vigilance... many students, parents, teachers, and administrators enter the school each morning feeling less secure. The schools no longer feel as safe as they once did and that is a direct result of the increased school shootings and massacres highlighted in the United States. Many schools now have added additional safety features such as active shooter drills, all doors always locked, and additional security officers.

He continued, *While the intention of these inclusions is a preventative measure and to have children feel more secure in the school, it often sends the message no place is safe. It is because of this that I strongly advocate for continued use of services in the school setting to give the child a place to process those fears and help alleviate the reality that the world can be unpredictable.*[8]

Why not take Dr. Blanco's suggestion to heart and advocate for more school counselors in the aftermath of these shootings, to teach children problem solving and emotional skill building? Anything that we can do to possibly prevent a child from growing up and feeling the need to kill is certainly worth a try. Especially if we are looking at increasing government budgets to include acquiring funds to hire more security. It doesn't have to be one or the other.

But, you want to know something scary? When we fail to recognize the importance of supporting children in all ways in school settings, we set ourselves up for a continuation of what many schools have become—school insecure and "school hardened."

Littleton, Colorado school counselor Sandy Austin knows! In a *Good Morning America* article where she speaks of Robb Elementary in Uvalde, she cautions us that security plans and school safety are important, *but prior to a school shooting, we must turn to the mental health plan that every school should have in place. This includes ensuring teachers and staff know how to talk to students about the trauma they just suffered in a developmentally appropriate way and having extra counselors ready to help.*[9] Simply put, we have to recognize that each child is unique with different needs. If we get back to the basics of looking at kids with a child development lens, it may be what works for them individually as well as in groups.

And help is what is needed in order to be our focus in talking with children about school shootings. Our responsibility is to equip kids with the tools needed to insulate themselves from tragedy driven trauma, both now and in the future.

In the following strategies, as a teacher, parent, director, or provider, adapt each one to fit your environment or need

ᛋStrategiesᛌ

1. Listen…while riding in the car, at mealtime or bedtime, or during playtime. You may hear misinformation or mis-perceptions about a school shooting and now you will be better able to make gentle corrections. I find that younger children often broadcast information more than they ask questions.

2. Focus on what they are saying, rather than thinking ahead about your response, or how you feel about what they are say-

ing. Use responses such as, "This is what I heard (or read or believe) and it's different than what you are saying, but that's OK." Or, "I hear what you're saying; here's another way to think about it."

3. Provide reassurance now and in the days to come, as they process stress and grief very differently than adults. Home should be a safe zone where talk about the shooting is at a minimum unless they bring it up. Breaks from television/news are needed; keep answers or guidance to a minimum, only answering what is asked—in one sentence if possible. And then we pause, and wait for the next question.

4. Watch for patterns of play, grief, play, grief. If you don't see this pattern, look for ways to get professional help from school counselors and play and family therapists. Play is critically important for children to "get back to" after they have experienced trauma.

5. Children need movement to process their feelings. It's time to plan some stress-reducing activities such as going camping, fishing, hiking, bike riding, going on walks, or playing in the park. Think about activities that your children lean toward, ask to do (a lot). What makes them smile? Also, avoid excessive screen time and stress producing activities as much as possible.

6. Practice problem solving with children. When we give our kids opportunities to figure things out, they become strong problem solvers. Try not to correct them (unless it is problematic, or dangerous thinking or behavior). "Let's think of some ways to solve this problem together." Or, "Show me what you would do first." And, "If you do it that way, what do you think will happen next?"

~20~
School Violence—Safety, Prevention, & Warning Signs

We've addressed talking about school shootings with children, but let's dive deeper and take a look at safety, prevention, and warning signs as they relate to school violence. Every time there's news of another school shooting, you are not alone if you ask yourself, "Are my own kids safe?" "What can I do to stop this?" And, "Should I home school my children now?" Some children will begin to wonder, "Will it happen to me?" And, "I'm afraid to go to school now." These are all signs of typical development in children, and rational thinking in adults.

We should take comfort in this key point when talking with kids about school shootings that comes from the National Association of School Psychologists. "Although there is no absolute guarantee that something bad will never happen, it is important to understand the difference between the possibility of something happening and the probability that it will affect you or your school community directly."[1]

We can reassure children that there's a great chance that it won't happen to them (the probability), and adults are always working to keep them safe. But, the possibility of another school shooting is more common than it once was so we wouldn't be totally honest with them if we say it could never happen. It's a really tough call.

And, understandably, those words will ring hollow to you if your child was killed, injured or witnessed a school shooting. But for all the kids who attend our schools every day, we have to keep on keeping on, reassuring them of our best efforts to keep them safe.

Think about your response if your child had been in an automobile accident and was afraid to get in another vehicle. You would use this same thinking to provide reassurance. Of course we can't predict another accident will ever happen, but a promise to do everything we can to keep them safe is our best course of action. "That's why we always wear seat belts; get out of the car curbside; or don't use loud voices in the car and distract the driver."

Jennifer Huber blogs for Stanford Medicine's SCOPE. She put school shootings in perspective when she wrote, "Like older adults who grew up with the threat of nuclear bombs during the Cold War, children are now growing up with mass shootings — the new normal."[2] Those of us who did not grow up with the threat of nuclear bombs don't have a reference point for that. But we are called to keep our children as emotionally anchored as we can. And that means being honest and filled with hope, but not overlooking the safety, prevention, and warning signs of school shootings.

Keeping Children Safe

"For decades, auto accidents have been the leading cause of death for children, but in 2020, guns overtook that and were the No. 1 cause," so says NPR's Dustin Jones.[3] About 10% of all firearm deaths (not just school shootings) were children in 2020, over 4000 of them. That's so hard to grasp. To put it briefly, we've made more progress in keeping kids safe in automobiles, but less progress keeping them safe from firearms.

I've referred to Dr. David Schonfeld before. As a developmental pediatrician and children's grief specialist, he travels to schools after mass shootings. He refers to adults as being the ones to go to for kids. "We want children to know we are an accurate source of information no matter what they've heard or seen on social media or television."[4] That's sort of how I look at us as being "in the trenches" with children, the ones who are always there but ready to get help for them if needed. WE are their safe havens, their secure bases, and their sheltering trees.

As children become aware of tragedy from overhearing conversations, the news, or from other kids, we know to take precautions. And many kids are very sensitive to the pain of others, even if they didn't know the victims. They attend active shooter drills and talks about school safety as if something will happen tomorrow to them. And yes, just as other causes of death increase for children, school shootings are happening more frequently in many schools around our nation, but gun violence outside of school is still the larger threat to them.

In my experience, even mentioning a drill will create anxiety in some children. I wish I had a hamburger for every time I announced a fire drill in my early childhood classrooms and at least one child responded, "So we're having a fire today?" or another started crying because they didn't want to get "burned up."

Active shooter drills can bring on the same anxiety; begin your announcement or conversation with an explanation of what is about to happen, or what constitutes a drill. Kids are tuned in to the word pretend from an early age. It's part of their play language. Use it to your advantage if you are a classroom teacher or parent doing drills at home. "We are just pretending, playing like there's a fire to learn how to be safe." Or, "Let's do our play drill and pretend there is something happening that is not safe, so we can know what to do just in case." Again, practicing how to respond during an active shooting can be treated like practicing how to respond in the event of a fire, tornado, or hurricane. Children should never be scared by these drills, but assured that we just want to be prepared. Using this three-step approach below for all drills with children is much more effective than something like ringing school bells without any advanced preparation:

Step 1: Talk about the upcoming drill and the reasons for having it. Go through the motions, giving the exact plan of action when an alarm is sounded. Talk about how to stay quiet and calm, using their quiet, deepest breaths, and staying focused on an adult/s.

Step 2: Practice going through the motions of what kids will do at school in the event of an active shooter or any threat to their safety. The drills will be different for active shooters versus tornadoes. Preparing in advance for the emotional aspect of drills will go a long way in alleviating anxiety in children.

Step 3: Review the experience with children soon after the drill and then periodically between scheduled drills. Talk about successes and challenges and how to make improvements next time. Talk about feelings. "What were some of our big feelings during the drill?" "How did we manage them?"

Prevention—What Kids Want Us to Know and Do!

We can't talk with kids about school shootings without talking about prevention. While researching this topic, I discovered there isn't one simple solution, but there are many possible steps that we can take, and most of them have to do with increasing the emotional wellbeing of our students intrinsically, rather than any extrinsic remedy. Kids who are emotionally okay don't kill other kids.

It begins with collecting additional current data to better understand what children in schools experience and then designing programs and implementing policies to identify kids who are at risk of harming others as well as self-harming. It's obvious that sometimes the professionals as well as the policies we already have in place are hamstrung. For example, school counselors tell me they need more time to work with children in groups and individually on social skill building but find their "time traps" are related to testing expectations.

We know that school shooting behavior begins early and has been identified in many kids who grow up to commit school shootings. Even if we have already given our attention to these types of actions, maybe it's time to begin again. Something isn't working. We must intentionally notice, pay attention to kids who are ostracized, left out, practicing bullying behaviors and being bullied. A bigger looking glass or microscope or whatever it takes to look closer, longer, and more intently is needed now. We have to ask peers, teachers, and families to immediately provide emotional assistance in the same way we would if kids were physically hurt.

Warning Signs

There are often warning signs before kids commit acts of violence in schools. These are indicators that help is needed, not just from others such as teachers, police, counselors, and doctors. It is needed from us and their peers. Most often, attacks are planned by those who kill and at least one other person knows of those plans. In Italy, Texas, a 16-year-old teen pulled out a semi-automatic weapon and shot another student at lunchtime while talking with her. He was described by a fellow student as someone they always talked about—thought could be dangerous. The local district attorney described him as "a young man with a history of disturbing violent tendencies toward animals and his peers. He had been afforded opportunities for rehabilitation and help, and nothing worked."[5]

This is not new information. I'm drawn to a report for principals and teachers from the US Department of Education that was written in August of 1998. It literally spells out all of the warning signs that we continue to see today in people who commit gun violence on school campuses.

For example, early warnings include emotional signs such as "social withdrawal, excessive feelings of isolation and being alone, and excessive feelings of rejection."[6] It's not enough to just know the signs; we have to talk with our children about them—how to identify someone who is hurting.

But, and I'll say it again, what we cannot do, is make kids afraid to be in American classrooms. We can all agree that we do need safer schools in the event of school shootings. But can we also agree that we need to give parallel attention to the root causes of shootings that happen long before a gun is purchased? And, while I'm on this soapbox, can we make it a priority to give more attention to all the ways our children are dying in America, in and out of school?

...

Let's review a couple of things. (1) Sometimes a super heightened anxiety that children feel can be attributed to us, the adults around them, as we process school shootings and then take so many precautions to keep them safe. (2) Let's remember that school shootings do not happen as often as other gun related deaths and a much smaller number of gun violence deaths occur on elementary school campuses than high schools each year in America. Most school shootings occur in school parking lots targeting older students. But because of the depth of the tragedies, how awful and tragic they are, it feels like they can happen every day in every classroom nationwide. I think one of the reasons school shootings get much attention is they are a portrayal of collective horror; they happen to many kids all at once and we see the grief of parents and others on live TV as well as on social media.

❧Strategies☙

For Survivors of School Shootings

1. Give yourself grace and don't try to go it alone. Use professional help for you and your child to process what has been witnessed. But know that a one-and-done conversation isn't sufficient, either. It takes as long as it takes. Things will never be the same but getting help as opposed to not getting help can make a huge difference in how you and your child go forward.

2. Children may struggle to go back to school after a shooting. Try to find the greatest barrier for them and work from there. Returning on an abbreviated schedule (part time) may be needed. Ask your school district to work with you.

3. Turn your anxiety into action. Form a parent group at the school or in your community. Invite lawmakers and law enforcers to address your concerns. Show your children that you are their first responder and best advocate.

4. Ask your school to form a student group to address questions and "next steps" to keep them safe.

5. Be ready for children to grieve long-term, well past the shooting. All of the other info that I've offered in this book about talking with children about death and dying will be useful for children who have witnessed a school shooting or who are concerned about one. The closer they are to people who died, the more long-term the bereavement may continue.

6. As teachers (and parents), allow children to talk to you in their

own time. Good listeners make the best companions for grieving children.

7. Your child may not show signs of trauma outwardly so intentionally look for opportunities to talk or just listen (without hovering). Check back in! Again and again.

8. If you struggle to allow your child to return to school after a shooting, try to follow the child's lead. Is she ready? Does he want to return? Listen to your professionals. What are they encouraging you to do that is best for your child?

9. Children are naturally social, need to be with peers, and need routines. As soon as they can safely return to school, they should unless you have made arrangements to home school them. Uvalde, Texas pediatrician Roy Guerrero-Jaramillo had succinct advice for parents about homeschooling after the school shooting in May, 2022: "If you do not feel that your child is safe going to school in the fall, then do not send them. They will still need time to continue with what is familiar—spending time with peers and visits to their teachers, even if they don't feel safe going back."[7]

10. Support animals can be a great addition to your child and to his school. After the mass shooting in Uvalde, Texas, support and therapy dogs were deployed to welcome kids back.[7]

11. Rethink active shooter simulations, a dangerous trend for children happening all across America. It's different than active shooter drills as it attempts to simulate or bring to life what it would be like to have an active shooter enter the school and classroom. According to Sandy Hook Promise©, these live-action simulations of fatal shootings can include shooting pellet guns at teachers and spreading fake blood to mimic the scene of

a shooting. Fake shooters pound on classroom doors and take aim at students. The sound of gunfire is piped into the audio systems.

The simulations can occur without warning or preparation, sometimes preventing kids and teachers from knowing if it is real. The former early childhood classroom teacher and the child developmentalist part of me is asking that you as teachers and parents look toward those who study early child development for guidance and answers to this trend. Will it do more harm than good, causing more fear and anxiety? Their wellbeing as well as learning environments must be protected for our nation's children.

Answering Questions About School Shootings For Others

1. Listen for incorrect statements children are sharing and do your best to allay their fears of a shooting happening at their school. Share statistics of school shootings with older kids. Again, it's important to remember that most school shootings happen at high schools, in parking lots.

2. Keep answers brief and allow children to process your words before providing more information. They may have "gossip" information that has been exaggerated, misconstrued, or is incorrect. Correct their information to the best of your ability. For example, a friend shared that his young child was confused when he heard the term guerrilla warfare on the news and asked, "What's 'gorilla' warfare?" Exactly.

3. Share as much about the shooting with children as you feel comfortable but avoid traumatizing them with gruesome details. Consider their ages and stages of development and match

the details with what they can understand and give only as much detail as needed. If they ask, "Did those kids die?," answer, "Yes." Then wait for the next question. "How did they die?" Response: "They were killed by a person with a gun."

4. Refer to other conversations about death and dying offered in this book. Many of those can be used for all talks about death and dying and school shootings are without exception.

5. Begin the process of talking about death and dying long before a school shooting occurs. The best time to start was probably the last time something or someone died. But it's never too late.

For Teachers

I gave information earlier regarding drills for keeping kids safe. But for our youngest children who can understand a very limited amount of information about school shootings, do these instead to prepare them:

Provide attention getting signals that contain a cue to go to a specific/special place in the classroom, prompted by a soft bell ringing, a familiar song, or turning the lights off.

Practice one or more of the following phrases in soft voices in the event of an active shooting or other warning/danger. Have children vote on one to use if ever needed:

    1. Teacher: "Ready set"; Students: "Go-go."
    2. Teacher: "1, 2, 3, 4—Get on the floor."
    3. Teacher: "Mouse, mouse"; Students: "In the house; Shh."
    4. Teacher begins soft clapping pattern. Students echo.
    5. Teacher: "A, B, C; Students: "1, 2, 3."
    6. Teacher: "One, two"; Students: "Eyes on you."

~21~

Talking About Death By Suicide

I will love the light for it shows me the way, yet I will endure the darkness because it shows me the stars.
—OG Mandino

Talking with kids about death is hard enough, but explaining death by suicide can be even harder. I wrote earlier about how the topics of death and dying are often taboo, but sharing the news of a loved one's death by suicide with children may be the most unspoken and forbidding conversation we can have. Grief counselor Gary Roe shares this with us, "Suicide leaves a path of destruction that includes guilt, shame, blame, and a whole lot of "What-ifs."[1] "What if my dad hadn't gone to the beach that day?"

And, as we are egocentric beings to some extent, feelings of loss can prompt us to ask, "Why didn't he let us help him?" Or, "If only I'd known." Feelings of rejection are common. "Why would she leave us? Weren't we enough?"

If we aren't careful, our guilt, shame and blame can overshadow the deceased loved one's pain. Death by suicide becomes hush-hush and considered by some to be an unnecessary death. And, we often become silent in our need to protect our children.

But kids notice the silence; they are curious by nature and hard wired to sense when something is wrong, or there is more to be told. Children will be relentless in trying to figure it out. Your grief is often theirs to bear, as well. Along with guilt, shame, and blame will be sadness and anger. I call that a Crockpot© full of emotional stew to deal with, let alone share with children.

Children also assume guilt, feeling that they could have done something to prevent someone from taking his own life. Older children tend to display this emotion more than younger children as their understanding of death by suicide will be increased. In some cases, children will mirror the guilt they see in the adults around them. The truth is, many who die by suicide have planned their deaths in advance and no one or nothing can stop them.

Should I Tell My Child Someone Died by Suicide?

Think about the children who are old enough to have questions about a loved one's death, and they will. Do you really want them finding out from someone else or on social media that someone died by suicide? You may not want to hold secrets that begin as untold truths and then manifest as children get older.

There are lots of reasons you may not want to tell your children about the death of a loved one by suicide. Understandably. First of all, it's really hard to explain. "He didn't want to live anymore so he took his own life." And then there's the how. "But how did he do it?" In any situation, the age and stage of development of the child will be critical in your talks with them.

After Alexandra Wyman's husband died by suicide, she wrote a book titled *The Suicide Club* where she talked about how you and your children may now be treated differently. I was so struck by her words: "Yes, this manner of death can bring out the absolute worst in people...I took a long time to figure out that these reactions were less about me than about the grief of those involved."[2]

I wanted to know more about how Alexandra addressed death by suicide with her children so I contacted her @forwardtojoy.

In my message, I wrote that I wanted something authentic from someone who knows, and how suicide is often masked because the truthful conversation with children may be just too painful. She graciously responded with permission to share the following:

For me, I am choosing honesty every time by finding age-appropriate words to describe what has happened. I do know, though, that in general, there is still shame and guilt that may cause others to choose to not be as honest or wait until children are older. Children are much more perceptive and understanding than we give them credit for.

She reaffirmed how we have to take into account the developmental nature of children, always. And, how everyone has to choose their own time path in talking with kids about death and dying, especially a death by suicide.

Other ways of dying such as cancer, accidents, or even murder are often better received than death by suicide. These seem to be more "acceptable" deaths as the deceased had no part in making the decision to die. They are easier to explain—if anything is easier to explain when talking about death with children.

I get what many health professionals like authors Michael Myers and Carla Fine mean when they write, "With children, honesty about suicide is not only the best policy, it is the only policy. You must tell your children the truth in an age-appropriate manner from the beginning, no matter how young they are."[3] Yes, and the term "age-appropriate" is critical here and throughout this book.

Amy Biancolli writes this of her husband's suicide: "Telling children their dad committed suicide—that yes, he loved them, yes, they'll get through this, and no, it wasn't their fault—is incomprehensibly harder. As though you would even try to comprehend such a thing until it happens to you. You wouldn't. There's no point. Stop trying."[4]

Defining Death by Suicide to Children

When talking about suicide, children may not understand its meaning when they are given the news or overhear adult conversations. It's complicated and many of us just need to know what to say. Let's get a good definition of death by suicide that we can percolate on and maybe move closer to discussing it with children.

In her book *Breaking the Silence*, grief counselor Linda Goldman provides a really good explanation for children: *"Suicide is when people decide they do not want their body to work anymore and they stop their body from working. They are so, so sad or so, so angry or so, so depressed that their mind becomes mixed up."* She tells us to keep open discussions where no question is off limits, and to teach them "to separate the person that died from the way they died."[5]

This honest and sincere approach signals to children that you are willing to answer; you welcome their questions, even though this can be complicated and difficult to understand.

Coping After Death by Suicide Loss—Do's and Don'ts

A common theme that runs throughout this book is honesty. But your answers and conversations will be different depending upon the ages of children and their developmental stages. In this situation, I want to share some DO'S & DON'TS to be mindful of when talking with kids about death by suicide:

DO:
- Keep it simple. You don't need to have all the answers. Use the "Ask One–Answer One" technique where your child asks one question and you only answer that question. You can then allow another question at that moment or even later.
- Follow their lead. Answer according to their understanding.

- If it happened to someone they don't know, they may ask you what it is. Use this as a good starting point to talk about dying by suicide.
- Always find out what they know or think they know and begin there. It's even okay to ask, "What have you heard?" Or, "How about you ask a question and then I'll try to answer."
- Tell your truth. Keeping someone's death by suicide from your child is another form of the "tabooness" of death that I write about in an earlier chapter. It is as if we don't think they deserve to know how someone died, just because it makes us uncomfortable tell them. Or, we don't know how to answer their questions. If it's too painful, and their grief is hard to bear, tell your truth anyway. Or, call on your "someone" to help. We all have those, waiting to step in when needed.
- Explain suicide as "When a person does something to make himself die." Use phrases such as, "You know how a person's body can be sick like with cancer, or COVID? Well, your dad was sick in a different way. He felt so bad that he didn't want to live anymore."
- Treat death by suicide as any other death without shame or blame. To children, it was a life treasured and deserves the same homage that we would pay to anyone else who died in a different way.

DON'T:
- Hide your feelings.
- Feel guilty or blame yourself.
- Feel rejected by the deceased and be angry.
- Ignore triggers that may come after the death of your loved one.

～Strategies～

1. When a child asks, "How did she die?" answer succinctly and in one sentence if possible and, just a reminder—answer only what they ask. They may not be ready for all details, but are curious for your response.

2. It may be more comfortable to say, "She took too much medicine," instead of, "She overdosed on drugs." "You can also avoid saying, "She took her own life," and "He committed suicide," and respond instead with, "Her car hit a tree and her body stopped working." Or, when responding to older kids when they ask, "How did he die?," you can say, "He used a rope to cut off his oxygen so he couldn't breathe anymore." Again, it's perfectly all right to say, "It's hard to know what happened. I just know he was ready to die."

3. Call on your village to help. Talk to your child's teacher/s and school counselor and let them know what your child is going through. They can play a large role in taking care of your child while at school.

4. Seek a specialist, maybe a play therapist who can use specific techniques for grief associated with dealing with death by suicide.

5. Listen for talk of self-harming and wanting to be with Dad. Also, watch for signs of withdrawal from friends and family, talking about wanting to die, or disappear, and changes in eating or sleeping habits. Seek help immediately from doctors, counselors, and therapists if your child shows any signs of extreme despair.

6. Pay attention to your child's drawings as these are often the

prompts that are needed to know when to seek help. Certainly not all drawings about death and dying are cause for alarm, but let's go back to my three "red flags" of knowing when to seek help: 1. Length of time grieving, 2. Intensity (how extreme the grief appears) and 3. How much or often the child shows grief.

7. Use storytelling, painting, drawing, working with clay, dolls for role play, etc. to help children bring their feelings forward. These are what author Linda Goldman calls "projective techniques."[6]

8. Find a suicide family survivors support group for your child and you if needed.

...

If you or someone you know is at risk of suicide, please call the U.S. National Suicide Prevention Lifeline at 800-273-8255 or text TALK to 741741.[7]

Part 3

CHILDREN, GOD, & GRIEF

-22-

Talking About God and Death

*To every thing there is a season, and a time to every purpose
under the heaven; A time to be born, and a time to die...*
—ECCLESIASTES 3:1-2

Flourish. To grow exponentially. To thrive. To prosper. It's what we want for all children. But talking with children about grief often includes answering questions about our personal beliefs which include a higher power, a creator, the universe, or spirit. "Where do we go when we die?" Or, "Is my Daddy in Heaven?" These are familiar questions of children who grieve—children who wonder.

In the pages that follow, "God" will be used to refer to all of the above. I am not associating God with a particular religion, but referring to a spiritual entity that most people recognize as their higher power with which to develop a relationship, a belief that something exists outside of themselves. These chapters on children and God are predominantly built upon the 90% of the US population who call themselves believers. But you don't have to be a believer for you or your children to benefit.

We know that children are born curious. They spend most of earliest years exploring everything in their path. And as they grow, they begin to express a curiosity in things that aren't tangible, and cannot be touched or seen. They begin to "believe" in things that can't be proven. There is much evidence that not unlike adults, children have a capacity to look for comfort outside themselves, especially during grief and loss.

For example, take the work of Harvard University Professor Emeritus Dr. Robert Coles. His worldwide research of children and spirituality brought about the book, *The Spiritual Life of Children*. He spent many years exploring how faith of our youngest begins and then develops throughout childhood.[1]

In his book, Dr. Coles chronicles his findings of similarities in children around the world of their need-to-know God. He says, "For children...death has a powerful and continuing meaning. They hear what their elders hear in sermons and stories, and in songs... they also experience death personally when grandparents and other people depart." This need-to-know God happens more easily for children as it comes from their sense of "wonderment" and imagination, something that some adults lose with life experiences.

We find that young children have a propensity or a leaning toward as well as the capacity to seek understanding about death and dying. This need for kids to understand and engage in supernatural thinking often leads to looking at grief and loss with a kind of spiritual lens that can offer solace to grieving children.

Born Believers

Belief in God can bring a sort of emotional prosperity in times of loss for children. It brings a sense of control when it seems everything is out of control, and helps children feel a little less powerless, helpless and alone. They find shelter in their own ability to believe in something that cannot be seen and heard which may provide courage to face the loss of a loved one.

Children are what developmental psychologist and anthropologist Dr. Justin Barrett calls, "born believers" who engage in what he also calls *natural religion*.[2] So how do children acquire "natural religion," setting themselves on the path to God? How are they "born believers?"

Dr. Barrett's idea of natural religion is not one of theology, or belongs to any particular religious group or sect. He claims that in time, a child's natural religion can become Christianity, Catholicism, Judaism, Hinduism, and other practices of beliefs and morals as children grow older and become more exposed and acclimated to religious practices within their cultures.

Dr. Barrett's research provides evidence, "that children might find especially natural the idea of a nonhuman creator of the natural world, possessing superpower, super-knowledge, and super-perception, and being immortal and morally good."[3]

In other words, they are "born believers" in things existing apart from them and being all knowing. "They naturally develop minds that encourage them to embrace belief in the god or gods of their culture...to believe in gods generally, and God in particular."[4]

His words truly aligned with my thoughts as I have forever been convinced that we need to know more about how young children develop their curiosity for what's out there, or believing in things that they can't see (faith) and then increasing it as they grow. We've long known how important it is to believe that something greater than us is in control, but also present to communicate with, protect and watch over us. But Dr. Barrett's idea that we are "born believers" takes it a giant step further.

This brings us to how children come to know about God and the way they begin to understand death as it relates to God. From this perspective, believing in God provides strength, bringing communities and families together of which children are a part. Practicing a particular belief through religion can be central to working through grief as it comforts and eases pain for many people.

In her most recent book, *The Awakened Brain*, Dr. Lisa Miller writes, "...spirituality is a consciousness for which all of our brains are wired; and, long term, the spiritually engaged brain is a healthier brain." She continues, "It is founded upon the premise of an innate spiritual nature all humans have, beginning at "day one" and how being spiritual can actually make us healthier and guard against depression and other types of "unwellness."[5]

As children grow and develop into adolescence, renowned child development textbook author Laura Berk reminds us, "Adolescents who feel a sense of connection to a higher being may develop certain inner strengths—including pro-social values—that help them cope with life's difficulties and resolve real-life moral dilemmas."[6]

Children's Concepts of God

Each culture engages in its own beliefs and practices that are beyond a child's real world—the supernatural side of being human. Santa Claus (at least 10 versions around the world), elves, cartoon characters, and the Easter Bunny are the friendlier variations and are easily accepted by children by ages 3 or 4. Imaginary friends or toys and other things that "come to life" are part of their natural inquisitiveness and include Disney© movies and fictional children's books.

Chris Boyatzis is a professor and researcher of psychology with an interest in spiritual development in childhood and adolescence. He writes how "mythical figures are like God concepts in that they include supernatural features and have widespread cultural endorsement."[7] And as children get older, they become enamored with other supernatural things such as Marvel characters, Harry Potter type books, angels, demons, gods, spirits, monsters, witches and ghosts. But by 8 years and even earlier for some, children will begin to question magical thinking.

Dr. Laura Berk says around 8 years, kids "distinguish magical beings from reality." In other words, they come to know what's possible and what's impossible. They are able to distinguish between living and nonliving things. A man in a red suit can't come down the chimney and bunnies can't hide eggs!

This really happened! When I was a junior professor at Texas Woman's University, I was contacted to write a piece for newspaper circulation regarding when children stop believing in Santa Claus. I found the exact same information as Drs. Berk and Boyatzis—at about 8 years old, children begin questioning Santa, Rudolph, and all the other magical characters and events at Christmas. Of course, many children will not admit they don't believe, depending upon the high stakes imposed by the family to continue.

While this is all happening, Dr. Berk clarifies, "At the same time they embrace other beliefs stemming from religion that are culturally transmitted or taught."[8] These are tied to children's natural development and can happen outside of any belief or non-belief in religious worship. In other words, there is capacity to believe; there is an inner strength that can be tapped in to—a leap of faith.

Author, minister, and professor J. Bradley Wigger researched children and imaginary friends where he found that children <u>without</u> indoctrination <u>or</u> a religious community supporting them could not only invent imaginary friends, but they could create their own invisible, superhuman agents/gods.[9] Imaginary friends are also considered a forerunner to a child's ability to believe in God. If kids can believe in magic or something imaginary, there's a likelihood they have the capability to form beliefs in something outside of reality.

The Supernatural Side of God

We often struggle to explain the "supernaturalness" of what most of us refer to as "God," as we may have difficulty understanding this concept ourselves. Our beliefs are often handed down through generations—stories and sermons, songs, and religious texts.

But if it isn't that hard for children, could this be a spiritual restlessness? It appears that wrestling with a concept such as "god" that is challenging to be scientifically explained seems much easier for children than for many adults. They easily accept there is something out there, other than themselves and intuitively invent imaginary friends and pets, or talk to trees and the stars. So, an invisible entity or being can become second nature to kids—even when they haven't had any teaching or training, or even when their parents are non-believers.

I mentioned Dr. Lisa Miller earlier, a leading researcher and expert on children's spirituality. In *The Spiritual Child*, she describes a "transcendent relationship...that may be perceived as a personal dialogue with God, or sense of oneness with the universe."[10] Your religious and non-religious experiences/beliefs may be different and include other stories and rituals that your children readily accept as truth. They practice along with you without question as your belief traditions will certainly play a part, and include your children.

Here's that benchmark again. By about 8 years old, most children want to know what happens when they or someone else dies. They are pretty good at understanding once the physical body dies, it is no longer available to them—it's gone, but what happens next? While they continue to believe a person can still hear them when they talk to them, especially if they had a really close relationship, there are still lots of gaps to be filled. There are more questions than answers. And, this isn't particularly associated with religious beliefs for younger children. It's part of their magical thinking.

But as they become older, when they are taught specific principles of faith, the gaps begin to fill in with information observed and often taught to them by the adults in their world. And, it is easier to transfer their supernatural thinking into a specific religion; especially one that believes our soul or spirit "exists separately from the body and continues to live" on past physical death.[11] Children seem to easily adopt whatever religious teachings they experience, as they are always looking for more answers. This causes me to pause and wonder. Are they, too, hoping that life continues beyond death as a comfort, as a way of not having to let someone go?

Trickle Down Religion

Even if they have a natural ability to believe, children's beliefs may come from what they feel and what they have been told, a sort of trickling down of religious beliefs from their parents, grandparents, and other influential people in their lives. Dr. Ana-Maria Rizzuto calls this, "God representation," or when children get their ideas about God and death from home, school, church, and/or community.[12] It is their nature to explore the world, wondering and looking for answers to questions about who and what they are in this life and after death. Ana-Maria notes, "Most western people either believe in, or have at least heard of, a personal God."[13]

While parents may bring religious rituals and observances to children, it is the child's own unique and individual version or understanding of God that matters to them. To a child, it's sort of like giving them a puzzle (of your beliefs) to put together and there is no intended outcome, no picture on the box to put it together. They choose the pieces that fit their beliefs and discard the others and it still makes a representation of their own personal God.

Where Do We Go When We Die?

As one child put it bluntly, "I know he's dead but where did he go?" This is a way that children continue to process death. Your faith may contain beliefs of an afterlife, so your participation in immortality and your answer will reflect your faith. "I believe he is in our hearts." Or, "We believe that we go to heaven when we die."

But remember how concrete children's thinking can be, especially for younger children. I've said before that we often need to determine what they appear to know before answering their questions. I heard this recently from an 8-year-old: "My friend says we go to hell when we die if we're bad." Another child said: "I think we turn into dirt when we die." And, finally, "We become butterflies when we die and come back to earth."

All of these responses warrant further discussion with someone they know, love, and trust, based upon family values. In my experience, younger children are usually making statements they want verified based on our beliefs, after hearing something from someone else. They are not asking questions. Sometimes, just reflecting back to them what they are saying, such as, "That's interesting. What do you think?" are all they need to hear. Or, "You think we become butterflies? What kind of butterfly would you be?" Depending on their age and stage of development, if they want more information, or want to continue their one-sided conversation, they will ask (or tell you more).

But what if you, the adult, don't believe in heaven or an afterlife or you really just aren't sure what happens when we die? Or, you aren't sure how to explain it in kid speak. Again, your answers will be based on your values and upon what your child believes. Keep it simple. You can say, "I don't know," or, "I think our bodies just stop working and it's like we are in deep sleep." And, "This is what a lot of people think, but we just cannot sure." Being open, honest and straightforward is the best you can offer your child.

If you are a teacher or a care provider, your best answer will be one that honors a family's culture or religion: "That's a great question. Let's tell your mom that you are curious and let her talk about that with you."

With children, it just may come down to this. Rob Bell, a former pastor and New York Times best-selling author has been on Time's list of the 100 Most Influential People in the World. Think about how he addresses this concept. As a Bible scholar, he wrote:

I saw how the Bible isn't a book about how to get into heaven, it's a library of poems and letters and stories about bringing heaven to earth now, about this world becoming more and more the place it should be. There is very, very little in the Bible about what happens when you die. That's not what the writers were focused on. Their interest, again and again, is on how this world is arranged.[14]

Whether you agree or disagree with Rob Bell, knowing children as I do, I think the essence of his message to focus on this world is a key concept to convey to our children. It's tangible, more easily and readily understood and keeps our focus on reality and our everyday lives. Because in reality, there's just so much we really don't know!

When Will We Die?

This is another tough question and discussion to have with kids. There are two main schools of thought for believers. I've talked with so many people who believe in the "soft blame" of God when death occurs. It's rooted in the Bible in Ecclesiastes 3:1-2: "To every thing there is a season, and a time to every purpose under the heaven; A time to be born, and a time to die...." Many interpret this scripture that we all have a specific, pre-ordained "time" to die, and because God knows when we will die, He takes us at that predetermined time. "God needed another flower for His heavenly garden so he picked her." Or, "God gained another angel today."

Others believe Ecclesiastes 3:2 simply refers to the birth and life of all things, but God doesn't choose the time or cause our death, just like a loving parent would not choose the time of death for a child. "Our days are numbered" (John 14:5-7). Yes, we will all die someday, so we have a certain number of days to be alive but things happen that will cause death. We don't get plucked or chosen because it's our time to go. There is "a" time to go, but not "the" time to go. Both are founded upon belief; there's no wrong answer.

The following *post from Melissa Radke, author and wise woman beyond her years, gives her perspective on God choosing when we die and a promise of eternity.[15] Many of her Facebook followers who have lost children have found it comforting. This passage came from a Facebook post that she wrote in response to the death of a good friend's young son:

I don't choose one over the other.
I never have.
I never will...
I don't "take" people—I, instead, comfort the broken.
I don't "allow people to live"—I, instead, build up the faith of the hopeless.
I didn't take that child because I "needed him"—I need nothing.
I instead provide a place of beauty and light and peace and eternal life because when the world says "this is the end," I say, "not even close."

*Facebook Post, October 2021 (Used with Melissa's permission)

Let's recap children's concepts of God. No matter your beliefs or questions about God, or non-beliefs, children form their own conceptions of "Godness." And that's okay. As young as preschoolers, they begin to act like little scientists as they develop/grow, and question how things come into being, or how they are caused.

These ideas can change or even diminish as we know many people who grew up believers and then lost their faith later on. This book is about capturing those moments when they are children, and walking with them on their individual belief/grief journeys.

Even when the strongest believers experience death and dying, "Having faith in a higher power will not prevent us from experiencing death, or hurt, or pain," says Dr. Bob Deits. He calls this "fire insurance religion...for the primary purpose of avoiding divine punishment."[16]

We all go through stages of grief as believers and nonbelievers. But for the sake of our children's well-being during times of loss, their best chance of thriving depends on how we provide love and support at this time. And it doesn't have to come from parents only, as grieving parents may be the most challenged to provide support to their children.

In his book, *Life After Loss*, Bob Deits reminds us, when we let go of "Why" questions such as, "Why did this have to happen?" we can replace them with "How" and "What" questions. "How can I find and give hope to my children in the midst of this tragedy?" And, "What can I do to help them through the heartbreak/loss?"

One of the many things I love about author and minister Remy Diederich's writing is how he understands that people feel they have been lost to God, often by acts of their own faith community. He says it happens through spiritually abusive situations...and not always by sinners, but by practicing believers. In the article, *Broken Trust*, he makes the point that we don't need to be religious or even faithful to go to a place of worship. "I encourage them to sit in the back row and let God speak to them in His own way."[17]

This got me thinking. To non-church-goers and church-goers, our "back row" can be the place where we pray, meditate, think—just be. It can be waiting in the car at soccer practice, sitting on the back porch, taking a walk, or cleaning house. And then, little by little, thought by thought, prayer by prayer, we move closer to the "front," finding our way to the God or source that once fed our spirit. Step by step you find the prayer warrior within you, and assume your watch as your child's angel keeper. But whatever your beliefs, consider a child's inability to think in abstract terms until they have better understandings about God and death.

๑Strategies๑

1. Begin where you are, even in a place with feelings of doubt and worry. Be honest with yourself and your children, especially when asked, "Are you okay?" "I'm not okay today. I'm having a lousy, sad day." "I'm gonna' sit with this feeling for a little bit."

2. Model phrases that give motivation to grieve and thrive, grieve and thrive, but also show your beliefs. Let your children hear, "I'm better. I'm getting better every day." "I have good days and bad days but I'm having more good days than bad." "We are strong. We get stronger every day." "We can do hard things."

3. Love them "to the moon and back." Belief in God or any higher power is not a requisite for healing. But, if the essence of God is love, then maybe that is all you need.

4. Believers and nonbelievers—use your village. Find a go-to person, or more than one for you and your child to reach out to when grief blankets you. Allow other family members and support from your community such as friends and schools to help you carry the load.

5. Teach your children to find their "back row" and sit as long as it takes to gain spiritual strength to move on up to the front"

6. Think about the word "flourish" the next time you talk with your kids about grief and loss. Let it be the guidepost of the conversation. "Am I helping them flourish?"

~23~

Faith Development & Children

*Truly I tell you, unless you change and become like
little children, you will never enter
the kingdom of heaven.*
—Matthew 18:13

We've talked about the possibility children are born with a natural sense of wonder, one that causes them to try and make sense of the universe about dying and death. If we could tap into their wonderment, I think we could see how effortless believing in something outside themselves is for many children, from the very youngest to the oldest; how they use that ability to make sense of death and dying as they grow older, and to find comfort.

Children's Concrete Thinking and Beliefs

One of our early pioneers in children's thinking, Jean Piaget (pronounced Pee ah zhay), concluded that due to concrete thinking, very young children showed signs of believing in God as a human, like their parents, teachers, etc. "They were incapable of having a true concept of God: they think of Him as a supersized, magical version of their parents."[1] I have followed Piaget's work for many years and interpret this to mean that children don't have the same abstract thinking that adults have, or are able to practice their faith the same way adults do. But, it does not mean children can't believe.

You may have heard the Piagetian term, conservation, which

simply means the way in which a child understands that things stay the same even though their appearance changes. It happens around ages 4-5. For example, if we fill a glass with water and then pour that water into another glass of a different shape and size, kids who understand conservation will know there is still the same amount of water, even though the glasses are different.

Or, in contrast, if two kids have the same cookie and one is cut in half, the child who doesn't conserve will think the cookie with two pieces is larger. So, how does this relate to children and spirituality?

If you grew up studying early childhood theorists like me, David Elkind was certainly someone you read about. He was a Piagetian scholar and studied the origins of religion in children, building upon Piaget's conservation theory. Elkind wrote, "One of the problems of conservation which all children eventually encounter, and to which they must all adapt is the discovery that they and their loved ones must ultimately die."[2]

Dr. Elkind explains, "Religion offers a ready solution" to this conundrum for children. "This solution lies in the concept of God or Spirit which appears to be religion's universal answer to the problem of the conservation of life. God is the ultimate conservation since he transcends the bounds of space, time, and corporeality [material or physical]."[3] By accepting the concept of God, the young person participates in his immortality and hence resolves the problem of the conservation of life."

We allow children their own opportunities to question the concepts of God, and interpret what they hear. It's best to avoid having grown-up faith as the ultimate goal for our children, having expectations of them to be mini-me's. They need space to speculate and think out loud without shame or patronizing corrections— space to percolate their thoughts. These opportunities to exercise their own faith principles and beliefs along with your loving kindness and gentle corrections will encourage them to share.

Benefits of Religion for Children

Again, it is well documented the many ways that religion can be beneficial to children as they grieve. It can provide a sense of community, gives wonderful rituals and routines like worshiping with others, attending Sunday School and church camps, as well as saying bedtime prayers and grace at the dinner table. These outer acts of communicating through prayer with others either inside or outside a church crystallize their inner beliefs in God.

Religion can provide the additional support that children crave when grieving; it provides "meaning making" or a way to organize their thoughts when in despair. "Actively religious people...enjoy more mental and emotional health, recover from trauma more quickly, have longer and happier lives...more than nominally religious or nonreligious people do," writes Simone De Roos.[4]

Other benefits of participating in religion with children are feeling a sense of belonging, security and connectedness with family, as well as establishing identities or who they are. However, not all religions are created equal and note the word "actively" above when I describe benefits. It seems it isn't enough to identify with a religious organization; it is necessary for our children to be involved to gain full benefits. But, involvement must include <u>positive</u> religious experiences that include shared beliefs and values as well as a common purpose where children are loved and honored.

Children and Morality

Caregivers and teachers spend lots of time talking and teaching about morality—appealing to children's understanding of what's right and wrong. Laura Levine and Joyce Munsch write in their book *Child Development*, that morality in children is mostly determined by the people around them.[5] That speaks volumes as to how important it is to take the best parts of our beliefs, the goodness and kindness, and "bathe" our children in them.

However you know God, your faith walk is yours and yours alone to experience. We all use our own life experiences to shape us and in turn to share with our children, shaping and cementing their principles during early faith development.

Even if you do not practice spirituality, or are a non-believer, you can still help your children grieve. Good parenting during times of grief is based upon loving kindness, no matter the source. There is no wrong way to love when it is given freely and unconditionally.

Children and Prayer

Prayer may be a child's first introduction to God, born out of a need for control in their own lives and those around them. Someone once said that praying is asking God to speak to us, trying to hear God's voice, and intuition is God communicating with us. Another way to describe prayer is simply talking to God—going beyond reality.

Nightly prayers, saying "grace" at the dinner table, and praying for others are all ways that we teach children to play out their spiritual nature, even when they don't know what the words mean. My (then) three-year-old granddaughter Vivian gave a perfect example. With little hands folded and eyes closed, she gave this rendition of what we southerners call "Saying Grace."

> *God is great,*
> *God is good,*
> *Let us thank Him for our food.*
> *'Y' His hands, we are fed.*
> *Thank you for our 'day-me' bread. Amen.*

Saying "grace" is part of the routines and rituals that are important to strengthening families. It provides grounding, and a family cornerstone for children to build upon, increasing their faith. In turn, faith can be displayed by having conversations with God, sending messages back and forth, talking to God and then listening to what He has to say. We often forget this part. Also, saying prayers can be born out of moments of danger and pain or just a need to ask for additional help.

But children's understanding of the words can be developing, depending upon their age. Prayers can be a combination of something learned or something spontaneous, just as Vivian added and subtracted words to make meaning.

Diane Long and others found, "At around the age of five, children begin to understand that God plays an important role in prayer...and thinking is involved." And, around the age of nine or ten, children begin to think of prayer "as a type of private conversation with God." But it isn't until they are about 9 or 10 that they can fully conceptualize prayer as a relationship to a higher power. [6]

We know that prayer lessens anxiety, reduces fear, and helps kids to lift their burdens and place them somewhere else for a moment or even longer. Prayer often defers, replaces sadness or loneliness so that they can get to their "next" thing. Prayers bring God to us, instead of "out there," in the sky, in Heaven, or just somewhere else.

It is so interesting that Jacqueline Wooley researched how closely prayers and wishes were related in young children's thinking and how their early concepts of prayer resembled their concepts of wishing. The magical part of wishing carried over into praying.[7]

Dr. Justin Barrett reminds us to include God/prayer within earshot of our children daily, in the mundane, day-to-day experiences like getting a good deal on tomatoes, or helping us find a parking place, to not only include God in terms of things done in the distant past such as Bible stories and scripture. He says that of course there are scientific explanations for everything, but they don't need to compete with God. "Multiple explanations may be true and helpful simultaneously."[8]

But What About Non-Believers and Children?

As a parent, you may not believe in God. Understood. But this book is an attempt to offer ways to talk with children about death and dying and the "God" topic is a common denominator of children's afterlife questions, regardless of their parents' worldview on religion and/or spiritualness.

There is much evidence that children have a natural receptiveness to basic beliefs that there is a god, but as a parent you have the right to teach your child your own beliefs about death and dying. As a child developmentalist, I lean toward being open to their questions and their ability to believe in the supernatural and spiritualness of life. But, I also believe in working hard to instill problem solving, and practicing soul-searching ideas that will be with them throughout life is the ultimate goal.

Conversations about God, death, and dying are no different than talking with children about race, gender, culture, sex, murder, suicide, etc. when our aim is to assist with emotional growth. Our answers must remain true to ourselves, but at the same time only answer or provide as much information as needed to satisfy their questions about death and dying.

Over explaining or even indoctrinating children with religious or non-religious ideologies at the time when they are curious grievers can be simply replaced with, "This is what I know," or "This is what we practice (or believe)." And, "But what do you think?"

You are or you may know someone who is resistant to anything godlike, who claims they have no belief in God. Atheists (non-believers) as opposed to "theists" (believers) may have been believers at one time and now have found reasons not to believe. It's possible they made a choice to practice atheism after giving up on God or becoming affiliated with other non-believers, or just choosing to go it alone with their grief. And there are people who are agnostic and just don't know if there is a god or not. They are "liminal" in their belief—not quite in and not quite out (there's one of my favorite words again).

There will always be cultural and social factors such as family and peer influence, as well as social relationships. There can be huge doses of anti-religion indoctrination that may contribute to non-believing, as well as environmental factors such as geographic location. Others have no need for a greater power or have found reason to turn away from or even curse God due to tragedy.

About 10% of the US population identify as atheists or anti-theist and sometimes believe in human power rather than God power. For them there is no existence of life after death.

My friend and colleague Leslie G. grew up with a pastor father, but is now a nonbeliever. She says, "When the brain dies, that's it. We can't think anymore so there's no us anymore. And I'm comforted by that because I don't have to strive to get to another place or fear going to a bad place." I asked her what she would tell children if they asked about where we go when we die and she responded, "We never really die because we live on the hearts of those who love us."[9]

Again, I think we can all agree that telling our "truths" to children, including we really don't know what happens when we die, but this is what "I" believe happens, will be not only to their satisfaction, but also a comfort.

Think about this one last thing. Children are often believers even when they have been associated with atheism, or see their parents turn away from God, or religion. Dr. Justin Barrett writes, "Often people underestimate how much information children are born already having or are predisposed to acquire easily and rapidly."[12]

As children grow older, the choice is theirs to act on faith, or to become a non-believer. But, if you were to ask a child if he or she believes in God, chances are he or she would say yes, even if the parents are atheists. Because believing in the supernatural comes so easy for them. Because looking for comfort outside themselves is an individual and necessary act as a human being. Because they may be born believers.

❧Strategies☙

1. Think about how children may be natural born believers. Make a list of 5 ways that you see their spirituality or faith blooming and how you can nurture it by providing guidance and support.

2. If prayer brings your child comfort, help her make a book of prayers to read and/or share routinely or on special occasions.

3. "What can we pray about?" "Who are we thankful for?" Allow children to decide and then lead the prayer. We don't have to be the ones to direct their prayers. One Thanksgiving I asked my grandchildren to take turns, thinking of someone they were thankful for and we could pray for. When we got to the youngest, who was six at the time, Zaidon thought for a second and then said, "We need to be thankful for the old people." Everyone broke out in laughter. Of course, I was the only "old" person there!

4. Religion has often been used to be a divider between us. Be cautious of teaching your child "religious otherness" as it can contribute to discrimination and prejudice toward those whose faith is different than yours. Teach children to celebrate differences and avoid an "us vs. them" way of religious thinking.

5. Introduce your children to various religious practices and those who believe differently. Visit different churches or celebrations to expose your children to more inclusion, and especially beliefs about death and dying.
6. Sow seeds of unconditional love and let your children watch them grow.
7. Don't do this alone. Use your resources, both physical and spiritual. I was assembling a shelf and at the top of the first page of the instruction booklet was a graphic of a person with a phone in hand and the number to call for any reason. I thought, how convenient. They don't want me to get frustrated and then return the shelf. The number wasn't buried somewhere. They weren't asking me to go to a website to find it or to read some FAQ's. It was there in plain sight, FIRST. What if we "call first," as soon as we need help from our "others" rather than trying to figure out how to put this "grief shelf" together for our children!

-24-
Spirituality and Children

The foundations of a person are not in matter but in spirit.
—RALPH WALDO EMERSON

In this final chapter on children and God, I want to take a deep dive into the concept of spirituality and how it connects to thriving—flourishing in children. If science now produces brain scans and evidence through research data that kids are born more spiritual than we once thought, then why wouldn't we adopt what Dr. Lisa Miller calls a "bedrock for thriving?"[1] Why wouldn't we want our children to have every available tool to flourish in periods of grief related stress? We do!

Dr. Miller, in *The Spiritual Child* calls it the borders of life—death and birth—and how children consider them "deeply engaging, important, and taken as the bedrock of their reality." As a scientist she found, "We enter the world prepared to have a spiritual life," and in truth, children are born with a kind of spiritual optimism, one that often sustains through adulthood.[2] Children come with the capacity to grow their spirituality, sort of like a package of seeds just waiting to be opened, planted and nurtured into full bloom. And it's not just kids. Most adults find comfort in believing in *something more* in times of loss. There's an element of anchoring or tethering involved in tapping into our more spiritual side as opposed to experiencing our grief "rudderless," or bobbing like a cork.

Dr. Miller extends the "born believers" concept when she writes, "All children are born spiritual. Children are born knowers, even when it comes to death." And, she says, as humans, "We are hardwired for a spiritual connection."[3]

Defining Spirituality

Without question, it is refreshing that science is catching up to what many have felt all along; that there is more to our existence than we once thought. But first, let's define it. Spirituality identifies the seeking in us, coming from wondering, and looking for significance in this life and beyond. It brings us back to center, to our best selves.

In Pastor Rob Bell's book, *Everything is Spiritual*, he writes, "There's no word for *spiritual* in the Hebrew scriptures (Old Testament). There's no word for spiritual because to call something spiritual would be to imply that other things aren't. In the Bible, everything is spiritual. All of life."[4] Rob describes all of life as being connected in one way or another, bringing us all together from the farthest reaches of the universe to the smallest cells in our bodies.

I followed Dr. Laurence Steinberg for many years during my college professor days and I trust his definition of spirituality: "The degree to which one places importance on the quest for answers to questions about God and the meaning of life."[5] Again, the word tacit comes to mind, as in difficult to explain but you just know that you know there is something greater, bigger than us!

French priest and philosopher Pierre de Chardin described it as, "We are not human beings having a spiritual experience. We are spiritual beings having a human experience."[6]

How Children Become Spiritual/Hardwired

We can't ignore any longer how science and spirituality are intertwining. I know that I sound biased on the science side of there being something else out there, a higher power, but I find it so fascinating. So, here is my best shot at presenting the opinions of trusted scholars/researchers on spirituality and children.

Dr. Lisa Miller's extensive studies of the scientific link between children's spirituality and their wellbeing. Very early, kids figure out that things such as the moon and stars, the sun, trees, butterflies and giraffes, lemons, etc. are created by someone or something other than humans (God or spirit), as opposed to things manufactured by humans (houses, cars, bicycles, etc.).

Along with all other aspects of growth and change, spirituality exists in the developing child. At an early age, it manifests as a deep sense of responsibility to others, a sense of awe and connection with nature. Just like everything else, children develop on a pathway of spirituality or knowing that things exist outside of us that are often beyond explanation. Lisa Miller says this pathway "begins at birth, day one, with a presence throughout their lives."[7] But here's the one thing to remember. If spirituality is at our core, then each child goes through life responsible for his or her "attunement" with, or "tuning up" the spiritual core. It can ebb and flow.

Dr. Andrew Newberg, a neuroscientist who studies spiritual experiences known as "neurotheology" was asked why we can never get away from God. He answered, "Because our brains won't allow God to leave. Our brains are set up/hard wired in such a way that God and religion become among the most powerful tools for helping the brain do its thing—self-maintenance and self-transcendence,"[8] both here and beyond the physical world.

In 2018, scientists who conducted experiments on spirituality at Columbia and Yale Universities found there is actually a spiritual part of the brain. They call it the "neurobiological home" and during brain scans of spiritual people, they found this area of the brain lights up during spiritual practices such as being in touch with a higher power. And, it was discovered religion was not required, only that we have a curiosity or wonderment about our world/spirituality on earth and beyond.[7]

When we step back, we can see parents fostering a stronger sense of spirituality in their children. Think of yourself as "spiritual ambassadors," says Dr. Miller[9], with special assignments to provide a loving relationship filled with trust and acceptance. Important others can also provide a backdrop where spirituality in children thrives. It is this environment that provides security and a home base for children when they encounter loss of loved ones.

Dean Hamer is an American geneticist and molecular biologist who studies spirituality and its origin from a scientific aspect. He writes in his book, *The God Gene*, "Contrary to what many people might believe, children don't learn to be spiritual from their parents, teachers, priests, ministers...nor from their culture or society."

In his research, he found that spirituality and instinct are hard-wired into our genes. We actually "inherit a predisposition to be spiritual--to reach out and look for a higher being."[10] But, we have to be cautious of religious instruction/indoctrination in children as it can lock out spirituality if presented as concepts or curriculum to be taught, rather than as a presence to be recognized.

Last one, I promise. Peter Benson and his colleagues write, spiritual development is growth in "the intrinsic capacity for self-transcendence, in which the self is embedded in something greater than the self, including the sacred... It is the developmental "engine" that propels the search for connectedness, meaning, purpose, and contribution. It is shaped both within and outside of religious traditions, beliefs, and practices."[11] Put simply, this is to become more aware of our place in the universe, regardless of a belief in a particular religion—even in the absence of religion.

Benefits of Spirituality

The benefits are plenty. A study by the Mayo Clinic found that "People who are spiritual are healthier, both physically and emotionally during tragedy and suffering." They have "stronger immune systems, reduced risk of disease, improved self confidence and even live longer."[12]

Spirituality can help us overcome hardships as we understand how all things in life are connected, begin and end, and grow in between. We teach our children that falling down and getting back up is part of life, just as everything ebbs and flows, lives and dies. Moving forward takes courage and self-encouragement, knowing that there is "the other side" or another shore to reach. Spiritual people constantly move ahead, finding meaning in life's challenges, and grasping hold of a higher power.

"Those who are spiritual are kinder, more forgiving, connected to community, and want to help others," writes Dr. Martin Seligman. If, "Spirituality is an untapped resource in our understanding of human development, resilience, illness, health and healing," just think of the possibilities to "tap" this valuable resource in grieving children.[13]

What Spirituality Looks Like

In children, spirituality can have many faces. When a child uses a mystical approach to understanding their world, when they engage in "wonderment," or when they have "satori" or 'aha' moments, that's spirituality on display. Children can experience things like awe and wonder on a daily basis when they look at grasshoppers jumping, flowers blooming and birds taking care of their young. Life seems magical to them and the more they see, the more they want to know about the world.

We need to understand this innate need for them to know more, to ponder and wonder as the outward expression of their beginning spirituality. Children are often on a quest to finding out what's "out there," what's beyond this life after death, and what is real. This includes asking questions about loved ones who died, continuing to talk to them, and believing they are somewhere listening.

Are There Differences in Religion and Spirituality?

There are differences! Spirituality may pertain more to the child and a relationship to the world, to our very existence that includes God, rather than the connections to a community of other believers who follow a particular religion. Kids don't have to be a part of a faith group to benefit from spirituality when dealing with death and dying, or even wondering about it.

Dean Hamer claims that one of his biggest challenges in writing the book *The God Gene* is attempting to separate religion and spirituality. He writes that it is challenging because religion is often founded on or derived from spiritual beliefs. In turn, spiritual beliefs are "usually expressed using the language and rituals of religion."[14]

And the lines often get blurred between religion and spirituality. For example, Robert Keeley, author of *Bridging Theory and Practice in Children's Spirituality* defines predictors of spiritual health in children as, "Bible reading, prayer, service in a church, mission trips, and listening to faith based music."[15] But I would classify those as religious practices. Spirituality may not be (necessarily) labeled with actions. It is (for me) much more existential or affirming existing in one's very being or core. Children's very existence houses a place for spirituality and a sense of "seeking" and they don't have to initially be taught or guided to be spiritual. It seems it is a divine part of them.

Even if children don't practice or engage in a particular type of religion, they can still wonder about their world, believe in God and expand that belief by connecting to a higher power.

Dr. Justin Barrett interviewed many children whose parents were atheists and yet their children believed in God. And, he wrote, what makes it even more confusing for children are those adults who claim to not believe in God, "but believe in ghosts, spirits, and many other cultural supernatural beings."[16] As concrete thinkers, children seem to have an "all or nothing" approach, but usually more *all* than *nothing* regarding spirituality.

In her book *Nurture the Wow*, Rabbi Danya Ruttenberg writes that she was an atheist until she had a series of experiences at age twenty-one that she could not explain. She "came to see the goal of spiritual practice was perhaps more truly about service to others, becoming a better person, not just chasing the next moment of feeling twinkly and high."[17] God became something that wasn't separate from her, "but rather the reality into which I could melt... the sense of my particular, small self falling away into something larger, enveloping..." Whereas, religion was more complex, developed into routines, rules, and rituals.

I'll leave you with one last thought about children's spirituality and death. In researcher Rebecca Nye's book, *Children's Spirituality*, she says taking children's spirituality seriously can significantly influence our view of children. And that children are no less spiritual than adults, often being more open to spirituality than adults.[18]

This may be hard to grasp, but there is much promise in helping children during the grieving process, especially when we are soul searching for ways to provide comfort and hope. If kids can buffer against emotional "unwellness" when a spiritualness, or belief in something greater than us is present, why would we not explore this path with them? For many, spirituality stands as a backdrop, a net to catch us as we are falling. We can follow the words of John

Burroughs, "Leap and the net will appear!"[19]

❧Strategies☙

1. Dr. Lisa Miller writes about a field love as the place where children learn spirituality.[21] Have children draw or write about a field of love by including all the people and activities that are important to them. For example, "If you were to draw a field, who are the people and things that would be in it?" Or, "Draw a big heart. That's your field. Now put all the people and things in it where you feel love."

2. Spirituality comes from an openness and curiosity. Cultivate what Daniel Seigel and Tina Bryson call a "yes brain" in your child.[21] For example, routinely make statements that model the "yes brain" mentality. "I'm going to try this new recipe and no matter how it turns out, I will be glad that I tried it." Encourage children to try something new, disregarding the result. Prepare them ahead of time to be accepting of the end result.

3. Give children "yes brain" scripts such as, "I'm worried about my spelling test tomorrow but I'm going to do my best." Or, "I don't really like broccoli, but I'll take one bite because it is good for me."

4. Create a "Hosting Council" where you ask kids to sit at a real or an imaginary table and invite anyone—living or deceased who cares for them now, or before passing. Then, allow children to talk about the person, remembering significant times with them or objects that remind them of their loved ones. (Adapted from the work of the late Dr. Gary Weaver).[22]

5. Be open to children's questions and conversations about spirituality. And, they may not be able to label those thoughts as

spiritual but that's okay, too.

6. Teach children to forgive through modeling, forgiving others. Forgiveness is good spiritual medicine for them and us.

7. Take 5-minute breaks to talk with all children about kindness, and older kids about what they want to accomplish, where they can best be of service, and how they can improve themselves, their community, and their world.

8. Show children a way to honor the memory of loved ones. Plant a memorial grief garden. Winter Ross says a "grief garden provides natural healing connecting you with those who are no longer living." Fostering connections to nature has been known to have healing power as you add one or more of the following elements to your garden: color, stone; wood, and water. (Adapted from *The Sanctuary Garden*.)[23]

Part 4

Grief Through a Child Development Lens

-25-

Grief and Loss–Developing Stages of Children

Once a child sees that death is final—irreversible, he is far more able to understand grief and loss. By age 8 or 9, most children are able to comprehend absent versus present, and real as opposed to not real. As they mature, they begin to understand alive versus dead, living versus non-living. But, developing the finality of death or the understanding that once something or someone dies they are not coming back, is much harder for younger children, and takes time.

It was the ancient Greek philosopher Heraclitus who said some 2,500 years ago, "Time is a game played beautifully by children."[1] I take that to mean they will emerge with an understanding of death in time as they leave magical thinking behind. They begin to pay attention to the world when they are ready, and embrace death as soon as development requires them to become participants rather than bystanders.

Over the years, I have encountered children in various stages of grief by observing them in lots of different venues such as school, home, funerals, parks and playgrounds. I have studied the works of child developmentalists such as Jean Piaget[2] and Lev Vygotsky[3] and agree with so many others that stages can take years to experience and develop. And, not all children go through all stages of any type of development, including grief, or have the same levels of understanding at the same time.

Not a "One Size Fits All" in Children's Development

James and Mary Ann Emswiler affirm this in their book *Guiding Your Child Through Grief*. They tell us, "Your child's grief will reflect his current stage of development."[4] Younger, more concrete thinkers usually stay in beginning stages until they can think more abstractly and older children work through stages more quickly, especially if they are already abstract thinkers.

But just a reminder—each child will approach grief along their own path, or what child developmentalists call a developmental continuum. And, this varies from one child to another. A one-size fits all approach does not work when looking at grieving children.

For example, after a recent school shooting, a family lost one child and two others were left behind. Each child grieved differently as one became withdrawn, holding feelings in while the other child began to take care of his sibling and others, appearing to displace his own grief and take on the grief of those around him.

Sometimes, as adults, we do not realize that development is different for each child. As their protectors, it is up to us to guide them through this uncertainty that is filled with confusion and misunderstanding on our part, but what makes perfect sense to them on their part.

Messy Grief

Grieving is anything but tidy—it is messy and sometimes out of control, frustrating and scary. Sometimes children's grief visits them again and again. In their popular book *I Wasn't Ready to Say*

Goodbye, Brooke Noel and Pamela Blair write about children growing and experiencing loss again and again at each stage of development, affirming that grief is never over or final.[5]

We can talk about death with children as young as three or even with our precocious twos, but the conversations about death can begin even earlier when we talk about dead leaves or dying flowers; dead bugs and birds; and even batteries dying or not "working" anymore.

The more children experience and embrace other types of loss outside of death, the better they manage their emotions when losing someone they love. For example, we can use real-life scenarios to practice loss such as when a parent has to go away, when children change teachers or care providers, or when they go to the dentist to "lose" a tooth. Kids learn that not all grief is disabling and they continue to carry on, doing the same things as before the loss. Again, it all depends upon their developing stages and experiences and how we, the adults in their world, approach loss.

❧Strategies☙

1. Keep a developmental checklist such as the one in my book *Developmental Milestones of Young Children*[6] to remember that as children develop, they make tiny bits of progress and then sometimes regress before moving forward again. Use nature as a conversation starter or common events about loss. There are many others available on-line as well.

2. Ask your child to set <u>short term goals</u> (to be completed in one month or less) where immediate progress may be seen. Then, implement the goals with your child until they can do them on their own. Look at some suggestions:

- Develop a new hobby such as playing a musical instrument; bike riding; horseback riding, or anything of interest to your child that is available and affordable.

- Complete a feelings chart for one week in daily check-ins or as their feelings have big changes. Talk about the findings with your child. "Look how you felt happy on four days last week when we checked in." Or, "You had three sad days and four happy days last week. Woohoo!"

- Try a new trigger buster. Decide what "triggers" your child's grief and the accompanying behaviors such as crying, whining, or anger due to a certain event.

- Increase sleep time; get them to bed earlier, if only by 10 minutes. Increase the time until they feel rested or refreshed the next morning, less cranky!

- Begin to curtail excessive screen time, if only by a few minutes each time. Make a schedule in words, pictures, or both and use it as a cue for children to let them know what's expected without you having to be the announcer.

3. Make <u>long term goals</u> (to be completed in a few weeks or months) with or for children with mile markers to achieve along the way. If you break the goal into smaller, achievable goals, the progress will be compatible with the way a child develops. One long term goal could be letting go (or giving away, donating, etc.) of something that belonged to the deceased. Another goal would be to move back into their room if they have been sleeping with a sibling or parent, etc. after the loss. Note that long term for children is different than for adults. Short term is

immediate and long term is "a little longer!"
- Attend play dates with children who are grieving.

- Practice a sport or skill. Use a daily or weekly calendar to record each practice. Do a weekly check-in to see how times the child engaged in physical activity.

- Create a weekly or monthly "fun" schedule with your child; fill in a calendar of things to look forward to. Have "count-down's" to the fun event.

- Increase your reading time together. Set a timer. Use a calendar to record the number of times you read together weekly.

- Take a look at your child's daily, weekly, and monthly schedule. Is there enough "down time" to grieve or too much active time to allow them to grieve? Is there too much alone time? Work with your child to make a schedule where both down time and active time are in balance.

~26~

Kids & Kübler-Ross' 5 Stages of Grief

Unable are the Loved to die, for love is immortality...
— Emily Dickinson

We have looked to Elizabeth Kübler-Ross for many years as a grief expert. She was a legendary, well-known physician who worked with thousands of dying patients in her lifetime and she gave us the internationally best-selling book, *On Death & Dying* in 1969 where she outlines 5 stages of grief.[1] She has brought order to such a vast topic as she outlines possible stages of loss:

(1) Denial
(2) Anger
(3) Bargaining
(4) Depression
(5) Acceptance

I consider her 5 stages an excellent resource, but I also know that stages of emotional development in children are never set in stone. They are guideposts and benchmarks intended to provide us with reasons for differences in children's development. And, just being aware of stages of children's emotional development helps us understand how children grow and change throughout their lives.

A Look at Kübler-Ross' 5 Stages of Grief and Development

The five stages of grief have gained much popularity over the past 50 years and were written to address all stages of grief and death as well as other types of loss. In their book *On Grief & Grieving*, Kübler-Ross and colleague David Kessler[2] tell us there is no correct way or time to grieve.

But here's the thing—Kübler-Ross and Kessler also write that these 5 stages "were never meant to tuck messy emotions into neat packages. Just as there is not a typical response to loss, there is no typical loss."[3] Honestly, it is hard to fathom how much there can also be in the "in-between" of those stages of grief.

So, if we want to get a better understanding of grief, note that these stages are not necessarily consecutive or linear. They are only guidelines for stages. They are meant to be a foundation or backdrop with the understanding that the stages are fluid, and sometimes even absent in each individual's experience with grief and loss.

In other words, children (like adults) don't go through them one by one, step by step. Some stages are not experienced at all and other stages may take a long time to get to (not through). It really depends upon each child's emotional resiliency, age, and stage of development; how well they bounce back every time they experience stressful situations; and, whether they are four years old or twelve years old (for example).

Five Stages of Grief and Loss

(Stage 1) Denial
You wouldn't think that being in denial of something would benefit us but in this case it does. Think about how children can protect their hearts when they first hear of the death of someone by telling

us, "Hey, there's only so much we can handle. Let me have time to process this news."

(Stage 2) Anger
Once reality sets in, many children become angry that their loved one has died. Blaming others and trying to understand why this happened to them and not someone else is common. This is an important step in the grief process because once the anger begins to subside, the work of healing can begin. So, it's okay for kids to be angry.

(Stage 3) Bargaining
This is the stage of deal making. Children think that if they can do something or make a change to bring their loved one back, it can happen. Although this is not based in reality, as we know death is final, children still hope.

(Stage 4) Depression
The stage of depression happens when kids begin to understand the reality of death, and their loved one is not coming back. Sadness replaces hope and the overwhelming feelings that kids have can bring on depression. But, depression and sadness aren't necessarily synonymous. Depression is a much deeper feeling of hopelessness and may require professional treatment.

(Stage 5) Acceptance
This final stage of acceptance brings a sense of "I'm going to be okay." And, there may be days of acceptance and then kids will revert back to any of the stages above. There are good days and bad days with grief. But the overall good days outnumber the bad days. You will see this stage in action as children begin to start engaging in the activities they had before the loss; playing with friends; and getting back to school, etc. They look more like their "old selves!"

NEW STAGE: (Stage 6) Finding Meaning
David Kessler, long-time co-author with Dr. Kübler-Ross, very recently published *Finding Meaning: The Sixth Stage of Grief.*[4] This new stage, written after Kübler-Ross' death, shows us how to look at grief as a growth experience, and helps us move forward by honoring our loved ones with more love than pain.

...

Let's take a closer look at grief as it often fits the definition of structured chaos, situations where there's lots of confusion and yet organization—cluttered but eventually tidied emotions where good things come from it. Can it be that grief has cloudy boundaries on the outside, but common or familiar (more static) middles we can count on, like sadness and love? Maybe. Keep reading as we take a look at my perspective on grief and child development.

My Child Development Perspective

I want to use my child development and early childhood education background and experience to offer thoughts regarding children and stages of grief. In addition to Kübler-Ross's stages, I will also focus on a more developmental stance or position on grief and how children move through it. In the pages ahead, we will take a brief look at each stage of grief through the eyes of children, and their emotions as we explore how children may approach Kübler-Ross' stages in different ways, betwixt and between working through a stage and moving on to the next.

In this book one of my goals/suggestions is to help you lay a footpath to healing for children as we begin with the first stage—*denial*, and conclude in the final stage of grief—*acceptance*. As you become more familiar with the stages of grief, you will recognize them as your child shows characteristics of anger, depression, denial, etc. Your knowledge will be your power.

❧Strategies☙

1. Use the information in this chapter to find characteristics of the five stages of grief and possibly identify (not label) your child's stage or stages of grief.

2. Keep a grief journal as you observe the stages of grief in your child. Look for reminders that children can experience the 5 stages of grief in any order, and they may even move forward and then regress to a former stage before making progress again. Consider that children have been known to experience all or some grief stages. And just a reminder—they can experience more than one stage at a time. Use the knowledge from journaling to increase understanding of children's behaviors.

3. Identify one step to take toward helping them manage their grief such as:
   - Giving children words to describe their feelings.
   - Provide coping techniques such as asking for help, seeking alone time; seeking friends and family time; and talking with someone about the loss.
   - Doing something for someone else. Your child will benefit but you may find satisfaction and even enjoyment as well.

...

This has been a quick overview; now, see Dr. Kübler-Ross' 5 stages of grief in more detail!

-27-
Denial-Stage One

When children first hear about the death of a loved one or an impending death due to illness, their first thoughts are often to deny it is happening. They experience confusion, shock, fear, and avoidance. For example, one six-year-old, upon hearing the news of her grandmother's death, screamed, "No, not Gramma!" "SHE'S DEAD?" Another child kept asking, "Where's Mommy? When is she coming back?" And another young child continued to look for his older brother days after his death. An older school ager wouldn't talk about the death of his sister at all and wondered why everyone was so upset. These are classic responses to the first stage of grief—denial, often accompanied by shock.

Other children in the stage of denial may not show extreme emotion related to the loss, but still have lots of difficulty believing someone is really gone. Younger children may deny the news with, "It's okay. He'll come back someday," or, "We'll see her again in heaven." And, our youngest children deny a loved one's death because they have a difficult time with finality, knowing that things will not return to their original state of being. Gone forever may not be in their wheelhouse of understanding, depending on how far they have traveled in growth and development.

Denial can last from moments to weeks, depending upon the emotional health and/or sensitivity of a child. It may be a constant strain as children take emotional turns when grieving, talking about loss and then playing or continuing everyday routines.

The time your child will spend in this stage can depend upon personal development as well as resilience factors, such as how well he already manages stress, handles adversity and everyday challenges. Some children make strides in overcoming denial while others may not.

Granger Westbrook, in his book *Good Grief*, says that once grief becomes overwhelming, we may become temporarily anesthetized, even though our brains are designed to accommodate pain and sorrow due to loss.[1] It is this anesthesia that may prevent children (like adults) from having to deal with such difficult news with full force, denying that it is happening. Children often shield themselves from grief as denial, in the form of disequilibrium or confusion, will take place until the child adapts to the loss.

From the Child Development Lens

Denial may have at its core what Jean Piaget called the egocentrism[2] of children and how they approach the world with "me, me" glasses. Their worlds revolve around themselves until about the age of 8 when they enter what Piaget called the formal stage of operations. It is at this stage they can usually reason abstractly (as opposed to concretely), but even then, most of their thoughts are centered inward. But don't confuse it with egotism or selfishness says Laura Levine and Joyce Munsch in their book *Child Development*.[3] Kids seem to be resistant to any change that brings unwanted emotions such as the pain associated with the death of a loved one. Their thinking is more rigid, lacking flexibility. Know any of these kids? I'll bet you do!

Being egocentric simply means they find difficulty in thinking outside themselves, understanding how others must feel. Until children are able to do some perspective taking, it is awfully hard for them to self-regulate or even show empathy or sympathy for others. We also find that denial can take the shape of avoidance, where not giving grief any attention is what's comfortable to children.

So, if your younger child insists, "Mommy's coming back," she may be practicing denial or avoiding the reality of death. And, if we can consider deference or putting something off until later a type of avoidance, children "defer" feelings as well. For example, when a child says, "We will see Grandpa in heaven so we don't have to be sad," this may be another way to ease the pain of grief, to defer or move it to the future.

From a development perspective, children are resistant to change because they have yet to develop the prefrontal cortex, allowing them to have emotion regulation skills. But, as they get older, their thinking becomes more adult-like and they come to realize that death is final. I'm not saying it's easier for them. It is still really hard to accept death and dying, especially about someone they know/love. But it usually happens to "others," not to them. And their understanding that death is irreversible is not equivalent to an absence of feelings about the death of a loved one.

But what about kids who pretend nothing actually happened and don't want to talk or attend to anything related to death? Practicing denial and avoidance allows them to continue to believe that everything is going to work out and will be back to normal soon. This is much easier to deal with than death. It's just the child's way of saying, "Hey, there's only so much I can handle!" Let's use the term *developmental selfishness* once more as it fits so well.

↪Strategies↩

1. Give your child time to accept the news of loss and to work through this initial stage. Look for signs of denial:
   - Shutting down and not wanting to talk about the loss.
   - Avoiding anything that is a reminder of someone's death.
   - Putting off dealing with death.
   - Excess activity to preclude thinking about or attending to the loss.
   - Saying "I'm fine" when their actions speak differently.

2. Accept that denial can be self-protection for your child in dealing with loss and a response due to age and stage development.

3. Prepare your child for the uncertainties that will accompany the death of the loved one if you know in advance by (1) being as honest as you can about the anticipated loss and asking others to help; and (2) letting them know that it's okay to not think about something so painful as death all at once.

4. Tell a quick remembrance of the one who died or refer to something they wore or used. "Here is Grandpa's walking cane. What should we do with it?" Or, "I think we will just leave Dad's car in the driveway for now. We can decide where to put it later."

5. If denial lingers or severely impacts your child's behavior and daily routines for more than a few weeks or even days seek professional help with a play therapist who is an expert in Child Centered Play Therapy[4]. Use your wisdom to decide, but if in doubt, call someone.

~28~

Anger~Stage Two

He isn't giving you a hard time.
He's having a hard time.
Breathe and repeat.
Be the light!
—UNKNOWN

Even when we don't mean to, we let our "grief guards" down. That's when anger sneaks in and causes us to lash out due to the pain of loss. It affects children in the same way. The good news is that anger is a typical behavior during grief. The bad news is this secondary or "next" emotion is happening for a reason and that reason is usually fear. It is the fear of powerlessness and inability to bring things back where they were. It is a fear of loss of control.

Anger can be described as emotional pain to loss, and sometimes after children experience denial of grief, they can feel the "bigness" of the loss settling in and understandably become angry. And, when your child displays big emotions such as anger, frustration, irritability, and anxiety, this also characterizes the anger stage of grief.

My long-time colleague and Texas Woman's University professor/family therapist Dr. Glen Jennings once told me, "You have to learn to see it (anger) coming like a tumbleweed and let it pass on by. Recognize it, honor it, accept it, and let it move on past you."[1] This is in stark contrast from avoiding anger, squashing it, or pushing it down. There's a far greater risk of expanding our children's anger when we encourage them to reject it—just get over it, or don't put it on display for others to see.

I love how children's author, Elaine Whitehouse addresses anger in her book for children *There's a Volcano in My Tummy*.[2] She writes, "We aim to help children to be aware of when they become angry in the early stages so that they have some choices about what they do with that feeling." If children use anger as a distraction, they avoid thinking about the pain (loss) that it causes, and turn their anger to others. Some children even harm themselves to numb the pain. But, back to Elaine's statement about helping them identify choices when they become angry—that's where we come in as their most trusted adults.

From the Child Development View

Beginning in infancy, children express anger. It is a basic human emotion that lasts throughout life just like surprise, joy, happiness, sadness, anxiety, or fear. But developmentally, angry outbursts in children begin to taper off around the time a child gets to kindergarten. I could see a marked difference in anger in the four- and five-year-olds that I taught in prekindergarten, versus my five- and six-year-old kindergarteners and first graders.

A closer look at anger in children shows us that it is often a reaction to one of three things: 1) distress; 2) fear; and 3) frustration. In my field, we don't view anger as good or bad unless prolonged to the point where it becomes harmful both physically and emotionally to children. It's considered an emotion that everyone needs to protect themselves from whatever is deemed harmful.

Anger provides the start-up for the fight-or-flight response in kids' brains, alerting them of impending danger—whether it's fear of loss, or the distress caused by so much sadness all around them.

Others often consider anger as a negative emotion, and I would posit that grief brings a hall pass to kids suffering from losing something, or someone they love. It's OK. It's one of the five stages of grief and not one of the stages is labeled as "bad."

Think of anger as little bits of emotional steam that must release, and the more we shut off the release valve, the worse it will be for children. Every day, when children are expected to control their anger, if we discount or rebuff their feelings, it can strangely enough rob them of their ability to move forward in building block upon block of healing and strength.

Dr. Kübler-Ross writes that, "Anger is a necessary stage of the healing process and the more willing we are to feel anger, the more it will begin to dissipate."[3] As children experience or recognize feelings of anger or any other emotion, they use the power of strong emotions to guide them forward toward calming. It is the powerlessness or out of control feeling that often brings anger in the first place.

As we struggle to figure out anger from grief, we know that during this stage a child may blame others for these feelings. And here's where it gets uncomfortable. Their anger can last for days, weeks, months and even years (and forever) if not dealt with. They get "stuck" on the anger train, riding it to places that won't bring them back to self-control and resiliency.

Anger cannot be "chosen" to feel or not to feel. It is a natural response to life's challenges based upon our need of "enoughness" or self-esteem and self-worth. It has its place in healing as sometimes it's the only emotion with which children can identify during times of grief and loss. Allow them to feel it as long as needed. But, as long as it (1) does not cause self-harm, and (2) does not cause harm to others.

Anger Triggers

Of course, self-regulation is the highest form of managing emotions, especially anger. It is a lifelong skill to learn, but children especially benefit from learning how to over-ride emotions with replacement behaviors. With help, kids can learn to identify what triggers their anger in order to "see it coming"—to think about what is causing their grief anger. You can benefit from knowing your child's triggers, too. It's another way you can provide support during grief and loss. I've included some typical triggers, but take time to observe / listen and watch your child's patterns of anger. Then try to associate angry behavior as a byproduct of one or more triggers below. For example, if your child is feeling left out, is their anger attached to that event? Use the Checklist to keep track of your child's triggers:

- ☐ Parents' anger
- ☐ Grief and loss of someone or something
- ☐ Left out
- ☐ Being talked about
- ☐ Large groups
- ☐ Left alone
- ☐ Criticized
- ☐ Not getting enough sleep
- ☐ Teased or harassed
- ☐ Loss of privilege
- ☐ Too much screen time
- ☐ Having to wait
- ☐ Embarrassment/disappointment
- ☐ Hunger
- ☐ Loud noises

My work as a teacher of young children also included an ABCs of anger behavior. The three components that follow were invaluable when assisting children in learning to recognize what made them angry. I encourage you to consider these three steps to map out a plan for grieving children. By trying to look at the before, during, and after behaviors between you and your children, anger associated with grief can be addressed in a more practical way:

A—*Antecedents* or what happens (the triggers) before the anger behavior. This is what "sets off" your child or has in the past. Is it a place, a person, a thing? Be prepared to do some coaching/preventive teaching prior to the event. For example, if you are going to deliver sad news, prepare yourself and the environment for your child rather than waiting for him to react.

B—Describe the actual *Behavior* such as hitting, breaking things, cursing, crying, doing self-harm, throwing tantrums, etc., rather than generalizing the behavior as misbehaving or acting out. Try to remove yourself emotionally from the behavior. We are asking a child to be the most in control during what may be the hardest thing (grieving) when they have no reference point, or "schooling" for this.

C—*Consequences* are needed that are non-punitive and will continue to provide support for a child. As you make consequences fit, or become equal to the unwanted behavior, work with your child to provide an opportunity to make a new plan of behavior for the next time she is triggered.

There are three types of anger that are commonly discussed in child guidance courses and textbooks: (1) outward anger; (2) inward anger; and (3) passive anger. Which one most typically describes your child's anger? All three are equal in that one isn't better than the other. All are often associated with grieving children

and deserve our attention:
- *Outward—Expressing their anger by shouting, pouting, being verbally or physically abusive toward others*
- *Inward—Keeping feelings inside, using self-harm, denying themselves with food or relationships*
- *Passive—Using passive-aggressive behaviors.*

So, we've looked at lots of information about anger, triggers and grief, but how do we cultivate a healthy relationship with grief and anger for our children? How do they get "unstuck"? Without question, it starts with acceptance and knowing that even though it may seem like an endless cycle, it will subside or dissipate as Kübler-Ross describes.[4] Children will recover from anger if we respond in ways that encourage them to allow it to "wash" over them, and then make its way back out to a calm sea.

⇜Strategies⇝

1. Talk about triggers of anger with children who are grieving. Give them cues for how anger feels and then how to work through to the other side of it.

2. Recognize your own anger and determine how it makes kids feel. Younger (and sometimes older) kids aren't yet developmentally prepared to process anger from others in a healthy way. Also, be on alert for siblings, peers, and other adults who get angry with your child. A child's response is usually to get angry too, due to their lack of emotional regulation.

3. Let children express the grief they feel, even through anger. It may feel a little risky, but offering private spaces to "un-bottle" these big feelings and talk about the loss, now and later, frees the child to deal with his anger and ward off emotional trauma.

I just can't say this enough!

4. Help your child recognize anger as a feeling and separate it from the behavior of acting out. "It's okay to be mad, but it's not okay to slam the door."

5. Anger Rules: Establish rules that focus on what they can and cannot do; use statements such as, "It's okay to feel angry, but it's not okay to hurt others, yourself, or things (Whitehouse)."[3] "Remember our rules. Let's figure out what you <u>can</u> do instead of what you are doing with your anger."

6. Teach children unstuck-ness. Model ways that you get unstuck. "I can't stop feeling angry that your brother died; I must be feeling stuck. I'm going to look at some pictures of him and remember something funny that he did."

7. Breathing Exercises—Help your child learn to take big breaths in order to calm himself when angry. Slow and deep breaths are known to reduce anger. Have them breathe slowly into the nose and out of the mouth for the best results. But, know that saying, "Just breathe" can be anxiety producing instead of anger reducing for some kids. Breathe with them; show them how to breathe through their anger or get to the other side of it.

8. Make an anger stoplight with red, green, and yellow circles. Have your younger child point to the light/color that represents how she feels in an anger episode. Stay with her, or keep checking on your child until she moves to Green on the stoplight. Note: Red stands for, "I'm really angry." Yellow stands for, "I'm feeling a little anger." And Green stands for, "I'm starting to feel okay now."

9. Create a "Feelings" poster with two columns—I'M FEELING & I WANT TO FEEL. Older children can create their own or assist you.

Some typical feelings they can write on the poster are:

> I'm Feeling—*Sad, Scared, Angry, Lonely, Frustrated*
> I Want To Feel—*Happy, Excited, Hopeful*

10. Read books about anger and how to work through it. These are some of my favorites that you can find at most bookstores:

    The Boy With the Big, Big Feelings

    Mad Isn't Bad

    My Mouth is a Volcano

    A Little Spot of Anger

    When I Feel Frustrated

    When Sophie Gets Angry—Really, Really Angry

    A Volcano in My Tummy

    How to Take the GRRR out of Anger

11. Anger Coping Skills—Make a poster or a list of things your child can do to replace angry behaviors such as "Tell funny stories or jokes." Place it in a handy spot to use when your child begins to get angry. Have your child use the following prompts to recenter when angry. Sometimes he will need your help and sometimes he can do it by himself. Of course, a child's list will depend upon the emotional development and age of the child.

    - I will ask you for a funny story.
    - I can feel angry but I will try to stay calm.
    - Anger can't drive my brain. I'm the driver.
    - Things don't always go my way but I don't have to be angry.
    - I will draw or paint something when I'm done crying.
    - I will take a walk to find my control again.
    - I will take 10 deep breaths to charge my control batteries.

- I will get in my magic bubble and go to my happiest place.
- I will find people who make me laugh.

12. Anger Bead Bracelet—String three beads of three sizes to make a bracelet. Help your child self-regulate by identifying how big the anger is by touching the largest bead, the middle-sized bead, or the smallest bead. Talk about what to do when he has the biggest anger feeling such as, find an adult to talk to, or take a time away (instead of time-out) and do something by himself. The middle-sized anger bead is a reminder to watch out for anger to get bigger. The smallest bead is a representation of beginning anger and how children can seek distractions for themselves when they feel anger coming. They can ask an adult for help or to talk to, or learn to identify triggers that can help anger grow if not addressed.

13. Sometimes you just have to walk away and wait; "let it rest" before trying to restore calm in your child. Or, keep talking in your calmest voice. Everything has a season, a time. Maybe you need time to calm as well, as your anger can prevent your child from restoring his center or getting back to calm.

...

For every minute you are angry, you lose
60 seconds of happiness.
—Ralph Waldo Emerson

-29-

Bargaining–Stage Three

*Guilt is often bargaining's companion. The "if onlys" cause us to find
fault with ourselves and what we "think" we could have
done differently. We remain in the past, trying
to negotiate our way out of the hurt.*
—Elizabeth Kübler–Ross and David Kessler[1]

Children use bargains to plead for a loved one not to die, or to come back after death. It is what my younger daughter described as trading. When we hear phrases like, "Please, God. Bring my mom back and I'll be good for the rest of my life." Or, "If you won't let my sister die, I'll never be mean to her again." When Kassi was six, I was in the throes of doctoral dissertation research. She was curious. "Mom, what do you do every day when you watch kids at the center?" This would be easy, right? Hardly. "Well, I watch children and how they let other kids play with them, or get to sit by them, you know, be with them." (I carefully left out words like rebuff and acceptance.) "Like hang out," she asked? She thought for a second. "Like trading!" She decided when you ask for something in return for something that you are willing to give, you are in "kid-speak," trading!

In this third stage, there is an attempt to regain control or squeeze a few more moments out of what has been our normal. We make the most bargains with those we perceive to be more in control or a more competent authority such as God. Children think by changing something (such as a behavior), they can undo or even prevent something happening in the case of anticipated loss. The vulnerability and helplessness they feel can cause them to bargain before and after loss, often as an attempt to get back to what is normal or familiar to them. Even though bargaining may be impossible to achieve where death is concerned, this stage represents a continuum of grief as kids negotiate or make deals (or trade).

Feelings of guilt (they couldn't stop the loss), shame (it wasn't them who died, instead, it was their sibling or parent); blame (God took my mom); fear and anxiety (Will I die too?); and insecurity (What will happen to me now?) are all possible before the acceptance of reality comes.

Bargaining also provides breaks from grieving, as waiting for the response from a higher power or someone in control can provide an intermission or a reprieve for them. As long as they can bargain, kids can refuse the reality of the impending loss or death. And, no child wants to experience constant emotional pain, so bargaining postpones sadness in many instances. Just know they are bargaining because they are clinging to strings of promise attached to spools of hope.

❧Strategies❧

1. Accept your own reality of impending loss as well as loss that has already occurred. It will be difficult for children to move on to acceptance if they see you continue the stage of bargaining

2. Give children time. Accepting the reality of loss takes time and your child needs you to patiently understand their need to continue to bargain. Allow them to share their thoughts and seek professional help if you don't see any movement toward accep-

tance.

3. Help children shift their focus to things they <u>can</u> control such as sports they will play, plans for trips or outings, projects to begin (or continue/finish), and resuming practice on anything they stopped while grieving.

4. Allow them negotiating power over things they can actually achieve, such as allowances for chores, what they can wear, and places they want to go

5. Include them in family decisions when appropriate. Again, we are giving them more control over their lives due to loss, where they have no control.

-30-

Depression-Stage Four

Sometimes, only one person is missing, and the whole world seems depopulated.

—ALPHONSE DE LAMARTINE

Dr. Bob Deits describes depression as a way of taking time out from working through grief. In his book *Life After Loss*, he says, "It is like lifting a barbell over your head. But there comes a time when the weight is too heavy… and you have no choice but to rest before trying to lift it again."[1]

When we think of depression in children we often think of prolonged sadness and feelings of hopelessness. Sometimes it's accompanied by irritability and changes in mood or fear and worry. Children may feel discouraged at this stage, coming to the realization that loss is final and the physical person they knew and loved is not coming back. They may be left alone without parental anchors and guideposts. Uncertainty overcomes certainty and children can become despondent and unresponsive to their normal routines (and even to us).

A feeling of helplessness settles in. And since depression can be disguised, we often have a false sense of hope and security of their wellbeing. "Although some fears and worries are typical in children, persistent or extreme forms of fear and sadness could be due to anxiety or depression," says Dr. Deits.[2] Just to be clear, occasional sadness and hopelessness is common in children who are grieving. It is the persistence of those feelings that are alarming.

For the moment, give some thought to the changes in behaviors below followed by the strategies, and how you can incorporate them into your child's daily routine. Just because a child is sad does not mean they are depressed. Depression lasts longer than occasional sadness, is more intense and often debilitating. And, many children skip this stage altogether or go through it briefly; keep that in mind as well.

Depression and Children — Changes in Behaviors

Depression in children is often difficult to diagnose and treat. Watch for the following behavior or activity changes in children as possible indicators or signs of depression, especially if prolonged or are extreme changes in the child's typical behavior. Share your observations with your pediatrician or family doctor to get assurance that you are giving a grieving child as much support as needed:

- Prolonged sadness
- Excessive crying
- Physical pains that weren't there before the loss
- Loss of interest in things that brought joy before
- Change in sleeping patterns—more or less than normal or typical, prior to loss
- Change in energy levels—with more or less than before
- Feeling guilty about the loss
- Changes in eating patterns—more or less than before the loss
- Greater difficulty paying attention or following directions

I can't encourage you enough to talk to your health care provider if your child shows chronic or sustained symptoms of depression and/or anxiety. And most importantly, feelings that accompany depression aren't always visible.

I'm a broken record, I know, but as important as we are in maintaining good emotional health for children, sometimes we just aren't enough. Your and your child's school involvement will be crucial in implementing a treatment plan from a health professional.

Sadness and Grief

Sadness is often an accompanying factor of depression. But it's refreshing to me that after sadness can often come the "next"—the other side—"the rainbow after the storm." This necessary sadness may be what makes us compassionate humans. It is truly a blessing in disguise. Funny how I never knew exactly what that phrase meant, but it fits grief with sadness so well.

Embracing the broken–heartedness of grief will most likely occur in each stage of grief, but especially in the depression stage. For example, Dr. Alan Wolfelt describes intense sorrow as a "hallmark symptom of grief, which is the consequence of losing something we care about. In this way, you could say that sadness and love are inextricably linked."[3] So, if losing someone (or something) that we love brings sadness, we can take that pain and lean in to it, sit with it, let it brew and stew. We have to take as long as it takes to work through any particular grief stage with all its sadness and pain. To look at sadness as a good thing such as when hope springs from despair, can be a necessary emotion.

Being heartbroken often makes us move from one emotional point to another; it plays such an important role in grieving. We see how it causes us to see clearer—to see who is left with us needing our love and care, particularly our children.

As we learn to lean in, get closer, we often model breaking through (not conquering) grief for our children. We show them how to re-adjust and re-cast a life now without a loved one, keeping their memories close. And, if you are like me, someone who always wants to know everything about everything—the end before the beginning—I find it comforting to look at stages of grief as messy, and yet having structure. I am also comforted by the possibility of a more tidy, final stage—*acceptance*.

༄Strategies༄

1. Are kids getting enough exercise and physical activity daily, especially sports? Or, has physical activity sort of gone by the wayside during this period of grief? Now is a good time to start or restart.

2. Take time to listen to kids when they are talking to you AND when they are talking to others! Really listen! My favorite is, "I've got 2 minutes. Let's hear it!" I found that what children need to tell me rarely takes 2 minutes, and usually only a few seconds, but is well worth my time.

3. Step up the nutritious meal planning and let them help. Has fast food become the staple of their diet? When you announce, "It's time for dinner!" do your children jump in the car?

4. Give kids a budget for their weekly or monthly snacks and have them shop for them or help you shop. Help them prepare "Must" and "May" lists before going to the store (or ordering online). There are snacks that are "Musts" such as fruits, veggies etc. to buy and snacks that are in the "May" category. You know the ones I'm talking about!

5. Are they getting enough sleep? The US Center for Disease Control says preschoolers need 10-13 hours per day, including naps and school agers need 9-12 hours per day.[4] How do your children's sleep schedules measure up to this suggestion? Take a first step to improve their schedules as you can.

6. Pay attention to what your child eats and drinks before bedtime. Eating and consuming any caffeinated drinks too close to bedtime (especially after dinner, or "supper" in my neck of the woods) can keep children awake, resulting in irritability, lack of focus, or crankiness the next day.
7. Use APPs (applications) with soothing nature sounds to help children fall asleep.
8. Provide relaxation time before bedtime, such as, reading, simple yoga breathing activities, or anything sans screen time.
9. Get them reading. Provide books to read such as picture books for our youngest and chapter books for older kids. Read with them as often as you can, even if it's a couple of pages per night.
10. Play soft music that signals bedtime; or, set up a bedtime routine. First, we take a bath; then we brush our teeth; then we read a book (or look at a picture book for younger children); and finally, we say our prayers / send good wishes and thoughts to our loved ones.
11. Check noise and light levels in your child's sleeping area. The darker the better for falling and staying asleep but children may need a nightlight for comfort. Along with producing less melatonin, sleeping with a light on (especially TV) can stimulate brain activity all night.
12. Help kids connect with other family members and children by returning to school as soon as possible; attending social events such as joining clubs, parties, performances, having play dates, and going to sleepovers.

-31-
Acceptance-Stage Five

Acceptance is often confused with the notion of being all right or okay. This is not the case. Most people don't ever feel okay or all right about the loss of a loved one.
— Elizabeth Kübler-Ross and David Kessler

Once children realize that death cannot be undone and begin to process grief, they may reach what Elizabeth Kübler-Ross and David Kessler describe as the fifth and final stage of grief— *acceptance*. They write, "Acceptance is often confused with the notion of being all right or okay with what has happened."[1] But this is not true. Our lives may not ever be the same as before the loss, but with nurturing and guidance, children can regain familiar routines and some similarity to what their lives were before.

A new relationship with the deceased loved one is now shaping and our children are being asked to continue living in a world where someone is now missing and never coming back.

I talked with Mary, a mother who lost her young son in a car accident over 20 years ago. She still remembers vividly how her other children were affected by his death. "The grief was too much," she told me. "My husband wanted to die, too, but I told him we had two other kids that needed us and we had to help them get through losing their brother and that takes time." Mary felt it just wasn't possible for her children to take in all that grief and loss at one time, and for this reason, there was a need for time to adjust, and time to accept this new information. The researcher in me is seeing a pattern here in Mary's words—time.

I'm pretty sure that time *doesn't* heal all wounds, but maybe it brings a new perspective of hope and promise to grieving children. When we take time to really focus on the children left behind, while continuing to remember the ones who died, we bring balance to the lives of the children still with us. Just maybe, time is the main ingredient for acceptance.

Gracie Bell

I remember when my grandmother Gracie Bell, whom we fondly called "Grace" at her request, died of cancer in 1971. "Grandma makes me feel too old," she would say.

We were pretty much strangers to death as she was our first close family member to die. She was 62. I, along with my siblings, Diane and Darryl and our 12 cousins were so connected to her that it felt like life would never be the same. And it wasn't/isn't. She made each of us feel as though we were an only grandchild. She loved unconditionally. Acceptance seemed as if it would not happen in our lifetime. Yes, it was Grace's time to die, and yes, it was our time to go on living. No, it wasn't fair. But death never is. Does your child have a "Gracie Bell?" I hope so.

Child Development Lens on Acceptance

Child development theorist Jean Piaget used the term *equilibrium* to describe when a child re-centers or gets back to a place of comfort, or, where we can understand new information based on what we already know. It's learning something new—a new norm that helps children understand and eventually accept death.[2] Healing?

Kübler-Ross and Kessler write, "Healing looks like remembering, recollecting, and reorganizing."[3] I would add that for children, due to their ages and stages of development, healing sometimes means shaping a new persona of the deceased, especially if they were very young when their loved one died, and, depending upon how attached they were to the loved one.

In earliest stages of development, our youngest children may not have memories of the loved one, but may create a fantasy person to fill in for the deceased, such as, "I don't remember my mom much, but I know that she was kind. My Grandma told me." Or, "She was beautiful 'cause I saw pictures of her."

And remember how brutally honest (egocentric) children can be. Their recollections don't always paint beautiful pictures of the deceased. Children are often blunt...crisp...do not sugarcoat their memories: "All I remember about my brother is that he was mean to me. But he let me borrow his baseball glove and I still have it."

Acceptance may be the final stage in Kübler-Ross' five stages of grief, but I'm wondering if it may be the hardest. It's too final. Too much of "the end" and grief has no end. Far from it. No one can tell your child to "just accept it; get over it."

I'll end this topic with a story from Dr. Garry Landreth's book *Play Therapy: The Art of the Relationship*. Garry is a renowned play therapist, author, and Professor Emeritus from the University of North Texas. He describes what speaks to me as moving through *stages of grief* from play therapy sessions with a six-year-old boy whose grandfather died two years before. Dr. Landreth wrote how the child and his mother would take trips to the cemetery to "talk" to his grandfather through the hole for a flower vase in the grandfather's headstone prior to coming to play therapy. But by the fifth play therapy session, the child could verbalize that his grandfather was dead, moving to what appears to be Stage 5: Acceptance—"My PawPaw died you know."[4] Dr. Landreth's book is a fascinating read in learning more about CCPT/Child Centered Play Therapy.

❧Strategies❧

1. Reassure children that acceptance does not mean they are finally over the death of someone or not allowed to grieve anymore. We can say things like, "Let's think of ways to keep remembering your brother," or, "What would he want us to do if he was here?" And, "We can donate that box of his things when you are ready. Let's do a check-in in a month and decide."

2. Make small changes toward acceptance. This new journey of healing means adjusting in order to be more accepting. "It's okay to stop setting a place at the dinner table when you are ready." Or, "You didn't cry today when you heard your mom's favorite song."

3. Help children accept loss by continuing to grieve alongside them. It may take months and even years (if ever) to work through acceptance.

4. What if love is a big part of what is missing when kids lose someone? What if love is what will bring them closer to accepting the loss of someone else? Pile it on in the form of us accepting our children.

5. Remember that kids think differently than adults. Try to see things from their perspective.

6. Acceptance is not replacement. One definition of acceptance is "tolerance." We can't replace the loved one but we can help children make new relationships; find new hope in everyday activities that are the "goings on" of life; and seek tolerance.

-32-

Emotional Milestones, Children, & Grief

The soul is healed by being with children.
— FYODOR DOSTOYEVSKY

Individual emotional milestones or benchmarks as well as strategies to kick-start children's development on this grief journey are the essence of this chapter. As adults, we can play a critical role in helping our children "grieve better" as we respond to their emotional pain in appropriate ways. We know that all children express their emotions differently, and it is unique to each child. Some show more emotion, or take longer to recover from intense sadness or fear. Other children show more optimism, emotional hardiness and grit. Luckily, either isn't good or bad. It's more about how tuned in we are to them, and how deeply the connection between us exists.

Puddle Jumping, Kids, and Grief

I like what Child Bereavement UK describes as "puddle jumping"—"The way children move in and out of grief, with the puddle being filled with grief."[1] It seems children can't stay in the puddles of sadness very long as they tend to jump in and out, again and again, finding distractions. It's as if they have to take breaks from their grief, unlike adults, "who feel a bit like being in a river of grief" and spend more time there. In truth, kids jump in and out of puddles of feelings in general. They don't seem to stay with any particular feeling for long. It's all part of a child's way of thinking—especially during periods of grief.

It isn't because children are disingenuous about their grief. It's really because they can't mentally and emotionally hold on to extreme grief and loss too long, and appear to jump in and out of it. And that's a good thing! The trick is to decide when to come out of the puddle of grief and jump back in when necessary.

As teachers and parents, we strive for ways to prevent emotional scarring that will last many years, or our children staying in grief puddles for too long. It's worth noting, just like our children, we take wrong turns, get lost on the grief highway. But most of the time we continue on, looking for that next stop or road sign that points us in the better direction. I call these emotional mile markers and it makes a huge difference when we become aware of them in children.

Emotional Mile Markers & Milestones

In the pages that follow in this chapter, my goal is to supply you with knowledge of children's developmental milestones aka "mile markers," and the impact on how they can be used to grieve well. Once you filter out the noise of everyone telling you how children should be grieving, you feel calmer and more certain of your own decisions and actions, using children's development at the core of your decision making.

We start this journey with Infants and Toddlers and then take a look at Preschool children, ending with milestones for School Agers. I draw from my book, *Developmental Milestones of Young Children*[2] for many of the strategies offered for each age group.

Infants and Toddlers: Ages Birth to Three

Maybe you haven't really thought about it, but infants and toddlers, too, have their own way of grieving. This age group is a special kind of mourner and needs as much or even more than older children from caring adults. Author Alan Wolfelt writes, "Yes, even babies grieve." And, "Any child old enough to love is old enough to mourn."[3] They can sense when something has markedly changed, such as an important person now missing in their lives. The people closest to them such as parents, grandparents, care providers, and siblings are now somehow different—sad, angry, irritable, stressed or distressed, or even depressed. Something is wrong.

Knowing our youngest children can detect a change in our emotions is key in addressing our and their grief. Their understanding of death and dying at this age is very limited, but their ability to sense stress and anxiety in those closest to them is in full operation.

Jennifer Lansford from Duke University shares that infants as young as one month can sense when a parent or caregiver is being affected emotionally, when something is different in how they are typically cared for. She writes, "While infants vary in their sensitivity, research shows that babies sense and react to their parents' emotional cues...they're picking up on what you're giving off."[4]

And what if you are giving off those signs that you aren't able to care for your baby? In *Developmental Milestones of Young Children* I write, "Babies can often tell when others are sad, happy, or angry by the tone of the voice." And, "The baby begins to cry or fuss as the family member or caregiver leaves his sight. He appears to notice the absence of the significant person."[5] This may happen when parents are unavailable to care for their infants due to making funeral arrangements and attending funeral events during the period of anticipated loss when a loved one is dying, or the days and months after a loss.

Changes

Infants and toddlers somehow know that things are different as other people may now be giving them attention when you can't. They grieve not only the deceased, but also what they knew and loved. Daily normal activities have been disrupted. Babies can sense the absence or even miss the sound of the loved one's voice, their smell, their smile, or familiar routines and become more fussy than normal.[6]

We cannot think they are too little to understand, or hope they won't be affected because they don't respond in the same way as their older brothers and sisters. Alan Wolfelt reminds us, "When someone they love dies, children of all ages need our time and attention if they are to heal and grow to be emotionally healthy adults."[7]

Infancy

Dr. Alan Fogel is a favorite author of mine. I often used his textbook when I taught the course on infant and toddler development at Texas Woman's University. He calls our responses to babies "contingency;" when we follow an infant's smile or coo, she will in turn repeat or mirror these behaviors.[8] Infants react to the emotions of the adults who care for them.

Our responsiveness to infants or simply talking with them will directly impact their mood and behavior. For example, when you smile at your baby, she responds (talks) to you and seeks additional smiles and interactions. Those responses are contingent upon your actions with her, and how much you continue to engage and communicate with her.

As young as one, a baby already has the expectation that their distress from something such as loss, will be met by someone with whom they love and trust. So, consider how the loss of someone with whom the infants were extremely attached can impact them, as well as the loss (at least temporary) of the interactions with the people who are mourning.

These "secure base scripts" from John Bowlby are strong as they trust you to come to their aid, even while you are grieving.[9] If you just can't, then use your village, your tribe of support! The more we can continue to be there for them, to keep the routines of our youngest intact during loss and grief, the better able we are to buffer adverse effects.

Toddlers and Stress

Toddlerhood is often described as ages 18–36 months and is a magical time for children. Some say toddlerhood begins when children begin to talk and walk. By any definition, toddlers are no longer babies. They have reached an important milestone of thinking, and they are beginning to understand that others exist outside of them.

Toddlers are now actively participating instead of passively receiving information from those around them. "They are becoming aware of their physical and psychological separateness from the caregiver."[10]

There is little written about toddlers and grief, but much attention has been given to toddlers and stress. Each child will react to stressful situations differently but will often try to find something to comfort themselves such as an adult, a blanket or toy, or a thumb or pacifier. But, Dr. Fogel reminds us that nothing (he calls them transitional objects) can replace an important adult when a toddler is in distress.[11]

Separation is known to be the most challenging and anxiety producing emotion in infants, but oddly enough, toddlers are beginning to understand that people will come back for them. You can see how this makes the death of someone loved so challenging for toddlers. They have just begun to trust that people will return and now this. It is critical that toddlers are around others they can trust if they have to be left during a time of loss.

❧Strategies☙

1. Be attentive to babies' and toddler's moods. Are they crying more frequently or less frequently than before the loss?

2. Be attentive to <u>your</u> moods. Are you visibly distressed, talking to and holding your baby less frequently? If your youngest are responding to your distress from an anticipated, impending, or recent death, it may be time to practice calming by giving more attention to your breathing. There are breathing "apps" on smartphones and watches that remind you to take deep, slow breaths every hour.

3. Check out Stress.org[12] for tips on breathing deeply (as opposed to typical shallow breaths) as it increases the supply of oxygen to the brain and stimulates the parasympathetic nervous system. Just by taking deep breaths, we can promote a state of increased calm. Try it. Your baby will thank you for it! (https://www.stress.org/take-a-deep-breath)

4. Make eye-contact frequently with your baby. Reassurance that you are there is a wonderful antidote to grief. Be as comforting as you can. Also, make physical and verbal contact, frequent holding and hugging; talking and singing.

5. Try baby massage for relaxing a tense infant or toddler. Also, placing infants on the chest of a caring adult provides something known as kangaroo or skin-to-skin care and can soothe and relax a crying infant. Keep routines the same as much as possible, even if you have to get someone to take your place for the moment.

6. Infancy to Age Two: Watch for anxiety, irritability, and marked changes in eating and sleeping. Give lots of physical and verbal attention in this age range as they are often looking for the deceased. They may become increasingly anxious if they are around strangers and will need that one significant other to cling to. They may even delay grief as infants focus on what happens now instead of how it happened or what happens next.

7. Toddlers Ages Two to Three: Be prepared to answer lots of questions, again and again. When younger children don't understand the finality of death, they will continue to ask you, "Where's my daddy?" Also, watch for regressive behaviors where they are acting in ways that are atypical for their age (bed wetting, tantrums, restless sleep).

Preschool Children: Ages 3-5

Preschool age children have left toddlerhood behind and entered early childhood. Our youngest preschoolers live in a pretend world with vivid imaginations. They show signs of concern during the death of a loved one, but as they grow, egocentricity, or "my way" of thinking has them seeing everything from their own viewpoint. Their sense of self is coming in to full bloom and only includes their world and those closest to them. Lots of time spent playing will be a preschooler's daily work, with questions about death sprinkled in between.

I have used Marjorie Kostelnik's textbooks on guidance for as long as I can remember and her knowledge of social development in young children is unparalleled as an author. She and her peers write in *Guiding Children's Social Development and Learning*, regarding preschool children, [they] "May not react immediately and may delay grief, with full understanding coming even years later. They may appear to be through mourning before they actually are."[13]

She and others bring home the point that young children are in the beginning stages of developing perspective taking or trying to feel what another is feeling. However, both empathy and perspective taking won't be fully developed until much later. And some of us struggle our whole lives to develop these two critical emotions. That's why it's so important to foster these in children, to try and speed up the process.

We do that by being trusted adults who model empathy, kindness, and look at other's different points of view. We ask preschoolers questions such as, "Can you tell me what you remember about

Daddy," and, "Can you name a big feeling that you are having?"

Know that our youngest preschoolers may not be able to articulate or explain their grief but can certainly feel the absence of their loved one differently than adults or even older kids. They are now able to identify feelings in general, so be prepared to link those feelings to their grief. I address this in *Developmental Milestones*: "At this age, the young preschooler is beginning to talk about how he feels and identify emotions as mad, sad, happy, and scared."[14]

Preschoolers, like toddlers, may have regressive behaviors where they temporarily revert back to something such as baby talk, thumb sucking, or bed wetting which act as coping mechanisms for dealing with stress. We respond without shaming or telling them to be a big boy or girl.

Again, validate their feelings and be patient. Ask if they need extra hugs or to be held. For bed wetting, simply help them fix the problem such as changing their sheets without criticism or even better, be prepared for mishaps by putting sheets and fresh pajamas out where older children can access them without waking you. If your child is reverting back to behaviors you thought were conquered and it becomes too much, is it possible to get help at this time so that you can divide the duties with someone?

Marjorie Kostelnik and colleagues tell us preschool children "focus on what happens now instead of what led to the death and how it could have been prevented. They demonstrate great curiosity about the detail, such as the funeral and the coffin."[15] They may or may not talk about their pain, but the separation from a loved one who is dying or has died is very real for them. It is just so important that we don't overlook our grieving preschool age children.

✒Strategies✑

1. Help preschoolers understand the body doesn't work anymore when someone dies and that death is permanent. We can use phrases such as, "Once the heart stops beating and lungs stop breathing, our bodies cannot live anymore and that's when we die." And, "Jacob died because his body stopped working and can't be fixed."

2. Kids need to know that death is universal—it happens to everything (flowers, plants, pets, etc.) and everyone. Talk about life cycles with sensitivity. Let them ask the questions that lead the conversation, and be ready to provide facts if you hear misunderstandings. "Johnny said we turn to dirt when we are buried." Your response: "I think he means dust, but that doesn't happen for a long time."

3. Answer only what they ask. Allow preschoolers to digest your answers and then come back to you when they have more questions or with the same question.

4. *Reflect* on what they say by saying back to them what you sense they are feeling. "You wish your brother didn't die. You miss him." Or, "It makes you uncomfortable to be around all these people (at the funeral, etc.)."

5. Encourage preschoolers to play. You can set up play experiences during initial grief and beyond. They process feelings through play, even play that involves re-enacting death.

6. Hold them tightly. Show them how important they are to you and to their family by offering extra hugs and attention. Use these terms to provide a name for what they are feeling. "I can

see that you are feeling sad (or scared, etc.). Can I sit with you (or hold you) for a little while until you feel better?"

7. If your child hits or uses any other aggressive behavior to show he is angry or scared, etc., "Use your words to tell us how you feel" is a great go-to. Teaching them to say, "I'm so angry" goes a long way in learning to express emotion. And, preschoolers learn to regulate by watching the trusted adults in their worlds regulate their own emotions.

School Age Children: Ages 6–12

School age children are our most mature grievers, as their grief mirrors those of adults much more than their younger siblings. They are better self-regulators and have more (developed) coping strategies. But, until the loss of a loved one happens to them, even though they can grasp the permanence of death, they perceive it as just something that always happens to someone else. Younger school agers may also believe that death happens to grandmas and grandpas, or only to "older people," even though they have a clear concept of death by this age. Everything lives and then it dies.

Developing the Death Concept in School Agers

School-age children may still show their "egocentric selves" when thinking about how death will affect them. They also assume that whatever they are thinking or feeling is the same as what other people are feeling. They also experience anxiety and fear, much like adults. Let me refer to my book *Developmental Milestones* once again. "This is the age when children may worry about things to come and show frustration or symptoms of stress but refrain from discussing their fears with adults."[16] Peer influence is so strong during the school-age years, and a need to seem "tough," even while grieving, may supersede their need to be comforted and reassured.

Still, our younger, less emotionally mature school agers may still believe their dog will wake up once they have been told the vet "put him to sleep." They will often have lots of follow up questions about the permanence of death and how death will affect them, especially causes of death. "How does he (God) choose who dies?"

and, "Will I die too, when I get sick?" may be asked. Also, "Where did he go when he died?"

Older school agers, between 7 and 8 and beyond, are beginning to put death into a "things that are final" or permanence category but ask very detailed questions in their quest to understand more. As they approach the age of twelve, they may ask more adult-like questions such as, "Why did it happen to her?" and, "Could it have been prevented?" Or, "Why didn't we do something?" And, "How did he die?" But, at the same time, they can understand causes of death as well as what is referred to as "applicability" or "death only applies to living things" better at this milestone.[15]

Even though some school agers may talk on an adult level and shy away from affection, they still need to be nurtured. Our love language for them involves listening unconditionally, acknowledging how very valuable they are with praise and acceptance, and spending quality time with them. They never get too old for that! Who has had a school ager on their lap? I raise my hand!

And finally, we have to check our own mental pulse. School-age children are always watching us to see if it's up or down, whether we are stressed or anxious, and approachable or off-limits. Also, they often mirror our pulse. It's okay not to be okay, and school agers are often old enough to understand. I've said this before. When someone asks, "Are you okay?," it's okay to say, "No, but I will be and thank you for your understanding and patience." I can think of no better modeling for children.

❧Strategies❧

1. What are school agers' anxiety or grief triggers? Once you figure some of these out, help your school ager recognize them. Activities can serve as cues, such as marking the calendar for

important dates that remind them of someone who died. This can reduce and/or address the stress that comes with a trigger.

2. School agers are curious and like details. Even if you don't know what happens at the funeral home after someone dies such as how a person is embalmed or what cremation entails, find resources together with answers to their questions. If this is a taboo topic for you, try to look at it as research, gaining information to help your grieving child. Chapter 44 in this book can help.

3. Model empathy; show them how to be empathetic and ask school agers in return to show empathy and care for others who are also grieving. Give them tasks to do to show empathy through kindness and concern such as delivering food to a grieving family or offering to do small chores for someone.

4. Allow them to cry. I know I talk about this at length in Chapter 15 about sacred tears, but I think it bears repeating here. Phrases such as, "Big boys don't cry," or, "Only babies cry" can be hurtful to grieving school-age children. Also, it's okay to let them see you cry.

5. A 7-year-old said to me after losing a pet, "Tell me something funny so I don't have to feel sad." Fill up your jokes and funny stories pool, especially those about the pet or someone who died.

Part 5

Resilience & Grief

-33-

Growing Resilience in a Grieving Child

Accept the good. Don't lose what you have to what you've lost!
—Lucy Hone

Resilience researcher Dr. Lucy Hone lost Abi, her 12-year-old daughter in a car accident and then turned her immense grief into helping others. In her book, *Resilient Grieving*, she set out to discover if her own knowledge could be used to enable the process of healthy grieving.[1]

As a professor, I have also researched and written about resilience and my focus has been on how we foster resilience in children. I learned that children who are more resilient, who learn to express their emotions in healthy ways are much more likely to bounce back after loss. They approach grief differently than their less resilient peers, as they have a sort of built in "grief-ometer" that tells them when they need to move to the next stage or even the next moment of grieving. In other words, they have grieved enough, for now at least.

Resilience looked like this in my then seven-year-old granddaughter Vivi, two weeks after her dog Brooks died: "I just don't want to be sad; I don't want to cry about it anymore." In her words, she had cried/grieved enough (for now). She had become wary of sadness, and being saturated in grief.

Certainly, she continued to grieve the weeks and months after, but for that moment, she had to become emotionally upright again, practicing buoyancy and coming back to the surface to maintain her emotional wellness. Later, her grief turned into acceptance which consists of reflection and recall of fond memories more than sadness of loss. That ability to bounce back in times of heartbreak is more common in some kids and less in others.

Dr. Kenneth Ginsberg[2] is a pediatrician and professor who specializes in fostering resilience in kids. He tells us that children who have vigorous amounts of resilience will understand that even though their loved one has died, the memories of that person will live on in them forever.

In your own family, each child may be different. One child may have copious amounts of resilience and another child shows less emotional hardiness. This reminds us to consider how all children are on their own developmental continuum i.e. age and stage pathway and our approaches may vary for each one.

Raising Resilient Kids

Resilient kids handle overwhelming feelings when faced with extreme loss. In order to maintain their ability to bounce back, they embrace their feelings, accept what has happened, and often with help, move through stages of grief and back again.

We know that children who are more sensitive, may have bigger challenges in overcoming grief. They absorb the feelings and emotions of those around them like little sponges, at the expense of dealing with their own. These are the children who can read our pages, know when we are in a bad mood, or are sad and just not ourselves and often become mirrors of our grief. Ultimately, children are the experts at guiding us through their needs.

Look at four factors that may explain why some kids are <u>more</u>

resilient regarding death and dying than others:

(1) When kids who have been raised in homes where adults/families are loving to one another and to them;

(2) When parents include children in their grief, making plans, and keeping them close by;

(3) When we have modeled and taught empathy (feeling badly for someone), and perspective taking, trying to understand how another person feels;

(4) When we have been open and honest about discussing death with children from their earliest questions.

What Resilient Grievers Do!

Resilient grievers do three important things most of the time in order to bounce back. According to author Kenneth Doka in his book, *Mourning Children. Children Mourning*, they 1) have an optimistic mindset, 2) believe that something good can come, and 3) keep positive memories of the deceased.[3]

Having an optimistic mindset is what Dr. Lucy Hone calls, "accept the good." She cautions us on not "losing what you have to what you have lost. You may have other family members, children, parents, and dear friends who will continue to need you."[4]

When we *believe that something good* can come from even the worst events, we practice our faith, or have confidence or trust that something or someone can help us. We seek people who give or share love, hope, and laughter and we welcome those who have positive emotions of inspiration. We need those who promote serenity to foster resilience.

Knowing that our children will benefit from those who can believe with us, we gravitate to them and ask them to stay close to us. If we are believers in a power outside of us, we let our faith magnets go to work in these darkest hours. "Draw nigh unto God, and he will draw nigh to you" (James 4:8).

In *keeping positive memories of the deceased,* we maintain a sense of control. Routines and rituals to keep their memories alive, even small ones, can bring a sense of calm over our lives that losing a loved one has taken away.

Children find predictable rituals and routines reassuring, giving them something to look forward to as well as to carry on when they become adults and have families of their own. I would add, the more children become resilient grievers, the more they overcome being emotional hostages.

Keeping positive memories alive benefit children even though you may feel that you died with the child, or husband, or parent that you lost. Bobbing (like a cork in water) is totally normal as your emotions are stretching and struggling to breathe through the loss. But, most children can ride the waves of uncertainty, keeping themselves buoyant as long as you show them glimmers of hope through attention, optimism, kindness, and love.

When we fail to realize that children are individuals first and will have their own responses to emotional grief, we may miss the boat in fostering resilience or assisting them in becoming upright, rebuilding their lives. We are the ones to provide the emotional life raft they need in order to move forward in the ongoing grief process. Notice that I use "We." I take daily doses of my own medicine.

You can't get this wrong if you are committed to fostering resilience in children—a mindset that will carry them through the next and then the next challenge. You (we) are "enough."

❧Strategies☙

1. Let children see you bounce back during this time of loss. The healthier you respond to the loss, the more resilient your child can be. Dr. Bob Deits says "...there are no lasting emotional scars" when adults, "respond in ways that help the child face loss."[5]

2. Read a children's book such as *The Tenth Good Thing About Barney* by Judith Viorst. Help your child think of 10 good things about the person (or pet) who died and draw a picture or write in a grief/resilience journal.

3. Teach children to become "button-proof!" Richard Carlson, author of *Don't Sweat the Small Stuff*, writes about life always giving us experiences that can push our buttons, but the goal should be to mentally shrug off those hurtful times. He wrote, "Here's another chance to build my strength (resilience)."[6]

4. Consider resilience boosting as a journey and not the destination. We can help our children make small changes, focusing on little things first, such as getting through one day or one hour without giving up or becoming emotionally hijacked. These little bits of progress can soon add up where grief may forever be in the background, but shows up often in the foreground.

-34-

Staying Upright During Loss

We can touch the pain directly for only so long until we have to back away. If we did not go back and forth emotionally, we could never find the strength to find peace in our loss.
— Elizabeth Kübler-Ross and David Kessler

What I love about kids who learn to express their emotions in healthy ways is that they are much more likely to be resilient. You can count on them to be the ones who are most verbal, the ones who can articulate their feelings, often paired with a story. By all means, keep them talking. Their ability to bounce back after a period of despair or tragedy can match adult resilience.

I was fortunate to hear Dr. Kenneth Ginsberg's presentation on resilience at a Military Child Education Coalition (MCEC) annual gathering a few years ago in Washington, DC. I was there presenting with my colleague, Dr. Ron Palomares-Fernandez regarding student teachers' approaches to working with military connected kids in public school classrooms. Dr. Ginsberg was the keynote speaker and his presentation was the highlight of the conference.

Dr. Ginsberg has a profound understanding of resilience and children who are grieving, calling resilience the fourth "R" along with "Readin'", "'Ritin'", and "'Rithmetic." His words ring true as he claims in his book *Building Resilience in Children and Teens*, "Even young children who may not understand death react to grieving parents."[1] This is a cue for us to realize that even though we think we are hiding our grief from them, we are not. We are at our best when we share our feelings with them, even if it is a peek at showing them our ability to move forward as we try to overcome grief.

While younger children may not understand the finality of death, older kids can understand death as the final experience in life. Again, Dr. Ginsberg tells us that children who have vigorous amounts of resilience will understand that even though their loved one has died, their memories will live on in us forever.[2]

Listening as a Resilience Booster in Kids

The last thing we may want to do or have time to do is give children our undivided attention, especially if we are in the midst of our own grief. But if we are truly committed to boosting our kids' resilience factors, and to their wellbeing and emotional hardiness, being there for them is a critically important act on our part.

And not just paying attention to their words. Being attentive to their whole selves as you let listening be your love language is a skill that some of us develop with lots of practice. It is actually defined as a process of receiving and responding to spoken and unspoken messages. It was Ernest Hemingway who said, "When people talk, listen completely. Most people never listen."[3] Maybe it's habit, but certainly unintentional on our part. I don't think any of us get up every day thinking, "I'm just not gonna' listen to my grieving child today." If setting a timer works better, sitting facing them while they talk to keep distractions away, or getting in a room or car with just the two of you, try it. Or plan date nights or excursions with your child where it's just the two of you. It takes effort I know. But it will be so well worth it in fostering resilience.

I always thought I was a good listener, especially with so much early childhood training. But my younger daughter Kassi at six years old taught me the importance of stopping what I was doing and truly listening. I was writing my doctoral dissertation and thought I was a master at multi-tasking while typing. I could type and listen to her at the same time. Right? One day after school, she began talking to me and when I didn't stop typing, she put her small hands on mine and said, "Stop, Mom. I really need you to listen to me." Point received. I'm still working on it—not the dissertation—learning to stop and listen!

We give our full attention to those we value. Just ponder that for a second. The more we value or cherish someone, the more likely we will listen and the more we boost their resilience.

❧Strategies❦

1. See the best in children. Resilience boosting occurs when we look for our children's pluses and not their minuses.

2. Practice good communication. We don't have to have the perfect words; we just have to be willing to hear.

3. Permit children to talk openly and without the answer we want to hear. As we open the door a bit more to emotional expression, we allow them to have healthy, but small eruptions rather than the need for volcanic ones.

4. Children often mirror or parrot our words. Listen to what they are saying. Do you recognize your voice? Say to them what you want to hear!

-35-

Risk and Protective Factors

*You know when I sit down and when I rise up;
you discern my thoughts from afar.*
—Psalm 139:2

When we talk about resilience in children, we have to consider their risk and protective factors. When they have high amounts of resilience, there are often lots of people in their environment who provide them with protective factors. Yet, when they are at risk, the opposite is often true.

If kids are already vulnerable or experiencing other physical and/or emotional stressors, they may crumble at the first sign of the hardship of grief. They have trouble coping with any loss which in turn gives them the opposite of protective factors—too many risk factors.

Let's dive a little deeper into these two resilience terms. They can mean the difference in living resilient lives or being at risk and lacking coping skills now and later, as they enter adulthood. We can become the linchpin in keeping the wheels on their emotions of grief. We do this by minimizing their risk of fear and harm, and adding protective factors wherever possible.

The Resilience Scale: Risk Factors

Losing someone they love is already a huge risk factor that we cannot control. However, we can help children gradually move forward by mitigating additional risks. I think of it as insulating our children from further trauma.

Kids can have high or low resilience quotients when facing loss. The good news is that support from parents, teachers, and the whole community aka their tribe, as well as their own coping skills can increase their emotional hardiness. Think of a scale with risk factors on one side and protective factors on the other. We want the scale tipped to the protective factors side to the greatest extent possible.

When experiencing relationship loss such as the death of a parent or close sibling, a child is already more "at risk" for physical and emotional illness that can continue on in to adulthood without support. And, unfortunately, this childhood bereavement often increases due to risks that were already in place prior to the loss.

Risk Factors

I've included some pre-existing risk factors that may be social and emotional, physical, or cognitive in nature and can increase grief after the death of a loved one.

Social and Emotional
- The deceased person had a terminal illness that caused high stress on the family as they anticipated the loss
- Parents were recently separated or divorced.
- Recent loss of another close member or friend.
- Behavior difficulties at school; recent move to new school or child care program; difficulty transitioning

Physical
- Pre-existing illness, chronic or terminal.

Cognitive
- Learning difficulties; attention deficit challenges; or problems concentrating

The Resilience Warehouse—Protective Factors

Several factors go into our resilience warehouse—sort of an emotional depot of things that help children grieve well. In particular, their age and stage of development is a huge component in how resilient they are while grieving, such as older kids versus younger kids, emotional maturity, and a whole host of other growth factors.

Another favorite author duo who write about kids and resilience are Drs. Robert Brooks and Sam Goldstein. In their book, *Nurturing Resilience in our Children*, they write, "By giving children choices, by modeling problem-solving behavior, by allowing them to experience success or failure as a consequence of their choices, children feel empowered and these are basic components of a resilient mindset."[1]

When resilience researcher Christie Eppler[2] explored the resilient traits of 12 school agers who had experienced the death of a parent, she found certain themes present in their stories about their grief. They identified feelings such as sadness, anger, fear, and happiness as well as themes of family and extended support. And, she found that looking at children's existing strengths and building on those was critical in fostering resilience.

Both risk and protective factors can be classified in three categories: (1) Child; (2) Family; and (3) Community, but let's take a look at protective factors in each category. If your child possesses many of these factors, you can give yourself a big pat on the back as there's a good chance he is protected. But if most factors are absent, your child may be more at risk in grieving.

The protective factors in each category below give a starting place to begin to attack those resilience busters. Note: Risk factors would be the opposite or absence of protective factors.

Child/Individual Resilience Protective Factors

- At least one stable and committed relationship with a supportive adult (this is the single most common factor in resilient children)
- Social and emotional skills
- Self-esteem or thinking highly of themselves
- Self-efficacy—knowing they can do things
- Problem solving skills
- Coping skills
- Perspective taking—seeing the other person's point of view
- Empathy—ability to attempt to understand what another is feeling
- Sympathy—imagining the feelings of someone else; being sad for them

Family Resilience Protective Factors for Children

- Most family members practice resilience
- Authoritative (firm but gentle) parenting
- Low family stress
- Sound parental mental health
- Absence of addiction in family
- Safe environment with no threat of homelessness or food in-

security; no threat of violence (domestic or neighborhood)

Community Resilience Protective Factors

- A supportive relationship with a mentor
- Positive school experiences
- Safe neighborhoods
- Close community
- Social support
- Part of religious or faith community
- Extracurricular activities

Because of your own bereavement, you may be still struggling with your grief and not able to focus on boosting the protective factors your kids need. That's okay. Boost your own protective factors first, and children can benefit from them as well. I urge all of us to consider counseling or therapy if the path is so dark we can't see the light anywhere.

Also, we should never, ever feel ashamed or embarrassed. Children may benefit from professional assistance right along with us. As a bonus, Family Therapy is keen on looking at the issue as a whole—systemic, and works to serve the entire family.

❧Strategies☙

1. Be as intentional as possible in observing children during this time. Do whatever it takes to remember to put your eyes on a grieving child. Place it in your smartphone calendar, write it in your planner, jot it on your wrist, or put it on a sticky note where you will see it often. We get so wrapped up in our own grief and taking care of all the business and emotional aspects

of it, we sometimes forget about grieving children.

2. Look for signs that more is needed from you or a trusted professional. Learn to read your child's "grief pages." Silence is a great indicator of your child's continuing grief. Some children are just the quiet type, so you may not easily recognize this as a sign of grief. That's why doing those check-ins is so important for all children.

3. Use open-ended/divergent questions that don't require a yes or no answer, but require a more developed response, verbal or nonverbal. "On a scale of 1—10, how are you feeling today?" "What was one thing that you did today that you did not want to do?" "How will you handle that next time?" These questions open the door for more conversation and are more thought provoking than, Mom: "How are you feeling today?" Child: "Good," or "Okay" (or even a shrug).

4. Teach problem solving skills by letting your kids watch you solve problems. A colleague once asked me, "Is everything okay?" I answered, "Not right now, but it will be." It's knowing that things will get back to some kind of normal that stokes resilience factors. We and our children may never be the same as before a loss, but life may become more "upright" when we give it time, and intentionally trigger our protective factors. Triggers work both ways, you know!

5. Use affirming phrases with kids such as, "I have faith in you. You can do it." "Do as much as you can and I'll help with the parts you can't." Or, "It looks like you are working really hard to get that done. Go as far as you can and let's see where you get stuck."

~36~

Bouncing Back, Moving Forward from Loss

*Who you truly are as a person is best revealed
by who you are during times of conflict and crisis.*
—Karen Salmonsohn

Bouncing back is a term I've often used when addressing the needs of children to return to a degree of what was known before faced with heartbreaking loss. There will never be a true return to normal, or what we thought of as normal before death occurred. Their lives will be forever changed. But bouncing back is the closest thing to finding their "way back" to a life that's more familiar, more do-able.

Although we may have varying amounts, I think resilience is at our very core, always bringing us back to our North Star when we allow. I know this because I've worked with so many children who are striving to get back to a place that is sheltered, safe. Just like adults, children don't like grief. It is "the uncomfortable." Most children begin to bounce back as soon as they can find their way. They are the ultimate thrivers and strivers, the bouncers.

And that's where we come in. Again, we are the *path lighters*, the pointers to the way back. In holding the torch for them, we just may find our own way back, or maybe forward is better.

But, in some cases, we become the learners, the observers. If we let them, resilient children can teach us how to bounce back, how to thrive and strive in times of our greatest challenges.

Bouncing Forward

It's true. We want children to return to what was familiar to them by learning to bounce back, but what if we also taught them to bounce forward. We can teach them new ways to problem solve, to become even stronger than they were before the loss, becoming even more resilient to face the new challenges ahead.

Several years ago in an article I wrote for early childhood professionals, I provided my top ten strategies for teaching children to bounce back. I wrote, "Children are able to overcome adversity to bounce back before social and emotional harm is done, even after being exposed to extreme risks."[1] I still believe this is true but now, I would prefer "bouncing forward" to bouncing back. (There's a link to the article in the Notes section at the end of this book).

And remember the famous resilience mantra written by Lao-tzu almost two thousand years ago: *"The journey of a thousand miles begins with a single step."*[2] Steps go forward, right?

❧Strategies☙

1. Routines and rituals are great bounce back aka forward activities. If you don't already, why not establish some in the memory of your loved one and in honor of your other children? It can be as simple as placing flowers on the grave (if and when possible) of the loved one on their birthday or other important times of the year or having a butterfly release at the grave site or any other special place.

2. Cooking their favorite meal, wearing their favorite color, playing their favorite song or game in memory of them helps chil-

dren to maintain a connection with the deceased. These memory markers can be small but wonderful as they celebrate the life of the loved one instead of focusing solely on their death.

3. Look toward the coming months and how you can make a point of keeping the loved one's memory alive in a very casual and natural way. Use Grandmother's favorite china or put hot chocolate in Grandpa's favorite coffee cup. Have a birthday party or a "death day" party for the deceased. See their favorite team play and wear an item of clothing to match for the game.

4. Children love keeping memories alive by recalling stories about loved ones. Even when children did not know someone well, we can use those stories to provide a sense of connection/of belongingness to family. My grandchildren and I often tell "Mamaw Dorothy" stories such as the one where she slipped off her chair onto the floor at our Thanksgiving table but quickly said, "I'm okay" as she burst into laughter, or as we say in Texas, "busted out laughing!"

5. Choose one or two bounce-back activities to get started. Don't put pressure on yourself or your child to grieve quicker, faster, better. Give you and your child as much time as needed and know that resilience doesn't come in linear steps. Two steps forward and one step back are normal and even typical. And, sometimes it's just one step forward, stuck for a while, and then one more step forward.

6. Read author/artist Allesandra Olanow's book of illustrations, "*Hello Grief.*" She reminds us that even though we strive to make progress on a grief path, "*You don't have to bounce right back!*"[3]

Part 6

HeARTful Activities for Grieving Children

-37-
Bridging Home and School

Having children is like having two souls at the same time.
—UNKNOWN

Transitioning back into the routine of school is often challenging for kids and takes patience and understanding on our part. Some children may want to return to school soon after the funeral in order to carry on with sports or activities that were in place before the loss. Other children may want to stay close to home for a longer time. And then others may not want to return to school at all and prefer or even need to be home schooled for now, if possible. In all of these instances, we have to account for differences in our children, their varying amounts of resilience, their emotional development, and just as importantly, your circumstances.

But here's the catch. No matter when you send your child back to school, listen to the timeless words of early childhood specialist Dr. Sue Bredekamp, "The school must be ready for the child rather than the child getting ready for school."[1] It is as important for those on the receiving end (school) as it is for those on the sending end (home) to accept that children need equal support from both. Creating a safe environment sounds a little cliche so what does it actually look like for grieving kids?

Safe Environments
Think of a safe environment for grieving kids as one that is more

emotionally and socially focused—one where children's feelings are not only tolerated, but embraced. Teachers and caregivers who are schooled in grief literacy are ready to help grieving children and their peers. They are equipped with tools and knowledge to make the transition back to school super inviting and supportive.

Reliable support systems are incredibly important in this process, and that's where those of us outside of school can help by building a strong communication bridge between home and school. The safest environments contain dedicated advocates for children, those looking out for them as their "earthly grief angels."

When children are grieving, it may be more difficult for them to maintain social connections due largely to the fact that other children just don't know what to say or how to act toward a grieving friend or classmate. What were once close connections between peers/friends may be frayed or even diminished because of an inability to know what to do. And it's not only kids who don't know what to say. Many adults struggle to find the right words. We feel deeply, but our words don't carry the message to the griever.

When sending grieving kids back to school, there are lots of strategies for parents to try. There are so many it was hard to choose as I wrote the list below. I apologize for the long list but I hope that you find them helpful. They are written for parents, teachers, and providers, so choose those that are needed for your particular circumstance. As always, hone in or choose one or two to start, and then add others as time permits and need allows.

↠Strategies↞

1. Meet with your child's school counselor. Share as much as you feel comfortable about the child's loss. Ask if they are schooled on grief counseling and if not, can they recommend someone?

2. Ask the school counselor to routinely check-in with your child, even if it is a quick chat with the homeroom or classroom teacher. Note: Even while homeschooling, your public school district may provide access to public school counseling. Call your child's school and if possible, take advantage of it.

3. Contact a local university department of psychology, counseling and/or family therapy and ask to speak with a clinic director, professor or program director of school counseling and play therapy. Universities often have clinics where professors oversee play therapy internships for students. The cost is usually more affordable and on a sliding scale according to family income. And, professors, graduate students, and clinicians may have private practices outside of the university. Just ask!

4. Write a letter or email to inform the school of your child's recent loss to continue conversations and support for your child. You can call, but putting the information in writing provides a stronger voice and starts a paper trail of advocacy that is harder to overlook or get misplaced. Never forget that you are your child's first advocate!

5. If your child is currently seeing a therapist, ask if signing a release (if you are comfortable) is possible so that the teacher and therapist can communicate and support one another. As a former classroom teacher, I always wanted to do everything that I could to work with others on behalf of a child in my classroom. "It takes a village." As the teacher, I could provide anecdotal information to better inform the doctor / therapist of how the child was transitioning back to school after a loss.

6. Provide coping strategies that your child can use or say throughout the school day, such as:

- It's okay to be sad. Ask for a time out or break if you are feeling sad and need to leave the group to journal, write stories, draw, or, if you just need some time to be alone.

- Talk about your feelings when you can to your teacher, a friend, or the school counselor.

- Remember that sadness is like a wave—it will wash back out to the ocean after it comes to shore.

- Play with friends. Get lots of running and moving activities when you can.

- Reach out to others for help and remember to help them too.

7. In extreme cases where anxiety and/or depression are present, home school your child, if at all possible, even if it is just for a little while. Your school may have itinerant teachers who make home visits for children who qualify. Or, ask if there are on-line assignments for grieving children.

8. Provide happy memories that your child can share at school such as artifacts (photos, possessions, etc.) or stories of the deceased. Be sure to contact the teacher first to make it okay.

9. Donate children's books on death and dying to your child's classroom library or the school library. You'll find titles for all ages of children at the end of this book in the Bibliotherapy Book List. Or, ask the provider / teacher or principal/director to purchase books on death and dying for classroom and library use. Ask if you can check the books out.

10. In some cases, your child may benefit from an emotional support animal to help when going back to school. Ask if your child's school has therapy dogs. If not, think about getting your child's pet certified as a support animal. A prescription is needed from

your doctor stating that your child needs support because of extreme grief and the pet will provide assistance. There's a national certificate for support animals as well. Contact the ADA National Network[2] to find out if your state allows service animals in schools or contact your state education agency.

11. Let your child slowly get back to a school routine. Begin with abbreviated school days if necessary, and then let your child work up to staying a full day. Some children just can't handle a full day at first. They worry about the family members left at home, and coping with the enormity of school and all the interactions and expectations can be too much. It may just be too "peopley!"

12. This is a hard one. Try to set limits on screen time, if you don't already. Some new research from San Diego State University provides a link between screen time and mental health problems such as anxiety and depression. Doctors Twenge and Campbell write about the associations between screen time and children's emotional well-being: "Even after only one hour of screen time daily, children and teens may begin to have less curiosity, lower self-control, less emotional stability and a greater inability to finish tasks."[3] Also, the American Academy of Pediatrics website gives recommendations screen time limit based on the age of the child. A link can be found in Notes at the end of this book.[4]

~38~

Grief Play

*All of the arts (creative movement or dance, drama, music,
and visual art) incorporate creative problem solving,
playfulness, and the expression of feelings and ideas.*
—Joan Koster

Children who have such a profound loss that returning to their "roots" with what they know or play, may be the best pathway to moving forward and getting unstuck with grief. This kaleidoscope of feelings cannot be addressed in any other way. Finding the way back for these sometimes-forgotten mourners can be challenging, but the more we stay close to what they already know and do, the more helpful we are.

In this section, I want to focus on play and something I call "grief arts" at home and school. There are no better tools or medium for healing a grieving child. Whether they are playing alone or with others, children need this comforting, innate, and authentic response to their world because all across cultures, we intuitively embrace play for ourselves and for our children. You see, in a child's world there are only two gears—playing and not playing. It is the number one thing we tell them to do. "Go play!" It can be directed or free play, but still has the same meaning—a break from "not playing." And when they are not playing, they want and need to be.

When Grief Play is Lost

But what about children who get lost on their way to play? Grief has painted a dense, thick fog all around them. The "on" switch for playing may be broken or stuck. That's where we and others (parents, teachers, peers, friends, etc.) are needed.

I wrote an article in *Young Children,* the journal for NAEYC, based on researcher Barbara Rogoff's concept of "guided participation." I explored how much time we spend on the "ABCs and 123s" but we often fail to address the emotional and social needs of children.[1] Children need guidance to get back on their play tracks, to join the play with others, and to deal with their grief.

They deal with distressing events by playing out their feelings, but we can be the "guides" to nurture and comfort them along the way. Learning social and emotional skill building for grieving children during play is a wonderful example of *guided participation* between parents, teachers, care providers, and children.

I learned from my play therapist colleagues that talking through grief during a counseling session is not the main objective for children. Activities such as pounding clay, drawing and painting pictures of the deceased, and dramatizing their understanding of death through pretend play are all ways that children can process grief. I learned from Dr. Garry Landreth's work that child directed play therapy doesn't even have to include death talk. Children can find their way by playing/addressing everything that is important; every thought and idea becomes fodder for play. And making strides in overcoming grief become the jewels of play therapy.

Observing their play and listening is far more important, as children are often challenged to verbalize their actual feelings about death and dying. Instead, they bring them to the surface through a true dance between the child playing and the play therapist observing and guiding.

In the Meantime

The following "heartful" (or artful) activities are meant to help your child find moments of joy and happiness through play, especially when grieving. I like to think of one focus of this chapter as something I came up with years ago—an "in the meantime," things that you can do along the way, <u>before</u> you decide if your child needs professional help aka counseling or play therapy AND things that you as a parent or teacher can do <u>while</u> a child is working with an outside professional. It occurred to me that children can only spend a minimal amount of time with a play therapist or counselor, but in the meantime, they have us—teachers, care givers, and parents.

Dr. Joel Muro, a play therapist and colleague at Texas Woman's University and I often discussed how there are many things that are similar to what we can do to extend what a play therapist does in sessions with children to the classroom. The child gets the benefit of both settings when we work together.

We then, co-wrote an article with a doctoral student (now Dr. Maavis DakoGyeke) on this very idea for the Journal of School Counseling where we provide lots more information about bridging play therapy and the classroom. If you find this idea intriguing and want to read the article, there is a link to it in the Notes section at the end.[2]

There is no right or wrong way to use heARTful activities, as long as a child responds in a way that invites growth, and a way back from grief. The arts have long been used to provide play for grieving children:

(1) *Art*
(2) *Journaling*
(3) *Music & Dance*
(4) *Books*

(5) Pretend or Dramatic Play

...

I hope that in the days to come, you can support grieving children and they may find comfort in activities in the following chapters, and that you take to heart the words of Picasso ,as you "let art wash the dust of everyday life from your child's soul!"

❧Strategies☙

1. Observe children's play. Does it include related role plays of the death and dying experience? You can redirect or assist through offering play props such as dolls, people figures, stethoscopes, bandages, masks, thermometers, transportation toys, etc.

2. Ask children open ended questions with lots of possible answers, such as, "What's happening here?" or, "What happened to him?" Another great prompt for children is to plant yourself in their play and offer assistance by taking on a pretend role: "Can I help? I can be the nurse that checks the patients in," and, "I can drive the ambulance." But, let them lead the play theme.

3. Seek the help of play therapists who can provide professional guidance when your child is "stuck" or perseverates on the details of the trauma again and again.

4. Use phrases and questions to show children you value them and to give them a chance to process their experience with grief:
   - Tell me about what you built (made, created).
   - What was one thing you liked best about building that?
   - What will you create (or work on/make/etc.) next?
   - Why did you choose _____ over _____ for the wheels (or color, materials, etc.)?

-39-

Using Art to Heal a Broken Heart

Art washes from the soul the dust of everyday life.
—PABLO PICASSO

While I love art therapy, I know that we don't have to be therapists or artists to help our kids grieve in a therapeutic kind of way. Using art <u>as</u> therapy is different from receiving art therapy with a trained art therapist. It's available to everyone and does not require specialized training. Therapeutic art by people like us (non-therapists) is used to help children explore their emotions as well as promote healing and a sense of well-being. This tiny act of self-expression can be so helpful to children, even cathartic. And, let me add that if you have access to an art therapist, all the better. But "in the meantime" they have you!

After Hurricane Katrina devastated our Gulf Coast, University of Texas' Dr. Joe Frost, early childhood professor, researcher and author, found that children were "helped through the intervention of adults and the natural coping mechanisms of play, work, and the creative arts."[1] This innate sense that most children have to thrive, even in the most devastating times of grief and loss, is unlike anything else in human resilience.

Art making such as painting, drawing, sculpture, pottery making, digital art, and photography has long been used to express feelings and emotions, especially to allow children to relieve stress by creating.

I've written extensively about how the destination or final product should not be the most important part of creating to the grieving child. The journey or the actual doing/creating can be more beneficial as it is without pressure to produce something of value, or to be seen by others. Process over product!

When children create and make something from nothing, they tap into their core strength—their resilience. They gain a sense of control of their emotions as they take them from inside (their hearts and minds) to the outside (on paper or wood or canvas). So it just makes sense that their therapeutic creations are not to be judged or critiqued, graded or scored. Feelings often get "clearer" when children create to bring their feelings to light. This clarity is needed in order to process grief.

In her book, *Growing Artists: Teaching the Arts to Young Children*, Joan Koster writes, "All children find emotional release through arts activities, so it is not surprising that some children may use art to work through traumatic experiences."[2] Using art to cope is not only beneficial, but it may be necessary to restore their sense of balance and calm.

We know that art fosters emotional expression and children display their feelings during the process of creating art. It can replace the need for words from our more linear left brain, and activate the creative right brain, where images help them express and release their own feelings. Robert Schirrmacher & Jill Fox, in their book, *Art and Creative Development for the Young Child* write about how children can benefit from nonverbal forms of art therapy while adults find strength in verbal forms. It couldn't be clearer as they write: "Our aim is to provide a vehicle for emotional expression and release."[3]

Happy Accidents

Using therapeutic art, look for opportunities for your children to experience what art therapists Peggy Dunn-Snow and Georgette D'Amelio call "happy accidents."[4] For example, when paint spills on the drawing a child has been working on for what seems like hours, or a coloring page tears, or a play-dough sculpture gets smashed by baby brother, rather than throwing creations away, help her reconstruct her work.

Find ways to salvage or rescue accidents to grow them into something more than before. Some examples are tearing the coloring page into additional pieces and putting it back together like a jigsaw puzzle, or turning the painting with spilled paint into a new painting by adding more "spills" or brushstrokes of paint. These happy accidents are often a pleasant surprise if we help kids look hard enough.

This process helps children to slow down, see patience working in us as we gently guide them back to the creation and the chances it now has. Happy accidents. These are moments where a child made something new from something ruined, or stained, or torn, or broken. This can be the satori or "a-ha" moment where a child sees that all is not lost. We can move on to the next thing, and the next, grieving loss or disappointment, but looking forward to new possibilities.

Kids Need Grace, Too

I began this book talking about how we need to give ourselves grace. But, as you probably already know, our children also need grace. You've heard the phrase, "Perfection is the enemy of good." This "grief-time" is a time when nothing needs to be perfect. Expectations and deadlines may have to be put on hold while a child grieves. Goals and plans become flexible. Starting anything new may be overwhelming for children.

To give additional context to open-ended questions, I'm reminded how early childhood specialists/teachers have long practiced asking divergent questions about children's art—questions for which we do not already know the answer, such as, "How did you work it out," and "Can you think of a new way to do it next time?" These enable a child to take ownership of their artwork and proudly answer, knowing they can't get it wrong. We don't pass judgments on their art, but receive it as simply their creation. Grace!

Children do not typically suffer from perfectionism unless they inherit this trait from adults or they have acquired what I call "not good-enoughness." Without their work being constantly critiqued or prompted to be better, they are happy enough to belong to the good-enough club! I'm reminded of author Sarah Ban Breathnach, who wrote, "Upon completing the Universe, the Great Creator pronounced it, 'Very good.' Not 'perfect.'"[5]

Think about adults who begin creating at a much older age because they don't worry about what others think. They are finally in a position to just explore a new avenue of creating without the expectation of perfection. And then there are those of us who, even still, suffer from creation paralysis!

Dallas contemporary artist Carolyn Joe Daniel (@carolynjoeart) is absolutely one of my favorite, and I love what she says about the creator in all of us..."Just quiet the voices in your head that tell you it's no good; there's a lot of grace in painting. You can always paint over your canvas and start over."[6] This advice is not only good for us, it's probably one of the best tools that we can give grieving children, and not only about art, but about life!

The following strategies may help your child explore and express the feelings that occur during the grieving process, a way to have their feelings speak louder than their words.

❧Strategies☙

1. Encourage and accept all efforts from children to make art. Think process over product with children, especially when grieving. No effort to create is too small.

2. Set up an art corner in your home that you and your child can use weekly or even daily to paint, draw, create collages, and sculpt. Art therapists agree that children respond much better to these activities if they have someone to do it with them.

3. Provide activities that can be completed quickly for children who need more immediate gratification, as well as long term projects for kids who seek more in-depth creations.

4. Encourage scribbling as a means to a response to death and dying. Even though they don't make sense to us, scribbles can be a child's way of putting their thoughts and feelings on paper. Post them where they can be seen if space allows.

5. Children can create visual memories for loved ones who died. Family and friends find much comfort in seeing tributes to the deceased, such as drawings and paintings to share. Kids can create artwork to include in the funeral or memorial program/brochure. Older children can create photo montages for the funeral or memorial service.

6. Kids can make collages as a great way to pay tribute to someone who died. They can collect sources (with help and permission) from the following areas:
   - Outside—photos of the funeral and graveside; leaves and flowers.
   - Home—mementos or artifacts from the deceased, their travels such as post cards, photos, t-shirts; and clothing such as

t-shirts, work shirts to use for fabric scraps, hats, etc.
- Crafts—thread, fabric, paints, glue sticks, string, newspaper clippings, extra funeral programs, assorted paper for collage backgrounds, shoe or small boxes to place collage materials inside, sponges for sponge painting and printing, and small toys with wheels dipped in paint for making tire tracks. Find a replica of a toy truck or car that the deceased drove. And, for more tracks or prints, toy horses, dogs and cats as well as other pets will make this fun for children.

7. Sculpting and modeling—Provide play dough, modeling clay, putty, etc. to knead and form representations or globs. Any remembrance of the lost loved one will be the focus of this activity for the child. Also, experimenting with soft mediums can be stress relievers.

8. Mobiles—Attach photos or memory objects to string from a clothes hanger or other base.

9. Use Masters' paintings as great inspirations for painting remembrances or artifacts from the funeral and other events. Paintings such as *Starry Night* by Van Gogh and by *Bouquet of Roses* by Renoir provide color palettes for our youngest artists. For simple and vibrant color palettes, artist Georgia O'Keeffe, is our go-to. I visited her museum in Santa Fe, New Mexico and was mesmerized by the colors and detail in her floral paintings. What if you or your child took a close-up photo of one flower from the casket spray or other funeral flower arrangements (if possible) and used it for a model to copy the shape or outline of the flower? Provide a canvas and paint to match the colors of the flower. Encourage them to give the painting a title.

10. Create a "Maker Space" that contains "no-tech" tools and re-

sources for your child to use in creating art. Use the following checklist to create a space for children:

- ☐ *Large sketch pads (9 x 12; 11 x 14; or 14 x 17)*
- ☐ *Crayons and colored pencils*
- ☐ *Oil pastels or Cray-Pas© & felt-tipped markers*
- ☐ *Paints (acrylic, oil, watercolor, and finger paints)*
- ☐ *Brushes of all sizes*
- ☐ *Canvas and watercolor paper*
- ☐ *Sketching paper and journals*
- ☐ *Scissors and glue*
- ☐ *Magazines*
- ☐ *Cardboard boxes*
- ☐ *Soft wood for woodworking*

11. Make a "When I'm Sad" chart/poster and list the following art activities that your child can choose from independently and with your help. Have the child check off each after completion:
    - ☐ *Memory boxes*
    - ☐ *Coloring books with mandalas*
    - ☐ *Memorial scrapbooks*
    - ☐ *Clay/dough play/sculpting*
    - ☐ *Painting*
    - ☐ *Drawing*
    - ☐ *Sketching*
    - ☐ *Photography*
    - ☐ *Printmaking*
    - ☐ *Paint pouring*
    - ☐ *Ceramics*

(Add to the list as you find more activities.)

12. Give children a camera and let them photograph their "grief

world" to show us their thinking through photos. Help them make a digital album or an old-fashioned photo album.

13. Use plain sheets of paper to make two rows with three columns or boxes in each. After the funeral, ask your child to draw what happened in 6 steps. Hint: Use fewer steps for younger children. Focus on processing and storytelling to make sense of emotions and experiences through death. Ask if you (and others) can join in the activity.

14. If you are able to visit the grave site, take paper and a soft pencil or crayons for your child to do a "rubbing" of the headstone or monument, a nearby tree, or anything else. Surprisingly, I learned that this is called "frottage." Kids are much more interested in "doing" something rather than "seeing" or visiting it.

15. Tell a Story—Norman Rockwell is known for telling stories in his paintings. Find examples of his work on the Internet or books from the library and talk about storytelling through art. Young children may need prompts or story starters; older kids may be able to paint a story without telling it to you first.[7]

...

I'll leave this chapter with more words from Picasso.

"Every child is an artist, the problem is staying an artist when you grow up!"

-40-

Journaling Their Way Through Grief

Fill your paper with the breathings of your heart.
—William Wordsworth

You continue to search for meaningful ways to help your child grieve as they dip in and out of sadness and loss. Good for you! Let this book be your guide and cheerleader!

Journaling is a way to manage anxiety and reduce stress for adults and brings ease and comfort to children as well. Attaching thoughts to words and pictures to feelings is the first step in journaling. Getting in touch with the deepest emotions and thoughts causing harmful stress from loss is step two.

Your children may need anchoring, or re-attaching to what is familiar and comfortable after loss. They may feel an uncertainty about what the future holds and how to become grounded again. They cannot put these feelings into words, but the feelings will be very real.

Putting thoughts and feelings on paper can bring comfort to a child whose feelings have been fractured. Using journaling as a companion to a grief support group, or to the many other suggestions in this book may be the one thing that resonates with a child, where other things that you have tried do not.

You may be familiar with Albert French's famous saying, "There is power in the pen!"[1] When a child needs to really get at the heart of something distressing such as losing a loved one, writing about it can often help to re-center, and become more resilient and powerful over loss. Putting grief filled emotions into words is giving freedom to shackled feelings. It's as if the burdens of the heart are unchained and lifted, then placed on paper.

It's not true that we have to be great writers to journal. The empty page in a notebook can be daunting, but children can begin by making marks. Older kids can copy jokes, poems, quotes or stories.

Think about the following journaling strategies as ways to gently lure children forward in grief-bearing.

❧Strategies❧

1. Create an area that's convenient for children to journal, anywhere their writing tools are easily accessible. Younger children may want their writing space to be close to you, but older kids often want more privacy while writing, and a space to keep their journals somewhere safe/private.

2. Journaling isn't just about writing. Children can draw, doodle, color, paint, or sketch to put feelings on paper.

3. Include special pens, markers, paints, etc. in the writing space along with different kinds and sizes of papers. And! Journaling doesn't always have to be in a journal.

4. Encourage consistent journaling, especially all through the grieving process. Some say that having a routine time of day to journal works best and others encourage children to journal "in the moment"/spontaneously, or whenever they feel the need. Journal alongside them if it encourages progress.

5. Help children make a memory box of things that remind them of the deceased. Use the items as "story starters" when they

journal, as a prompt to get started, especially when they say, "I don't know what to write about."

6. Purchase 2 copies of a grief journal such as Mia Roldan's *How I Feel Grief Journal for Kids*,[2] one for your child and one for you. Journal alongside your child; set a specific time to journal.

7. Make a "How I Feel Today" book or poster and fill in the guided prompts below:
   - What I'm Sad about Today
   - What I'm Grateful for Today
   - What I'm Angry about Today
   - Why I'm Happy Today
   - What I'm Afraid of Today

8. Try "word-storming" by brainstorming words around a particular topic such as, "Things my _____ (loved one) liked to do," and, "Things I miss the most about him."

9. Journaling can be hard when getting started. To make it easier, purchase a blank notebook and fill it in with word prompts on each page, or have older kids fill them in. Journaling isn't graded! We have to encourage children to let the words flow, without concern for spelling or grammar errors. Expressive writing is for them to share or not. Take off our "teacher" hats!

10. Get a writing and drawing pad with space on top to draw and lines on bottom to write. There are powerful connections between journaling and drawing. The more we allow and encourage, the more children will take risks and write/draw. I think of it as purging and pruning the emotions of grief.

-41-
Music as Therapy During Grief and Loss

You've gotta' dance like there's nobody watching;
love like you'll never be hurt;
sing like there's nobody listening;
and live like it's heaven on earth.
—WILLIAM W. PURKEY

Music—another tool for our heARTful activities toolbox to help children cope with death and dying! Children can use music to replace words during and after the loss of a loved one. Avery Hart and Paul Mantell write about music and how it relates to feelings. "Feelings take sound and spin it into pure music magic; feelings are the fuel that make all music move; feelings fire music up and make it fly."[1] The restorative power of music may be just the thing to help them heal during loss or death.

One of the best things about providing music to listen, play or dance by is that it helps to break down a grieving child's emotional barriers in constructive rather than destructive ways. And you don't have to be a music therapist to provide an environment that helps children cope with grief. Music takes them to a place of comfort and security they won't ordinarily feel by just talking about their grief. And, maybe it drowns out the silence that children hold when asked to talk about death and dying.

We teach children that the death of someone does not mean the end of happiness and joy in their lives, even though it may feel that way. Music is a tool that can have a powerful effect on emotions, making kids feel happier and more creative. Soothing sounds can help children connect to others, relax and refocus as music and feelings go together.

And here's a "brainy" fact. There's a strong connection between the brain, music, and grief as it can trigger parts of the brain to "talk" to one another. Between the auditory cortex and emotion centers, music can provide children with calm and control. It allows us to release feel-good neurotransmitters or endorphins that cope with pain and sadness. Simply put, music provides an emotional release that kids need all the time, but especially during loss.

Kids can express those big emotions through singing, moving, or playing an instrument. They learn to regulate emotions by self-regulating and soothing as they bounce back from adversity, become more resilient from big feelings like sadness, fear, and anxiety. Music allows taking a break from those feelings that seem too big to handle.

Singing, playing an instrument, dancing, writing songs, and listening are all ways that music can be therapeutic, but without the therapist. You, the parent and teacher become the therapist, the healer, the one to provide the remedy. And, the child can become his own healer as he uses all things musical to agitate his emotions to get back to the core of the heart.

Now (again), I'm not delimiting the abilities and experiences of all the wonderful music therapists in the world. But, I am saying, because we are there in the "long time" as opposed to therapists who can only see our children in a "short time," it is up to us to offer as many heartful/coping tools as we can, such as the ones below.

✥Strategies✣

1. Have children bang away on drums; learn simple tunes on the piano or keyboard; and use rhythm band instruments such as bells and shakers to take breaks from grief.

2. Extend your maker space with music resources and activities. For example, make instruments at home or school with things you already have, such as canisters for shakers, tin can drums, cereal box guitars, paper plate tambourines, paper towel tube rain sticks, and any kind of dowels or sticks to make rhythm.

3. Make music together. It will be good for your soul as well. We know that music is a natural painkiller for those who are physically injured, but how about those who are emotionally injured, too?

4. Stir up some memories of a loved one by playing a song that was his or her favorite. Create two playlists: (1) your child's favorite songs, and, (2) songs that fondly remind your child of the person who died. Make new memories by playing songs from both playlists.

5. Take turns with your child as you choose music for listening—at home, in the car, and while out walking/exercising.

6. Sing! It helps kids to synchronize their breathing and feel more connected to others, deceased and alive. Turn on their favorite song and sing with them.

7. Move to music! Creative movement helps release emotions, and become what child developmentalist Lev Vygotsky identified in this way: "It is as though he were a head taller than himself."[2] Children can also release negative emotions through movement to music.

-42-

Books to Help Grieving Children

BOOKS: Happiness, sadness, bravery, anger, shyness . . . our hearts can feel so many feelings! Some make us feel as light as a balloon, others as heavy as an elephant.
—Jo Witek

Books can become the bridge between words and feelings when used with children, either before or after loss. Not only are we providing an emotional outlet for our children by reading to them or them reading to us, we are providing the connection they need by spending time with them. It is within books that children can be encouraged to recapture their sense of wonderment and break from the reality of grief.

If books were an important part of your child's life before the loss, they can now play an important role in bringing back things that are comforting and familiar. We know there is no going back to normal anymore, but books can provide a new sense of security and control if you are using them for the first time either in anticipation of, or after a death. Since our goal is finding more ways to communicate with grieving children, books can be a perfect tool.

Books as Therapy

Bibliotherapy or the use of books for a therapeutic benefit is a long-standing practice that educators, counselors and play therapists have used to help children learn about complex aspects of life, including dying and death. How many times have teachers used books about death and dying such as, *When Dinosaurs Die, The Tenth Good Thing About Barney,* or *My Grandpa Died Today* to get the conversation started or to at least recognize loss?

Parents can join in, too. Reading with your children is central to their development, even in the absence of loss. So why not make it an important practice before, during loss and beyond? Children can find characters in books that are going through similar challenges of death and dying. Books can help identify different emotions that make us feel what children's author, Jo Witek calls, "as light as a balloon...And as heavy as an elephant."[1]

...

Note: Be sure to always pre-read any book that you will share with children. Become familiar with the content first to ensure that it fits your children's needs and then decide if it is the appropriate age book for your child before reading.

All books included here as well as lots of others with authors' names and suggested ages can be found in the Bibliotherapy after Notes at the end of this book!

❧Strategies❧

1. Foster a greater understanding of death and dying with books such as, *The Fall of Freddie the Leaf: A Story of Life for All Ages,* or *The Dead Bird.* Allow books to provide the language that your child needs to illicit emotions and feelings.

2. Use a story's message to draw comparisons between the death of a pet and a person by reading, *I'll Always Love You; Goodbye, Mitch,* or *The Tenth Good Thing About Barney.* Help your child identify with the characters in a book who have worked

through fear and grief.

3. Plant flowers in memory of a loved one. Read Jane Preskin Zalben's book *Pearl's Marigolds for Grandpa* and see Jane's website with this and other activities here: http://www.janebreskinzalben.com/pearl.php.

4. Read *The Memory Box: A Book About Grief.* Sometimes you can gain further insight into their emotional challenges by reading and talking about books like this one.

5. Help your child acquire coping strategies such as continuing bonds with the person who died. *When Someone Dies* attempts to describe "gone-ness" created by death. Also, *A Story for Hippo* answers difficult questions and how to keep the spirit of our loved one alive.

6. Allow books to provide the language that you need to discuss sensitive issues, especially with younger children such as *Something Very Sad Happened: A Toddler's Guide to Understanding Death*. This book is also appropriate for preschoolers to 7 years.

7. Read books that can help children gain greater insight into death and dying, such as, *I Miss You.*

8. Keep your child emotionally safe by using books to keep a healthy distance between the real or actual event and their feelings such as *A Terrible Thing Happened* or *Where's Jess?*

9. *Rachel and the Upside Down Heart* can help your child to know they are not alone in their journey from overwhelming grief to healthy childhood development/wellness.

10. *Chester Raccoon and the Acorn Full of Memories* can help increase your child's understanding of the concept of death and how to process the natural end of life.

11. Discuss the dying process and the act of saying goodbye by reading *Badger's Parting Gifts* or *Thank You, Grandpa*.

12. Share memories and focus on the positives of remembering a loved one by reading, *And What Comes After a Thousand?* about a little girl who loses an elderly friend and learns how important memories are.

13. Use color and line to show a book character's emotions and mood. Molly Bang's book, *When Sophie Gets Angry--Really, Really Angry* is a great example (adapted from Galda and others).[3] Provide bright, medium, and pale colors of crayons or paints to portray children's emotions. Make two drawings; paint or color one happy, and the other sad or angry. Talk about particular colors for the different feelings in the paintings.

14. When books are "too young" for older kids, why not have older children read the books presented here to younger children, forming bonds through grief. You can start out by reading to them and then letting the older child take over. Or, begin by asking your older child if he or she will read to the younger child once a week. Choose from the books in the Bibliotherapy section at the end of this book to build your grief literacy library. Librarians as well as on-line and local bookstores can suggest others.

15. Read a book to a child and make a list or highlight words that are special or evoke special memories. "Let's find five words that remind us of Mommy." Place the words in a journal to write about and keep as reminders.

Part 7

Saying Goodbye

-43-
When Kids Say Final Goodbyes

And God shall wipe away all tears from their eyes;
and there shall be no more death, neither sorrow,
nor crying, neither shall there be any more pain...
—Rev. 21:4

We've looked at children through ages and stages of emotional development and how they typically approach grief. We've also looked at how child development experts tell us that grieving comes in stages, just like all other development. It is age related as it affects younger children in markedly different ways than it affects older children. It affects all children much differently than adults, and yet some facets of grief are common to all kids. That brings us to this—*Saying goodbye is just so hard for children.*

I've found that in any new situation, children need preparation, but how do we prepare them for final goodbyes to loved ones? Our number one priority must be to protect them from any added and unnecessary stress that can be avoided, while including them in the events related to their loved one's passing. Funerals, visitations, celebrations, and memorials can cause less heartbreak if we "make ready" our children in advance.

As an early childhood teacher turned college professor and researcher, I've spent most of my life working directly with or on behalf of children and I've noticed this lack of "death literacy" continues to exist. But now maybe it's time to do something.

Children, Funerals and Memorial Services

Why not make funerals and memorial services a time to include children in a celebration of life for the loved one who died? Ceremonies can be private with a few family and friends or large gatherings with people paying public tribute in words and song.

The most recent funerals I attended were a small graveside service due to COVID restrictions and a large service with over 1500 people. In both instances, children were present but played a spectator role. My culture reserves funeral and memorial services for professionals primarily, to speak, with occasional adult members of the family and friends participating. But what about the children? Could they play a greater role in saying goodbye? Your culture may already address this need of children. But for those that don't, here's something to think about. Maybe it's time to include children to play a bigger part, even if it is a small one, in saying goodbye to loved ones during memorials and funerals, as well as other rituals.

Funerals often serve as a sort of reunion or homecoming of relatives and friends that we seldom see. It's a time when families and friends bind together, knowing these services are for the living more than the dead—a time for getting to know or feel closer to family members and friends rarely seen.

Differing Cultural Experiences

Throughout time, cultures have always provided contrasting experiences in funerals, memorial services, and other religious services as beliefs vary widely. In the southern part of the US where I'm from, we routinely have open-casket services and viewings where family, friends and acquaintances may see the body one last time, even touching it before interment. Some feel that it brings more closure, or a way to say goodbye at this final event. Others have a harder time letting someone go and this is their way of holding on, savoring every last drop of presence with their loved one. Think about your culture and how it is the same or different.

Being respectful of cultural differences, we can see there is no right or wrong way to say goodbye. But if viewing the dead at a funeral will be difficult for your child, you can always call the funeral home and ask if the casket will be open at the service. In fact, a funeral services director shared with me they always know in advance whether the casket will be opened or closed at the funeral and/or visitation and are happy to give out that information to parents when called.

In many cultures, it is not considered morbid or unwholesome at all to touch the deceased. Others do not allow touching the body due to religious or cultural preferences or because of the way someone died. Also, much preparation by the funeral home often goes into presenting the loved one, and bodies of the deceased can be fragile.

Children's Perspectives

In any event, think about it from the child's perspective. There will be lots of questions. For memorial services, your child may be curious and want to know where the body is. The more questions that you can answer prior to the service, the fewer questions the child may have at the service, such as those about preparation of the body, cremation, and burial.

Whether children can endure any service may depend upon the emotional tone of the service and length, number of people, and even the noise level. If it becomes too difficult, be sure to have a back-up or "rescue" plan. Bring someone along who can take children outside or away from the service. Watch for signs of restlessness, anxiety, extreme sadness, or even acting out in order to get your attention.

When Children are on the Outskirts of Grief

Some children are on the outskirts of grief when they aren't closely connected to the deceased, but they are very attached to someone who was. As they accompany their parents, they too feel the need to say a final goodbye and often get a sense of how others cared for the loved one, seeing up close what grieving looks like, and participating in cultural and social traditions. Maybe they haven't been given a choice about attending due to lack of childcare. And, from time to time, children want to attend out of curiosity. I've also known children to come along to feel part of the group of mourners.

No matter the reason, even when on the outskirts of grief, kids can gain a sense of belongingness by participating in funeral rituals. They benefit by being a part of the experience, even if it is as a bystander or something similar to an "extra" in a play or movie. I'm not the only one who believes in the power of rituals. Best-selling author of *Atomic Habits*, James Clear says, "When someone you love dies, people feel lost, they're grieving and they don't know what to do next. But because we have (funeral) rituals, it somehow makes the next decision easier; it's a system for courage."[1]

I can see how the busy-ness of planning a funeral, the "getting on with 'it'," and moving forward can be comforting to us and especially our children. They love motion, action and need an act of doing something with grief that brings back a steadiness they crave, even when they are on the outskirts of grief, watching others grieve.

ᛋStrategiesᛌ

1. Before attending a funeral service where the body will be viewed, paint a "verbal portrait" for your child of what the service may look like or involve. Think of anything that may be shocking or unsettling to your child and then preview it for

them by describing it briefly. Answer questions honestly and truthfully as this may be a turning point for your child in deciding to attend or not.

2. There is no shame in a child not wanting to attend a funeral or memorial service. If at all possible, let them decide. I will continue to build a case for more child participation, though. It just might be the deciding factor for children to be more comfortable in attending goodbye services.

3. Children often meet other family members and friends for the first time at services for someone who died. Reunions in some cultures aren't as popular as they once were. This brings a closeness and familiarity for some children but a discomfort to others. Think about how to ease their anxiety by making a family tree with the names of relatives and photos that your children will meet. Tell stories about family (and friends) to give children a way to identify and connect prior to meeting them, as well as remember them.

4. Include children in planning the funeral and other events surrounding the death of a loved one. If they are able and willing, have kids participate in the funeral program by reading a scripture or poem, telling a story about the loved one, singing a song, playing an instrument, or any other custom for which children can be a part.

5. Plan age-appropriate events especially for children to attend before, during, or after funeral/goodbye services. Consider their needs when planning celebrations of life for the deceased.

~44~

Funerals, Burial & Cremation

*Any child old enough to love
is old enough to mourn.*
—Alan Wolfelt

❧

The quote above by children's grief expert, Dr. Alan Wolfelt, gives traction to the idea that kids mourn too. As you talk about saying final goodbyes with children, explaining the final process of burial or cremation is bound to come up, and can be challenging. If these two events are very unfamiliar or at least uncommon to children, take this opportunity to explain how they occur. Don't worry. You can do this even if you are a bit uncertain or even squeamish about what happens before and after a body is prepared to be laid to rest.

You know children are naturally curious. They question just about everything, and burial and cremation are topics that aren't often at the top of our list of things to talk about with children. In fact, "A parent or family member who would gladly help a child with his science homework may be uncomfortable answering the same child's questions about death, funerals and cremation," according to Dr. Wolfelt.[1]

Giving children this opportunity to grieve by understanding what is happening to a loved one is another way to help them say goodbye, to know that their grandpa, brother, friend, or pet wasn't able to be with us any more, as life on earth had come to an end.

The most important thing is to let your child take the lead and ask the questions. You only have to answer what is asked, and not feel that you need to school them on burials and cremations. This chapter is intended to give you some basic information and strategies to walk and talk you through this difficult time with your child. Let's take a look at both burials and cremations individually to try to get a better understanding of how to talk with kids.

Talking About Burials

Children may want to know that, in most instances, burials take place in cemeteries or a "graveyard" as we often say. There are also instances where families bury their deceased in graves on private properties and create their own private cemeteries.

In some states, there are no state laws prohibiting home burials, but each local government has its own laws, so we are cautioned to check those first (Texas[2]). Interestingly, at the time of this writing, only three states have outlawed home burial on private properties: California, Indiana, and Washington state.

There are also times when bodies can be buried at sea if they are in open US waters and not in a casket, especially when someone had a strong connection to the ocean or requested to be buried there. Older children may want to access *The Environmental Protection Agency* website in the US for information regarding burials at sea.[3]

Taking into account a child's growth and maturation progress, kids may ask more challenging and thought-provoking questions. Here are some basic answers to use for your child's questions about burial. Revise them to fit your beliefs:

"At the funeral, Uncle Joe's body will be in a special box called a casket or a coffin."

"At the cemetery, Uncle Joe's body will be placed in a metal box called

a vault and then placed in a deep hole in the ground."

"At the cemetery we will have a graveside service where we will sing songs and say prayers. Then we will say our final goodbye." (This varies according to one's cultural and religious practices; also, military honors can be an added event at services.)

"After we leave the cemetery, the caretakers will lower the casket into the hole that has been dug."

Note: Some family and friends elect to stay and watch the casket lowered into the ground and then covered. This is a ritual for a family member of mine to stay until the final moments of the interment. At a recent funeral for our beloved Aunt Ella ("Sissie"), my cousin Travis told me that as a child, he watched his Daddy do this and now he is carrying on the tradition to honor our deceased family members in his dad's absence. Acts of love like this one are what make families strong, bound by tradition and love as well as providing rituals for children to anchor them in times of loss and grief.

Talking About Cremation

Children may be naturally curious when they hear the word cremation as more and more people choose to be cremated, even though it has been around for thousands of years.

The key to holding meaningful and age-appropriate conversations about cremation is to treat this topic in the same way that we talk about other aspects of burial—using non-dramatic and direct language. Even if we think that cremation is too challenging a topic to discuss with children, not answering their questions may bring even more curiosity and possibly anxiety and worry.

Again, when children asks questions about death, we get a better idea of their understanding. You will be the one that a child turns to for answers if you have been open to talking about lots of things that are often difficult, not just death and dying.

Keep it simple. Use words like remains or cremains to talk about the deceased if they are being cremated. You can try these key phrases when answering questions about cremation:

"Cremation makes the body like sand by using very high heat."

"Cremation doesn't hurt because the body can't feel anything anymore."

"It happens at a special place called a crematory."

"Grandpa's <u>body</u> was cremated, but not Grandpa." (This refers to the body and the memories of Grandpa.)

"The remains or cremains will be given to us in a small box or container called an urn."

"The remains will weigh about 5 pounds."

"Some people bury the cremains, some people spread them in a place that was important to their grandpa, and some people keep the cremains."

"This is what Grandma wanted and we want to honor her wishes."

As long as you keep your answers brief, simple and to the best of your knowledge, your child will benefit. You don't have to know everything to all at once, and it's always an opportunity for shared learning to say, "I don't know; let's look it up!"

Giving Children a Choice — Is Your Child Ready?

Once children are old enough to display self-control in public places, the option to attend a funeral or other events surrounding a death should be theirs. You will be allowing them to grieve independently, to participate in events for which they feel prepared. This also helps them to become better decision makers and feel more power and control over their lives, knowing their choices and opinions matter.

Decide which opportunities are available regarding the funeral and the arrangements that must be made, but in the end, let kids decide if and when to become a part of this very important process.

Of course they should be invited to services, but forcing children to view or touch the body of someone who has died may have lasting, harmful effects.

Children will appreciate your effort to include them. It will be a precious memory for years to come. Death will not be a onetime occurrence and by giving children a choice in their earlier years, they may become much more comfortable in attending funerals in their later years.

My granddaughter Vivian was overwhelmed with grief when my mother died. She was six at the time and chose not to attend the funeral. She talks about her great-grandmother often, looking at her pictures and remembering stories we've shared. I asked her a year later if she wished she had gone to her funeral. She quickly said, "No, it was too sad." We were fortunate that she had Grandma Kreugh to stay with and it's comforting to me that we allowed her to choose. And, think about how you want children to remember their loved one.

When Children Should Not Go to Funerals

Okay. I said to let them choose. And I vote for children to play a larger part in goodbye ceremonies. On the other hand, there are times when children just should not attend funerals. And there's a good reason. They may have higher levels of sensitivity in just about everything, especially sadness. Harriet Lerner in her book, *Why is My Child in Charge?* cautions us about highly sensitive children who are often fearful of new situations and can be more anxiety prone. These children are tuned in to everything and everyone around them and "are triggered to experience stress more quickly, getting overwhelmed by their big emotions and out-sized reactions... which results in more frequent and intense meltdowns."[4]

If you have a highly sensitive child, funerals may be the emotional overload they cannot handle. For additional information, I turned to someone I knew to be an expert. I asked my friend and Regis University Counseling Professor, Dr. JoLynne Reynolds if children should attend funerals. As a long time play therapist, she said, "It's up to the family, but it may be too scary for younger children. It is important for adults to provide children with an understanding of death and the life after death that is in line with their family's cultural and religious views and their sensitivity levels; but attending funerals is a personal decision to be made between parents and their children."[5]

For sure, overly excitable children may experience different stages of grief by leapfrogging into acceptance in the beginning, and then going back to anger, denial, etc. later. Their sensitivity to the emotions of others will also be challenging for them as well as the need to take in and process the environment around them.

Other children may be at different stages of cognitive and emotional development and may have special needs that you cannot attend to during a funeral service. Or, you may not be available to provide the support they need because of their age, as well as your involvement in the funeral rituals. Also, some children cannot attend funerals because of health issues or health mandates.

As I am writing this book, we have been affected by a pandemic that has taken over a million lives in America, especially the elderly. Many children like Daylen have lost more than one friend or family member to COVID-19 and are experiencing death in an uncommon way, especially regarding saying goodbyes at the funeral.

If your child chooses not to, or cannot attend good-by services, there are other things that can be done to honor or remember the deceased. Ask someone to supervise young children that may require an adult's full attention during or outside of services. Dr.

Kenneth Doka, professor and psychologist, suggests a "shepherd or someone who is a trusted family member or friend for each child who could attend solely to the child's needs."[6]

That "someone" will be available to answer questions or take him out of the serviced if needed. With advanced preparation, children may attend a service for a specific part only and then leave to participate in something more developmentally appropriate for their age, such as playing with peers in a nursery prepared in advance with books, toys, and games.

ᛋStrategiesᛋ

1. Talk to your child about death being final; the body cannot feel anything anymore during cremation or embalming so there is no pain.

2. Help older children look up information about other cultures, especially those in some countries who still use funeral pyres for cremation. They will be curious to know that different cultures throughout history have parted with the remains of the deceased according to beliefs and customs.

3. Children as young as four can be included by selecting flowers and clothing and drawing a picture to place in the casket or have at the service. Older children can write something to include in the service program or speak at the service when possible.

4. Have a memory service where everyone present, including children, tells their best memory of the deceased.

5. Have a home candle lighting service with prayers, songs, and stories. Let children be a part of the planning.

6. Have older children write a eulogy or the obituary. Offer help, but let them take the lead. Ask if they can read it at the funeral.

7. Take photos (discreetly, of course) at the service and share with your child if they chose not to attend and are curious.
8. Bring mementos home to your child such as a petal or flower from an arrangement, or a copy of the funeral program.
9. Help your child select a small item to be placed beside or inside the coffin, or left at the grave site.
10. Plant a tree in memory of the deceased, at home or in an important place to the deceased. Some cemeteries even allow plantings at the grave site; be sure to call ahead for permission.

-45-

Don't Feel Bad, We'll Buy You a Puppy

॰

We want our children's pain to go away and we will do just about anything to make it disappear. Chances are if we were overindulgent parents (and grandparents) before our children suffered a loss, then we will continue that type of parenting after they have experienced loss. Maybe we'll get them a puppy.

But, allowing children space and time to grieve is the stuff of resilience that will bring them back to center. Buying them a puppy (and you can substitute anything for that) will not take the place of their loss, no matter how sad the child or how cute the puppy.

Eventually, the newness of the purchase will fade and the loss will continue on. What seemed like a great idea at the time may become more of a hardship than help. Masking feelings with something besides real, honest work on those feelings will be circumventing the grief work to be done.

Some call it "stuffing grief" and it looks like this. When a child pushes or stuffs down their feelings, they tend to compound the hurt by avoiding it. We don't know exactly why children (and adults) do this, but we have a pretty good idea. They don't want others to know about their suffering or feel sorry for them.

But avoiding grief isn't the answer either. That's when more complicated "stuff" happens, like physical and mental aches that will eventually manifest in one way or another. I think what I'm trying to say is that we have to be cautious about making rash decisions that have long lasting effects. Investing in physical things rather than helping children do emotional work will be a quick fix that can or may make us feel better in the now, because we are doing something, but those "action band-aids" won't always hold.

Take a magnifying glass to your heart. Will the puppy be for the child or will it be something that makes us feel better, something that shows you are trying to provide help or even rescue your child?

Now. Full disclosure. I like puppies. They bring so much joy at the right time. But, it really comes down to, are you ready to take on more responsibility as you aid a grieving child? Puppies or any other major purchase can't restore happiness or abolish grief. Helping children learn to grieve in healthy ways, without feeling the need to buy puppies etc., is the best we can give our children. You'll know when it's the right time!

❧Strategies❧

1. Let kids know they don't have to hide their feelings from you when you ask how they are doing; truth is better than pretense. It's okay to not be "fine." Buying a pet may be a quick fix now, but is such a long-term commitment that you have to ask yourself, "Who is it for?"

2. In order to make good decisions about knowing when it is the right time to buy your grieving child a pet or a new anything decide if it is the right time for you. Are you at a place in your grief that you can take on another responsibility? It will be a family responsibility as pet duty falls to the whole family, rather than to children to be responsible for their care.

3. Substitute anything else that you may purchase for your griev-

ing child for the word "puppy." It could be taking an elaborate trip, buying a new X-Box© or smart device, or an expensive toy that you would not otherwise purchase. Push "pause" and really think this through. Kids are not meant to deal with sadness alone. They need you instead of (fill in the blank).

4. Use time as a blessing. Henry Van Dyke wrote, "Time is too slow for those who wait, too swift for those who fear, too long for those who grieve, too short for those who rejoice, but for those who love, time is eternity."[1] Again, you'll know if and when it is the right time.

-46-

Grief—How Long Does it Last?

*We pick up our "grief case" again and again until it
feels lighter and we don't need it anymore.
Or, when we only need it occasionally.*
—UNKNOWN

Yes, this again! There's no timetable or "one-size-fits all" when grieving, or saying goodbye, in children or adults. It would be great if there was a crystal ball or a magic number of grieving days so that we could be more prepared, or just wait it out.

Because children grieve in different ways according to their human development timetable, nature and nurture experiences will shape how they approach grief now and later. When we are looking for a grief timeline, we usually come up empty. It's like asking a Magic 8© ball and getting my least favorite answer, "Cannot predict now!"

But to give some kind of answer to the question of how long does grief last, we can take a quick look at some grief studies. For example, researchers Holly Prigerson and Paul Maciejewski found that more extreme feelings of grief usually crest around 4–6 months after loss, and then begin to dissipate over the next two years.[1] In other words, grief may be acute in the beginning, but begins to wane or lessen from its original intensity in the coming months. They also found that "disbelief, yearning, anger and sadness" were the key concepts of grief and feelings reported from their participants. "As grief decreases, acceptance increases."[2] Do any or all of these sound familiar? But, what they did not find was that grief goes away entirely, ever.

John Bowlby researched attachment and separation between children and adults, by looking at children who had been adopted, enduring a loss of their mothers. He compared them with children who experienced the loss of a loved one through death and found many similarities in mourning both losses.[3] Maybe this speaks to my thoughts on how "grief is grief and loss is loss," no matter who or what we are grieving; there are so many similarities.

According to Bowlby, the earlier children experience loss, the longer the effect. But he also writes extensively about the strength of attachments—how close we are to our children and how they can count on us as being an integral part of their growth in all areas.[4] They have a greater chance of thriving emotionally if we, their parents, or other significant adults in their lives e.g. teachers and caregivers provide attachment opportunities at every juncture. Simply stated, we must perpetuate, continue, and make strong the love that we have with our children in order to help them through the grieving process, as long as it takes.

Some believe that grief comes in cycles. Others believe that grief comes in stages, like Elisabeth Kübler-Ross and David Kessler.[5] And still others like Sheryl Sandberg, COO of Facebook, and Adam Grant in their 2017 book *Option B*, tell us grief exists in states, not stages.[6] After suddenly losing her husband, Sheryl found herself going in and out of grief, sometimes daily, rather than experiencing stages in a lock-step fashion. She said she not only lost her husband, she lost her bearings. Adam and Sheryl looked at Kübler-Ross's work and determined a more appropriate and gentle way of grieving is to understand that the stages do not necessarily occur in a specific order.

Her use of the word "bearings" jogged a memory. My dad was a log hauler in East Texas throughout my childhood. I will forever remember how important the talk of bearings was to the man so many fondly called "Shine," as he maintained the wheels on many log trucks. "We gotta' keep those bearin's greased, or else they won't last," he would say. It turns out the noun *bearing* is derived from the verb "to bear" and its importance cannot be overstated. Bearings not only keep things turning, they support the weight of "things," metaphorically speaking. Exactly, Sheryl! We can all see why you thought yours were lost!

⁓Strategies⁓

1. Reset your child's "grief timer" as many times as needed. There are endless tries, no matter what.

2. Put your heart and soul into finding just the right group or just the right person if you need assistance to support your child.

3. The truest essence of the word therapy is not only about going to a therapist or counselor, but is really just finding ways of healing that help us find our way, get back on track, console others, and find relief. Explore your options in your area and beyond, online and in-house.

4. Something I call collective therapy, a collection of others as well as ourselves, can be the lifesaver when deciding how long one should grieve. What is the socially correct length of time to grieve? There isn't one! Who are your child's "others" to enlist for help?

5. Know that good grief or grief that is not debilitating or overwhelming for your child can last as long as it needs to last.

Kids and Grief

6. Think about this term—"invisible grievers." Sara Cormell, a licensed clinical social worker posted this on the Mayo Clinic Health System blog: "Children often are referred to as the forgotten or invisible grievers. You may not always see children's grief displayed outwardly."[7] I think of phrases like these to possibly depict invisible grief. "She's doing great. I thought it would be harder for her, losing her sister, you know, but she has really surprised us." And, "Oh, he's really doing better than the rest of us. I wish all my kids could grieve like him."

7. Be the lighthouse, the candle, or the torch to someone else during your and your children's darkness. Bring kindness, compassion, and grace to others who are struggling with grief and who are having difficulty finding light in their darkness. We can model these acts for children as we become beacons of inspiration.

8. "Instagrammer" Kimberly Geswein @kimberlygesweinfonts, posted this mantra and gave permission to use. She is an educator who writes about when you are afraid grief will never end: "Fear: thank you for the reminder I am about to do something brave."[8] Can you remind a grieving child that they are about to do something brave?

-47-
Seeking Help For Your Child!

*Then my mom, she said that grief is a suitcase that sits at the
end of your bed, and no matter what, without failure,
you have to pick it up every day, take it with you.
Some days it will be filled with rocks, and
you don't think you can carry it,
and then other days,
light as a feather.*
—CLAIRE BENNIGAN, The Whispers

The quote from *The Whispers*, a Steven Spielberg 2015 TV show, perfectly describes the ebb and flow of grief.[1] Lots of children go through stages of grief just fine, experiencing those "light as a feather" days, especially if the family members around them are grieving well. But if the grief is overwhelming, "filled with rocks," or goes on for a long period of time, you have to make the decision about seeking professional help for your child. I know, I've said this so many times in prior chapters in this book, but it's so important I've included a whole chapter to address when to refer.

You may also find it necessary to seek professional help for your own needs and in order to help your grieving child; you know, putting your own oxygen mask on first! So, the big question is, how will you know when it's time?

In their book *I Wasn't Ready to Say Goodbye*, authors Brooke Noel and Pamela Blair write that sometimes grief therapy or grief counseling (in a less formal group or setting) may be needed when a child has difficulty in separating from the deceased.[2] Also, therapists and counselors can help in providing continuous support when families have tried everything or just need additional coping skills.

Rose Arent, author of *Helping Children Grieve* tells us, "During the grieving process, to know when your child needs help is very dependent upon the changes that you see in your child."[3] These changes can be red flags/warning signs or important clues, depending how you look at them. But keeping a watchful eye on your child is key to noticing when more help than you can give is needed.

Kids, Stress and Trauma — Difficult to Understand

Certain things may happen that you consider as prompts or a signal that it's time to take action. Trauma presents itself in different ways, so, it is of extreme benefit (and I can't say this enough) to reflect on your child's behavior PRIOR to the loss or impending death of a loved one. What was a typical day like for them? Were they generally happy? How resilient were they when things "popped up" that did not go their way? How quickly did they bounce back?

And, here's my litmus test again! Are there marked differences in their developmental domains — thinking and talking, feeling, interacting with others, or physical? How extreme are those changes and how often do they occur, as well as how long has it been going on? I've placed these warning signs into 3 distinct categories:

(1) Degree

(2) Repetition

(3) Length of time

A closer look at each one is needed.

(1) Degree of Changes or To What Extent? How Great?

Grief brings changes to children's behavior. But the answers we seek are in finding the degree of changes—how great is the behavior and to what extent have the behaviors increased since the loss or impending loss of the loved one of a child? Signs of trouble often include the "bigness" of grief in children.

Take a moment to answer these questions on a scale of 1–10 with 10 being the highest or most challenging:

- How big is the feeling or emotion as in does it disrupt your child's day?
- How acute or difficult is the action that provides the clue for you that something is wrong? In other words, what is she doing that is an extreme difference from her prior behavior?
- Does it dominate everything that he does?

Remember that it isn't the event itself that may pose a problem, but the degree or intensity of the action. Certainly, talk of suicide, self-harm or even harming others is always a 10 on the red flag scale and immediate help is warranted. But follow your "gut" if it tells you to put this book (or any other information) into practice first, and then decide to seek help. I've said this before, I know, but even observing your child for a bit is so helpful for you and for a potential professional if you decide to seek one. Take notes!

The following specific child behaviors can be concerning and warrant seeing a health professional as you observe your grieving child. Think about each one in terms of degree of behavior, from the impact of the smallest intrusions or stressors to the largest:

- Creating non-stop stress and anxiety in the family or what may be called, holding the family hostage

- Feelings of hopelessness
- Emotional or mood swings are more exaggerated now
- Loss of appetite or marked increase in weight, either up or down
- Sleeplessness and sleepiness
- Extreme anxiety about things that did not affect him before
- Excessive crying or clinging to you or others

Your community will have some, if not all of the following health professionals either in person or online to choose from:

– Psychologists

– Psychiatrists

– Social workers

– Play therapists

– Family therapists

– Counselors (community and school)

– Pediatricians

– General practitioners

Note: I've experienced that starting with your child's doctor can be a great way to find appropriate help. Physicians may ask for anecdotal information to help inform their decisions, so be sure to take notes and ask your child's caregiver or teacher take notes, as well. These will be shared with professionals to provide additional evidence.

(2) Repetition of Events

We looked at the degree of the warning signs and then examples of behaviors that can range from small upsets to larger emotional strains on the child and others around him. If you see an extreme repeated pattern of the following behaviors in your child, it could be a sure sign that professional help is needed:

- Repeatedly expressing desire to join deceased person
- Talking to the deceased; pretending they are still here and denying they are dead
- Continuing to yearn for the lost loved one to the detriment of everything else, or a loss of interest in everything else
- Recurrence of bed-wetting or returning to other habits that are not typically age appropriate, and were curtailed or stopped months or even years ago

(3) Length of Time
How long a behavior lasts is as important as its intensity and repetition. There could be particular behaviors that seem to be ongoing long after the child should have curtailed the behavior or even abandoned it. Your child should have replaced the behavior/s already with more typical behaviors occurring before the loss. Look back at the behaviors found in "Degree" and "Repetition." Think about how long they have persisted. If you have the slightest fear that your child's behavior should have subsided by now, that's your cue. Call a health professional. There you are again—your child's first responder!

Depression

I've covered the topic of depression at length in the chapter on Elizabeth Kübler-Ross' five stages of grief. But I feel it needs to be addressed one more time as we make the decision to seek outside help for children. Or, if you skipped that chapter, here we go.

Just because your child is sad doesn't necessarily mean he or she is depressed. We need to be careful in making armchair diagnoses of grieving children. I often see the term (depression) tossed about very carelessly outside the medical profession. "He won't eat so he must be depressed." Or, "She isn't talking to me. I think she's depressed." And, "When she gets like that, I think that's her depression comin' on."

In truth, childhood depression is more serious and similar to adult depression according to many of my colleagues who are health professionals. It can be caused by life events such as the death of someone a child loves, but it can be caused by factors such as genetics, physical health, family history, and the environment.

Only a professional can truly identify the symptoms of depression. So, if you, a friend, a family member or a teacher says, "I'm afraid he is suffering from depression," you/they are probably expressing concern that the child has been showing serious and maybe frightening changes since the loss.

...

Some final words. Before talking to health professionals, begin notetaking, jotting down behaviors, dates, times, etc. that seem to "jump out" at you, or, something just isn't right. Then take these words to heart from Patricia McDonald, early childhood educator and researcher. She urges us to "be intentional when observing our children."[4] Although she directs this toward classroom teachers and child care providers, it is a great mantra for parents, as well as we help grieving children. So, be strategic. Be constant and consistent in watching for signs that your child needs help. Be intentional!

ᔓStrategiesᔕ

1. Use the signs given here in this chapter as a way to identify symptoms that your child may be struggling with grief as you decide if professional help is needed.

2. Schedule time to give them your whole heart. Molly Blake[5] was born to Ann, a fellow graduate school student in the 70's. I lost touch with Ann and Molly over the years, but in the meantime, I loved the name Blake so much I named my daughter Kassidy Blake after Molly. So you can imagine my surprise when I was asked to advise a graduate student at Texas Woman's University who looked so much like Ann! It was Molly Blake! She had become a master teacher for children with special needs in Dallas and was an expert in time management as my doctoral student. I recently asked her to share some wisdom as a child development specialist in giving children the time they need. She offers us this: "Schedule 10 minutes a week to sit face to face with your child to check on the temperature of their heart."

3. Make a checklist of red flags of behavior in this chapter and keep track of 1. Degree or Extent; 2. Repetition; and 3. Length of Time. Record anecdotes or evidence/signs of symptoms in case you decide to contact a professional. In my experience, they have always been very appreciative of any notes provided.

4. Make a decision tree to decide if a health professional is needed. Make a branch for each behavior that gives you angst i.e bed wetting, acting out, crying, or sleeplessness. Write a number between 1 and 10 on the behavior/branch that depicts the severity of the behavior in any or all of the categories: 1. Degree or Extent; 2. Repetition; and 3. Length of Time. Are the numbers mostly 1-5 or are there mostly 6-10's warranting professional help? (Adapted from Dr. Kenneth Ginsburg's decision-making tree for teens.)[6]

5. Draw a road that forks into two roads, one that seeks professional help and the other one tells you to wait. Make a list of all the possible outcomes from taking both roads in order to

decide.

6. Avoid striving for perfect kids, especially in times of loss and grief.

7. Refuse to see children as "broken." Even as I encourage you to observe your children to make a decision about seeking professional help, do your best to see your child as someone who has more positives than negatives and can be restored—brought back to a more up-right position of resilience.

8. Keep hope alive! Have your children draw three shapes on paper, etc. and fill each one with examples of these three things: (1) someone to love; (2) something to do; and (3) something to look forward to. Help them decide what is missing or what they need more of. Then, talk about practicing gratitude for the things they already have. (Thanks to my friend Emma Lee for sharing the three somethings). [7]

-48-

Left Behind

*Opening ourselves to the pain of others is always
such a challenge to our own longing to be
uncomplicatedly happy.*
— PEMA CHODRON

You made it through the funeral as well as you did because you and your children are loved greatly. There was lots of food, hugs, warm caring, and tears flowing like liquid love. You were surrounded by your village, your tribe.

And then the funeral was over. The next days and weeks brought less and less support, at a time when friends and families were probably needed the most. It's very common for them to do what seems like disappearing, once they have walked the initial grief path with you, doing what feels like leaving your children behind.

Pastor John Pavlovitz describes it like this. "The flood of support begins to subside, just as you feel the full gravity of the loss and get a clear look at the massive crater in your heart."[1] You find yourself and your children alone, looking for ways to move forward but the gauge is pointing to empty in your emotional gas tank. While our comforting friends and family have returned to their daily lives, we and our children are now left alone with their grief.

You find yourself sleepwalking or "grief walking" through the hours, days, months, and years ahead, he writes. You trip over your grief like a "Grief Zombie, outwardly walking but barely there."[2] Emptiness without your loved one makes the heart room feel so bare that it will never be full again.

But here's the thing. When our companions in grief just don't know what to say or do to make us feel better, maybe there's just an uncomfortableness that comes with uncertainty. Or they just get busy. One thing leads to the "on and on." Author Meghan O'Rourke writes about this very thing. After someone dies and the rituals are over, we are often left alone with our grief. There may be other annual follow up events to celebrate the loved one but for now, people think we "want to mourn privately."[3]

Most of us aren't taught these emotional caregiving skills. It's not that we are uncaring, but how can we know the days after the funeral can be some of the most unbearable? I think of it as leftover grief that no one should be asked to bear alone.

Tell them! Your village can't know how real your and your children's fears are that a loved one will be forgotten unless you tell them. They won't know how much you need them, still, unless you reach out. "But why should I have to be the one reaching out?" 'Cause you are. Because your children need you to. "But how long will I ask for help?" As long as you and your children need others to walk with you.

Let me end with another quote from Pastor Pavlovitz:

Grief has no shelf life; you will grieve as long as you breathe, which is far after the memorial service and long after people are prepared to stay. Again, they love you dearly, they just have their own paths to walk.[4]

⁌Strategies⁌

1. Ask family members to check in on you and your children when they can. "Y'all don't forget about us," is the prompt they may

need to be assured you welcome their calls and visits well after the funeral. "We'll be here!" and, as I say to my daughters, "I'll call you so you can check on me!"

2. Ask friends and family members to record or write stories about the deceased so you can read them to your children in their absence, after the funeral.

3. When children are grieving, make an effort to keep the love flowing from family and friends. Ask them to use email, texts, cards, letters, and phone calls to stay in touch. Tell them they don't have to know what to say. "I was just thinking about you," or, "Sending hugs your way," are good enough.

4. Ask your friends and family to plan visits to your grieving children as well as taking them on play dates when possible.

5. Comfort others. Have your children reach out to friends and family members by calling, sending drawings, short messages or thank-you notes, etc. And if it prompts them to return the communication, even better! It's sort of like saying, "Hey, we're still over here!" And you know what else? People still like to receive mail—the kind that requires a stamp!

6. Make a family and friends tree from the guest book at the funeral and/or visitation.

7. Have your children write thank-you notes to special friends and family for flowers or just coming to the funeral and sharing their grief. These contacts often spark return communication.

8. Yes. I get it. Some of us want to grieve alone. But children are very social—need action and distraction. Consider their needs to connect with friends and family during the days, weeks and months after the death of a loved one.

-49-

It's Not Over Yet—Signs Down the Road

There is no finite time for grief just as there is no finite time for love.
—Petrea King

The second you think your child has gotten past the major part of grieving, here comes the next wave. You've been taking a deep breath; enjoying a bit of your life returning to normal. And then, there it is! It's hard for us to understand why grief "rears its ugly head" down the road.

Nobody taught you to learn to see it coming. You weren't seeing continuing signs of grief you saw before, at the beginning of the loss. You may have been seeing little signs of improvement that gave you hope the worst was over. It doesn't mean the signs won't return. They can lie dormant for a while until an event or reminder—a trigger will bring them back around or pop them right in your direction.

But there's good news. In the education world, we call it a "teachable moment." It's a moment that presents us with the opportunity to go back to what we know works; begin again; make a new plan; learn to "see next" of the possibilities to come.

Most of us will want to throw our hands up and say, "This can't be happening again," but let the Mama Teacher in you go to work.

Know that the loss may take time to sink in, or your child's pattern of grieving revisits grief from time to time during long bouts of happy. Do what you do best. Come to your child's aid by getting him back on the track of grief and release; grief and release; grief and release.

There are lots of reasons grief gets "bigger" down the road. The events surrounding the death are over and there is more time to think about the loved one. Some even say feelings of grief can be delayed until the reality of death sets in. But, and this is a big "but," don't let those triggers call the shots.

Triggers of Grief

What are some of the triggers that can cause children to regress emotionally? Anything that reminds them of their loss and is germane to them only, not relevant to other grievers, can be a trigger. For instance, when they see a loved one's favorite color or meet someone with the same birthday, or, "Bonanza" comes on TV that Grandpa watched over and over can nudge the sadness right up again.

Triggers can rekindle unspent emotions or bring reminders that are welcomed and unwelcomed, necessary and unnecessary. Author Eleanor Haley calls these memory triggers, "aftershocks of the pain,"[1] just as smaller earthquake aftershocks come after larger or initial ones.

Regarding things that spring up on us, author and inspirational speaker Petrea King wrote a blog post entitled, *The Empty Chair at Christmas* [2], telling us:

> *Grief is often a private affair that others cannot share or perhaps even understand. Grief can spring out of drawers and cupboards, off shelves, from photographs, wafts to our nostrils upon a perfume,*

> *is precipitated by music, clutches at our heart,*
> *hollows out our insides and plummets us to the depths.*
> *It is indeed a strange beast to know and understand,*
> *to embrace, digest and assimilate.*

But maybe triggers aren't all bad. It's what we do with them that makes the difference. We can use them to spend extra time with grieving children as they need someone to share those memories, someone to reminisce with.

And, learning to recognize things that set off emotions in your children will better prepare them (and you) for whatever activates their grief responses. Although some things or events will always be surprising or seem to come from nowhere, there are many that you can prepare for.

Look at the list of events below that may be triggers for your child. Can they be used for opportunities to talk about grief?

- Father-daughter dances
- Parent night
- Birthdays
- Holidays
- Anniversary of death
- Donating or clearing out the loved one's belongings
- Grandparents' Day
- Weddings
- Family reunions
- Church christenings and baptisms
- Graduations
- Vacations
- Seeing someone who looks like the deceased

Letting Go of Timelines

When letting go of timelines for getting over the loss of a loved one, we can be more prepared for grief to last "its lifetime." We can make the grief more manageable for our kids when we "learn to see it coming" and are prepared to go to work in helping our children to look at these events, not so much as prompts or triggers, but remembrances and reminders of the one who died.

Now, I'm not suggesting we wear black for the rest of our lives to commemorate our lost loved one, as Queen Victoria did after the death of her husband, Prince Albert in 1861. Author Ruth Davis Konigsberg writes that during that time, "death was a process of being secularized or segregated as people were required to withdraw from society."[3] No. No. And No! Withdrawing is not necessary!

Keeping the emotional cords connected with loved ones provides healthy benefits. And, we make our grief visible so our children see that it's normal to continue to grieve; it's even okay to grieve on down the road.

Passionate Grief

Let's talk about a different kind of grief—passionate grief. It's normal. It's hard. It involves a lot of crying. As I've written before, crying together and crying often has its benefits. But the good thing is there are health benefits that come with healing ingredients. Continuing to prepare children for a future without their loved one is another one of life's important jobs. It can be exhausting and rewarding at the same time. How is that even possible? But, it is!

We make progress by yoking ourselves to our children; by asking them to help us in the planning and "how to" for the next event and then the next and the next. We make progress by talking about how it will feel when Daddy's birthday comes or their sister's

Christmas stocking will be hung just like always.

We move onward by knowing a new normal is coming and the old "normal" is gone forever. We make progress by knowing time cannot erase the memories we have. We move forward by keeping our loved ones close, now and on down the road. And, by having gratitude for the time we had with our loved ones and the memories to share with our children.

I'm inspired by this quote from M. J. Ryan's book, *Attitudes of Gratitude*. "At each level of gratitude our soul's capacity deepens, starting with contentment to meaningfulness, and finally, to pure joy."[4]

৯Strategies৶

1. Continue to use feelings posters or cards at least weekly with your children, as part of their check-ins or check-ups.

2. Post those special days I talked about earlier on your calendar, such as the birthday of the loved one who died, anniversaries, graduations, and other milestones that were important to the deceased.

3. Make an events poster visible to your child that you can change according to upcoming sparks or triggers. Place photos, and mementos such as seasonal cards and stickers on the poster. The idea is to get out ahead of what can be a grief prompt by reminding kids before it happens.

4. Place sticky note reminders around the house of upcoming events that could otherwise become triggers. Again, the idea is to use prompts and cues so that children won't be emotionally hijacked by an event.

5. Remember that children may progress through grief faster than

adults. They may not want reminders or check-ins and that's fine too. Our older kids tend to feel crowded, so be sure to "unsubscribe" when they ask!

6. Be a "hugging post." Stand still and ask for and receive all the hugs you can! Take turns. Ask your child if he can be the hugging post.

7. Remind others not to tease or taunt children who continue to announce what may be triggers for others. "Not again. Is she going to say that every time she sees that sign that's Dad's favorite beer?" can be answered by, "Of course. It's her way of keeping that memory alive." Or, "Every time we pass by the church does she have to remind us that's where Mom's funeral was?" You: "For now she does. It's her way of holding on to Mom with that memory."

-50-

Continuing Bonds

Her absence is like the sky, spread over everything.
—C. S. Lewis

Children often continue a relationship with the one who died. They live in a more tangible, concrete world of images, things, and reminders. These are acknowledgments that grief is ongoing. It never runs out of fuel. In 1996, authors Klass, Silverman, and Nickman introduced the theory of "continuing bonds" in a book of that same title, prompting us to explore how we continue our relationship with the person who died.[1] Their book includes a look at children's responses to loss, and how important it is to allow them to maintain connections/bonds with the deceased.

With continuing bonds, we are urged to hold on to our loved ones, keeping memories for ourselves as well as sharing with others. We can expand our soul's capacity by having a healthy connection with our loved ones. This ongoing attachment helps children cope with loss, as it provides comfort and strength in the days to follow. Someone once wrote, "We don't leave our deceased loved ones behind; we carry them with us throughout our lives." Continuing bonds allow us to do this when we don't stop talking to a loved one, saying goodnight to their photo, and holding on to some of their belongings. We visit places where we used to go with them, retell stories about them, pass on habits or traits to remaining family members, or serve a favorite food on special occasions. Just thinking about them can also be a continuing bond.

Seeking Balance

A study by Terrah Foster and others looked at the importance of continuing bonds between children and a deceased sibling. They found that children, like adults, also seek reminders by keeping personal belongings. Siblings in this study talked about how they felt closer to the child who died by hanging on to photos, toys (a Thomas the train engine), cell phones, and even clothes. They described staying in touch by talking to them or remembering them in a special way.[2] But can continuing bonds be a bad thing?

Some may think it morbid or out of touch with reality to keep memories alive in this way. I think it depends on how we balance the memory keeping and the keeping on. Even the authors of *Continuing Bonds* remind us, "Life is for the living and the children left behind may take note if we spend more time on keeping the deceased alive rather than focusing on them."[3] Want me to repeat that? It's a gem.

We achieve balance by carving out time to remember, share, and even communicate with our loved ones, but not at the expense of our "others" who need us so very much now and always. While there will never be a getting back to what we knew to be normal, there will become a new normal or a new understanding. The loved one is no longer here, but the memories are strong and important to maintain.

Allowing/encouraging children to stay attached by talking about, thinking about, and wondering about the deceased are positive ways of practicing continuing bonds. Communicating with loved ones, continuing relationships and hanging on to precious mementos are preferred over "letting go" and "moving on."

Avoiding Grief

Gradual, "baby steps" are needed for children in the lifetime grieving process rather than hasty removals of life and love which can hinder the development of continuing bonds.

Years ago, a friend told me a story about two children at her school who lost their mom to illness. After their mother's funeral, their father tried to protect his young children by sending them to stay with grandparents over the weekend. When they returned home, all physical traces of her were gone. He cleared away photos, clothing, and anything else that might remind them of her.

In his defense, maybe grief was so immense he thought he was protecting his children and felt this was the right thing to do. But, throughout this book I've built a case for children needing to grieve their loss. They need continuing bonds to provide a linking thread to the past as they move on into the future. If given the chance, kids will redefine what their new relationship will be with the loved one who died. Although perceptions of the deceased may shift over time, children can still remain connected through continuing bonds as a normal, positive way to grieve.

❦Strategies❦

1. Make "Memory Bears." Natashia Robbins posted this wonderful idea on her Instagram page *@rootedgriefrising* and gave permission to use it. After her husband died, her girl's grandparents had memory bears made for them out of their dad's work shirts. They also had blankets made from his t-shirts. Natashia graciously shared, "Dave lived in work shirts like these, Monday through Friday, so just touching the fabric feels so comforting and brings back memories."[4]

2. As children create a new "normal," they want to include—re-

member the deceased. Keep mementos or "linking objects," reminders for children, but take care to avoid building altars or shrines to the one who died out of respect for your living children.

3. Be patient if they continue to want to "locate" their deceased loved one. "Where did she go," or "Where is he now?" are very common questions from children. Consistent, tangible answers such as, "He is at the cemetery," or, "Mama's ashes are in the urn that we got from the funeral home," can be given.

4. Kids sometimes claim they have a continuing connection with the deceased. Their perceptions or beliefs <u>are their reality</u>. Some children feel strongly the deceased is still here, ghostlike, making appearances or contact with them, and even watching over them. Tune in ever so intently to their reports, make eye contact, but don't feel pressured to agree or disagree. It's their story. Stay in our lane!! They are taking risks by sharing and maybe only asking for acceptance rather than agreement. Or maybe they are simply telling a story.

5. Take a trip the loved one always wanted to take or revisit a favorite place of the deceased with your children.

6. Take photos of your child in a place that is featured in a past photo with the loved one.

7. Children may not wish to have continuing bonds with the deceased. They may be following the social norms of their culture and don't want to look crazy, silly, etc., or they may be continuing a relationship in private. But, the more open we are about continuing bonds, the more freedom we give children to choose.

Final Thoughts on Children and Grief

*To leap, you take some steps
backward and then run forward.*
—Kenneth Ginsberg, MD, PhD

By now you've been totally inundated with thoughts from this book such as, "There is no finish line to cross;" "no timed event for each stage of grief;" and "no correct way to grieve."

You may wonder, "Where do I begin?" You begin where you are, and where they are—where your child sits on the continuum of emotional development. You recognize how full or empty his emotional toolbox may be.

You realize that grief is an ongoing, perpetual, never ending, and always changing process. Your child's emotions will often seem up, down, and even sideways. There may never be a time that your child is completely without grief. But, if allowed to explore each stage or state of grief without rushing, without having expectations beyond their ability, there will come a time when a child can begin to make sense of loss.

It is important that in a book such as this, I leave you with hope. It is important that I leave you with the promise that you will be able to help your child row his little boat through these challenging waters of grief. Your oar is bigger!

The tragedy that seemed unbearable can become more "bearable" with a distant shore that gets more and more visible as your child travels toward it.

Humor me one last time as I borrow a financial term for loss—re-balancing—to describe this process of looking at grief as part of life. There are years just like the economy, where life is more volatile, where death and dying occur. And then there are times when we use that volatility and the losses that come with it to stop and take a look at what's in our children's "portfolio" of grief. There will be days of pluses and minuses. That's to be expected.

I hope this book has given you ways to re-balance, to learn from loss, to move forward, find courage, and be brave alongside your children; that you eventually have more plus days than minuses.

Keep unpacking your and your child's griefcases, little by little, day by day. Keep moving forward without shame or blame. Find others who can show you their lighted pathway from their own experience. Find your village, your tribe.

As you do, you will be the catalyst for progress in children as they draw from your strength and create their own pathways of courage. You will help them use loss as a process that helps us to cherish life in this moment and beyond. And sometimes, you just have to "leap and the net will appear!"

Karen Petty, PhD

Notes & References

1 Graced
1. Stuart Scott, "Counseling the Hard Cases," *B Academic*, (2012).
2. Megan Devine, *It's Okay That You're Not Okay: Meeting Grief and Loss in a Culture That Doesn't Understand* (Boulder, CO: Sounds True Books, 2017): 3.
3. Saint Elizabeth Ann Seton was a wife and mother who became the first born American to be canonized as a Saint.
4. Deborah Serani, "The Do's and Don'ts of Talking with a Child about Death: Parenting Tips to Help Grieving Children" https://www.psychologytoday.com.
5. Julia Cameron, *The Artist's Way. A Spiritual Path to Higher Creativity* (New York: Random House, 2016): 193.
6. Melissa Radke, *Eat Cake. Be Brave* (New York: Grand Central Publishing, 2018): xvii.
7. Linda W., mother of Laura, personal communication.
8. Rick W., grandfather, personal communication.
9. Justin Barrett, *Born Believers* (New York: Free Press, 2012), 146.
10. Maria Kefalas, *Harnessing Grief: One Mother's Quest for Meaning and Miracles* (Boston, MA: Beacon Press, 2021): 67.
11. Joanne Cacciatore, "Appropriate Bereavement Practices After the Death of a Native American Child." *Families in Society*, 90(1), (2009): 46-50.
12. Julia Cameron, *The Artist's Way. A Spiritual Path to Higher Creativity* (New York: Random House, 2016): 9.
13. M. J. Ryan, *Attitudes of Gratitude* (Berkeley, CA: Conari Press, 1999).

2 Finding Your North Star
1. Martha Beck, *Find Your Own North Star: Claiming the Life You Were Meant to Live* (New York: Three Rivers Press, 2001): 159.
2. Ibid.
3. Dan Buettner, *The Blue Zones, 9 Lessons for Living Longer* (National Geographic, 2012): 282.
4. Hector Garcia & Frances Miralles, *Ikigai: The Japanese Secret to a Long and Happy Life* (New York: Penguin Life, 2017): 35.
5. Ibid.
6. Dan Buettner, *The Blue Zones, 9 Lessons for Living Longer* (National Geographic, 2012): 282.

3 UFO's (Unfinished Objects)
1. Pauline Clance & Suzanne Imes, "The Impostor Phenomenon in High Achieving Women: Dynamic and Therapeutic Intervention," *Psychotherapy Theory, Research and Practice* no. 15 (3), (1978): 1.
2. Austin Kleon, *Keep Going. 10 Ways to Stay Creative in Good Times and Bad* (New York: Workman Publishing, 2019): 1.
3. Pomodoro Method, https://francescocirillo.com/products/the-pomodoro-technique.
4. Cal Newport, https://calnewport.com.
5. Emma Lee, friend—personal communication.

5 What Kids Want to Know About Death & Dying
1. Elisabeth Kübler-Ross & David Kessler's *On Grief & Grieving: Finding the Meaning of Grief Through the Five Stages of Loss* (New York: Scribner, 2005): 160.
2. Maria Shriver, Foreword in Elisabeth Kübler-Ross & David Kessler's *On Grief & Grieving: Finding the Meaning of Grief Through the Five Stages of Loss* (New York: Scribner, 2005): xi.
3. Ibid.
4. Erikah, mother of Daylen, personal communication.
5. Tim VanDerKamp, *Assimilation and Integration of Grief*, https: choosegrace.org/blog_post/assimilation-and-integration.
6. Kahlil Gibran, *The Prophet* (New York: Alfred A. Knopf, 1923): 80.

6 Death and Life—So Closely Related
1. Tammie, mother of Elizabeth, personal communication.
2. Mary Oliver, *Devotions: The Selected Poems of Mary Oliver* (New York: Penguin Books, 2020).

7 Don't Dodge the Questions!
1. Emily, prekindergarten teacher and former student—personal communication.
2. Tim Elmore, *12 Huge Mistakes Parents Can Avoid* (Eugene, Oregon, Harvest House Publishing): 166.
3. Karla Jac, grandmother—personal communication.
4. Dr. Leslie Guditis, personal communication.
5. Maribeth Ditmars, https://maribethditmars.com/4-keys-to-talking-to-children-about-death-and-heaven/ & Personal Communication. Maribeth is an author, blogger, and speaker. Contact her at https://maribethditmars.com/speaking/.
6. Bob Deits, Life After Loss (New York: Hachette Books, 2017): 161.

9 Why Death is Such a Taboo Topic
1. Allana Canty, http://childsplayqld.com.au/https://choosegrace.org/blog_post/assimilation-and-integration/.
2. Tammie, mother of Elizabeth—personal communication.
3. Cousins Bob, Travis, & Debbie—personal communication.
4. Katherine Sleeman, Cicely Saunders Institute. Professor and Inaugural appointee to the Isobel Laing Michal Galazka Chair in Palliative Care.
5. Amanda, mother of Hannah — personal communication.

10 Children Will Grieve in Their Own Way
1. Mitch, Albom, *Tuesdays with Morrie* (New York: Warner, 2000), 174.
2. Karen Petty, *Deployment: Strategies for Working with Kids in Military Families* (Minneapolis, MN: Redleaf Press, 2009).
3. Mia Roldan, *Navigating Grief: A Guided Journal* (Rockridge Press: 2021
4. Emma Lee, friend—personal communication.

11 Grief—The Good and the Bad
1. Jack Kornfield: https://jackkornfield.com/meditation-grief/
2. Gaultiere, Bill & Kristi Gaultierre, *Journey to the Soul: A Practical Guide to Emotional and Spiritual Growth* (Grand Rapids Michigan: Revell, 2021). https://www.soulshepherding.org/good-grief-a-process-of-emotional-healing/
3. Goleman, Daniel. *Emotional Intelligence Why It Can Matter More Than IQ* (New York: Bloomsbury, 1995).
4. Kassidy Blake, younger daughter of Karen Petty.
5. Warm Place. Grief Support Center for Children. 809 Lipscomb Street, Fort Worth, TX 76104. (817) 870-2272.

12 Yes, Kids Can Anticipate Loss
1. Elisabeth Kübler-Ross, *On Life After Death* (Berkeley, CA: Celestial Arts. 2008): 1.
2. Ibid., 163.
3. Turner, Victor. *Liminality, Kabbalah, and the Media* (New York: Academic Press, 1985).
4. Keith Smith, *Mourning Sickness: The Art of Grieving* (Resurrection Press, 2003): 60.
5. Maribeth Ditmars https://maribethditmars.com/4-keys-to-talking-to-children-about-death-and-heaven/ & Personal Communication. Maribeth is an author, blogger, and speaker. Contact her at https://maribethditmars.com/speaking/.

13 Sheltering Trees and Secure Bases
1. Samuel Taylor Coleridge, *Youth and Age*. Poetry Foundation. https://www.

poetryfoundation.org/poems/44000/youth-and-age-56d222ebca145.
2. Charles, Swindoll, https://insight.org.in/friendship/a-sheltering-tree/.
3. John Bowlby, *A Secure Base: Parent-Child Attachment and Healthy Human Development* (New York: Basic Books, 1988).
4. Haim Ginott, *Between Parent and Teenager* (New York: Scribner, 1969).

14 When Pets Die
1. Bob Deits, *Life After Loss* (New York: Hachette Books, 2017).
2. Marty Tously, *https://www.vetmed.ucdavis.edu/grief-counseling/helping-children-understand-pet-loss*.
3. Pet Compassion Care Line, https://www.gatewaypetmemorial.com/pet-compassion-careline/.
4. Lap of Love: https://www.lapoflove.com/our-services/pet-loss-support
5. Association for Pet Loss and Bereavement support groups: https://www.aplb.org/.
6. Bob Deits, *Life After Loss* (New York: Hachette Books, 2017).
7. Alice Villalobos, Quality of Life Scale: *Assess Your Pet: Is it Time to Say Goodbye? https://www.pethospicevet.com/wp-content/uploads/2021/02/QualityofLifeScale.pdf.*

15 Children's Tears are Sacred
1. Paul Ferrini, *Love Without Conditions* (MA: Heartways Press, 1994).
2. Juan Murube, "Hypotheses on the Development of Psychoemotional Tearing." *The Ocular Surface 7*, no. 4 (2009): 171-175.
3. Heather Hawk Feinberg & Chamisa Kellogg, *Crying is Like the Rain: A Story of Mindfulness and Feelings*. (Tilbury House, 2020).

16 Understanding Your Child's Grieving Style
1. Marty Tousley, *Finding Your Way Through Grief: A Guide for the First Year* (Phoenix: Hospice of the Valley, 2008).
2. Kenneth J. Doka & T. L. Martin, *Grieving Beyond Gender: Understanding the Ways Men and Women Mourn* (New York, Routledge/Taylor & Francis Group, 2010).

17 When Grieving Children Act Out
1. Bob Deits, *Life After Loss* (New York: Hachette Books, 2017).

18 How Culture Shapes the Way We Grieve
1. James Gire, "How Death Imitates Life: Cultural Influences on Conceptions of Death and Dying." *Online Readings in Psychology and Culture*, 6(2). https://doi.org/10.9707/2307-0919.1120. 2014.
2. Juanita Jacob, "Maori Children and Death: Views from Parents," *The Australian Psychological Society* 24, no. 1 (2012): 118-128.
3. kidsnationalgeographic.com https://kids.nationalgeographic.com/cele-

brations/article/day-of-the-dead.
4. Sandra Smidt, *The Developing Child in the 21st Century* (New York: Routledge, 2013): 97.
5. Dr. Cheryl Mixon, Early Childhood Specialist, personal communication.
6. Famous quote by the late Marcus Garvey.
7. James Gire, "How Death Imitates Life: Cultural Influences on Conceptions of Death and Dying." *Online Readings in Psychology and Culture*, 6(2). https://doi.org/10.9707/2307-0919.1120. 2014.
8. Dr. Tamara Banks — personal communication.

19 *Talking About School Shootings*
1. Jamie Howard, Child Mind Institute. https://childmind.org/article/anxiety-school-shooting/ Grief and Loss—Developing Stages of Children.
2. Rachel Ehmke. https://childmind.org/article/anxiety-school-shooting/ Grief and Loss—Developing Stages of Children.
3. Brene' Brown *The Gifts of Imperfection* (USA: Hazelden 2010): 98.
4. David Schonfeld & Thomas Demaria, "Supporting Children After School Shootings". Pediatr Clin North Am. 2020 Apr;67(2):397-411. doi: 10.1016/j.pcl.2019.12.006. PMID: 32122568.
5. Kimberly Mata-Rubio, activist and mother of daughter Lexi, killed at Robb Elementary in Uvalde, Texas https://www.youtube.com/watch?v=eceBpL4A5GQ.
6. James Alan Fox https://www.city-journal.org/article/sorrow-and-precaution-not-hysteria.
7. David Osher: https://www.npr.org/sections/
8. Dr. Pedro (P. J.) Blanco, Tarleton State University, Stephenville, Texas. Play Therapist. Personal communication.
9. Sandy Austin: https://www.goodmorning america.com/news/story/grief-counselors-columbine-parkland-sandy-hook-describe-school.

20 *School Violence-Safety, Prevention & Warning Signs*
1. National Association of School Psychologists, "School Violence Prevention: Tips for Parents & Educators". https://www.nasponline.org/resources-and-publications/resources-and-podcasts/school-safety-and-crisis/school-violence-resources/school-violence-prevention/school-violence-prevention-tips-for-parents-and-educators.
2. Jennifer Huber. https://scopeblog.stanford.edu/2018/04/20/184574/
3. Dustin Jones, NPR. https://www.NPR.ORG/2022/09/08/1121343954/Uvalde-School-Shooting-Texas-Homeschool-Education?FT=NPRML&F=1101183663.
4. David Schonfeld, "Talking with Children About Death". *Journal of Pediatric Healthcare*. 7, no. 6 (1993): 269-274.

5. Patrick Wilson, Ellis County Texas District Attorney: https://www.cbsnews.com/texas/news/mahkayla-jones-italy-high-student-shot-shooter-chad-padilla/.
6. US Department of Education: https://www.edweek.org/leadership/school-shootings-this-year-how-many-and-where/2022/01.
7. NPR:https://www.NPR.ORG/2022/09/08/1121343954/Uvalde-School-Shooting-Texas-Homeschool-Education?FT=NPRML&F=1101183663.
8. David Schonfeld & Thomas Demaria, "Supporting Children After School Shootings". Pediatr Clin North Am. 2020 Apr;67(2):397-411. doi: 10.1016/j.pcl.2019.12.006. PMID: 32122568.

21 Talking About Death by Suicide

1. Gary Roe, *Aftermath: Picking Up the Pieces After a Suicide* (2019): 160.
2. Alexandra Wyman, *The Suicide Club: What to Do When Someone You Love Chooses Death* (Houndstooth Press, 2022). @forwardtojoy
3. Michael Myers and Carla Fine, *Touched By Suicide*, (Gotham Books, 2006).
4. Amy Biancolli, Staff Reporter for Mad in America.
5. Linda Goldman, *Breaking the Silence: A Guide to Helping Children with Complicated Grief—Suicide, Homicide, AIDS, Violence and Abuse* (New York: Routledge, 2001): 35.
6. Ibid.
7. National Suicide Prevention Lifeline: https://988lifeline.org/?utm_source=google&utm_medium=web&utm_campaign=onebox

22 Talking About God and Death

1. Robert Coles, *The Spiritual Life of Children* (Boston: Houghton Mifflin, 1990): 112.
2. Justin Barrett, *Born Believers* (New York: Free Press, 2012).
3. Ibid.
4. Ibid.
5. Lisa Miller, *The Spiritual Child: The New Science on Parenting for Health and Lifelong Thriving.* (New York: St. Martin's Press, 2015): 9.
6. Laura Berk, *Child Development 9th ed.* (New York: Pearson, 2012): 498.
7. Chris Boyatzis, "Examining Religious and Spiritual Development During Childhood and Adolescence". In: de Souza, M., Francis, L.J., O'Higgins-Norman, J., Scott, D. (eds) *International Handbook of Education for Spirituality, Care and Wellbeing. International Handbooks of Religion and Education*, vol 3. Springer. https://doi.org/10.1007/978-1-4020-9018-9_4, (2009).
8. Laura Berk, *Child Development 9th ed.*(New York: Pearson, 2012): 498.
9. J. Bradley Wigger, "See-Through Knowing: Learning from Children and Their Invisible Friends," *Journal of Childhood and Religion* 2 (2011).

10. Lisa Miller, *The Awakened Brain: The New Science of Spirituality and Our Quest for an Inspired Life* (New York: Random House, 2021): 153.
11. Ibid., 161.
12. Ana-Maria Rizzuto, *The Birth of the Living God* (Chicago: University of Chicago Press, 1979): viii.
13. Ibid., 4.
14. Rob Bell, *Everything is Spiritual: Who We Are and What We're Doing Here* (New York: St. Martin's Essentials, 2020): 62.
15. Melissa Radke, Author and Instagrammer @msmelissaradke. Facebook Post, October, 2021.
16. Bob Deits, *Life After Loss* (New York: Hachette Books, 2017): 152.
17. F. Remy Diederich, "Tragedy and Loss: Don't Over Spiritualize It" (readingremy.com, October 21, 2018).

23 Faith Development & Children

1. Jean Piaget, *The Construction of Reality in the Child* (New York: Basic Books, 1954).
2. David Elkind, "The Origins of Religion in the Child," *The Review of Religious Research* V 12, No. 1 (1970). 35-42.
3. Ibid.
4. Simone A. De Roos, Jurjen Iedema, and Siebren Miedema, (2001) 'Young Children's Descriptions of God: Influences of parents' and teachers' God concepts and religious denomination of schools', *Journal of Beliefs &Values*, 22: 1, 19-30.
5. Laura Levine and Joyce Munsch, *Child Development: An Active Learning Approach* (New York: Sage, 2018).
6. Diane Long, David Elkind, and Bernard Spilka, "The Child's Conception of Prayer," *Journal for the Scientific Study of religion.* 6 (1967). 101-109.
7. Jacqueline Wooley, "The Development of Beliefs about Direct Mental-Physical Causality in Imagination, Magic, and Religion". In Karl Rosengren, Carl Johnson, and Paul Harris, Eds., *Imagining the Impossible: Magical, Scientific, and Religious Thinking in Children* (New York: Cambridge University Press, 2000): 107.
8. Justin Barrett, *Born Believers* (New York: Free Press, 2012): 247.
9. Dr. Leslie Guditis — personal communication.

24 Spirituality & Children

1. Lisa Miller, *The Spiritual Child: The New Science on Parenting for Health and Lifelong Thriving* (New York: St. Martin's Press, 2015): 16.
2. Ibid., 3.
3. Ibid.
4. Rob Bell, *Everything is Spiritual: Who We Are and What We're Doing Here*

(New York: St. Martin's Essentials, 2020): 61.
5. Laurence Steinberg, *Adolescence*, (New York: McGraw-Hill, 2011): 301.
6. Pierre Teilhard de Chardin, French philosopher & Jesuit priest, quote.
7. Lisa Miller, Iris M Balodis, Clayton H McClintock, Jiansong Xu, Cheryl M Lacadie, Rajita Sinha, and Marc N Potenza. Neural Correlates of Personalized Spiritual Experiences *Cerebral Cortex*, Volume 29, Issue 6, June 2019, Pages 2331–2338, https://doi.org/10.1093/cercor/bhy102.
8. Andrew Newberg, http://www.andrewnewberg.com/research.
9. Lisa Miller, *The Spiritual Child: The New Science on Parenting for Health and Lifelong Thriving* (New York: St. Martin's Press, 2015): 16.
10. Dean Hamer, *The God Gene: How Faith is Hardwired into Our Genes* (New York: Doubleday, 2004): 10.
11. Peter Benson, Roehlkepartain, E. C., & Scales, P. C. (2012). Spirituality and positive youth development. In L. Miller (Ed.). The Oxford handbook of psychology and spirituality (pp. 468-485). New York: Oxford University Press.
12. Mayo Clinic, https://www.mayoclinicproceedings.org/article/S0025-6196(11)62799-7/fulltext.
13. Martin Seligman, *Character Strengths and Virtues: A Handbook and Classification* (Washington, DC: American Psychological Association/New York: Oxford University Press): 204.
14. Dean Hamer, *The God Gene: How Faith is Hardwired into Our Genes* (New York: Doubleday, 2004): 49.
15. Robert Keeley, *Bridging Theory and Practice in Children's Spirituality* (Grand Rapids, MI: Zondervan, 2020): 13.
16. Justin Barrett, *Born Believers*, (New York: Free Press, 2012). 200.
17. Danya Ruttenberg (Rabbi), *Nurturing the Wow* (New York: Flatiron/Macmillan Books, 2016): 260.
18. Rebecca Nye, *Children's Spirituality: What it is and Why it Matters*. (Church House Publishing, 2009).
19. John Burroughs, "Leap and the Net Will Appear". Source unknown.
20. Lisa Miller, *The Spiritual Child: The New Science on Parenting for Health and Lifelong Thriving* (New York: St. Martin's Press, 2015): 137.
21. Daniel J. Seigel and Tina Payne Bryson, *The Yes Brain* (New York: Bantam. 2018): 2.
22. Gary Weaver, "The Yes Brain." In Lisa Miller, *The Spiritual Child* (New York: St. Martin's Press, 2015).
23. Winter Ross, *The Sanctuary Garden*-Christopher & Tricia Forrest.

25 *Grief and Loss-Developing Stages of Children*
1. Heraclitus "Time is a game played beautifully by children." <a href="https://kwize.com/Heraclitus-quotes">Heraclitus</a>, On Na-

ture (c. 535 – c. 475 BCE).
2. Jean Piaget, *The Construction of Reality in the Child* (New York: Basic Books, 1954).
3. Lev. S. Vygotsky, *Thought and Language* (New York: John Wiley, 1962).
4. James P. and Mary Ann Emswiler. *Guiding Your Child Through Grief* (New York: Penguin Books, 2000).
5. Brooke Noel and Pamela Blair, *I Wasn't Ready to Say Goodbye* (New York: Sourcebooks, 2018).
6. Karen Petty, *Developmental Milestones of Young Children* (Minneapolis, Minnesota: Redleaf Press, 2015): 18.

26 Kids and Kübler-Ross' 5 Stages of Grief
1. Elisabeth Kübler-Ross, *On Life After Death* (Berkeley, CA: Celestial Arts. 2008).
2. Elisabeth Kübler-Ross and David Kessler, *On Grief & Grieving: Finding the Meaning of Grief Through the Five Stages of Loss* (New York: Scribner, 2005).
3. Ibid., 7.
4. David Kessler, *Finding Meaning: The Sixth Stage of Grief* (New York: Simon & Schuster, 2020).

27 Denial—Stage One
1. Granger Westbrook, *Good Grief: A Companion for Every Loss* (Minneapolis MN: Fortress Press, 2019).
2. Jean Piaget, *The Construction of Reality in the Child* (New York: Basic Books, 1954).
3. Laura Levine & Joyce Munsch, *Child Development: An Active Learning Approach* (New York: Sage Publications, 2021).
4. Garry L. Landreth, *Play Therapy: The Art of the Relationship 3rd Ed.* (New York: Routledge, 2012): 254-255.

28 Anger—Stage Two
1. Dr. Glen Jennings. Family Therapist. Professor Emeritus. Texas Woman's University, Denton, Texas. Personal Communication.
2. Elaine Whitehouse, *There's a Volcano in My Tummy: Helping Children to Handle Anger* (BC Canada: New Society Publishers, 1998).
3. Elisabeth Kübler-Ross, D. Kessler, *On Grief & Grieving: Finding the Meaning of Grief Through the Five Stages of Loss* (New York: Scribner, 2005). 11.
4. Ibid., 15.

29 Bargaining—Stage Three
1. Elisabeth Kübler-Ross, *On Life After Death* (Berkeley, CA: Celestial Arts. 2008).

30 Depression — Stage Four
1. Bob Deits, *Life After Loss* (New York: Hachette Books, 21): 161.
2. Ibid.
3. CDC—Center for Disease Control (2022)./https://www.cdc.gov/violenceprevention/childabuseandneglect/riskprotectivefactors.html.
4. Alan Wolfelt, *The Depression of Grief: Coping With Your Sadness and Knowing When to Get Help* (Fort Collins, CO: Companion Press, 2014): 21.

31 Acceptance — Stage Five
1. Elisabeth Kübler-Ross and David Kessler, *On Grief & Grieving: Finding the Meaning of Grief Through the Five Stages of Loss* (New York: Scribner, 2005): 24-25.
2. Jean Piaget, *The Construction of Reality in the Child* (New York: Basic Books,1954).
3. Elisabeth Kübler-Ross, D. Kessler, *On Grief & Grieving: Finding the Meaning of Grief Through the Five Stages of Loss* (New York: Scribner, 2005). 26.
4. Garry L. Landreth, *Play Therapy: The Art of the Relationship 3rd Ed.* (New York: Routledge, 2012): 378-379.

32 Emotional Milestones, Children, and Grief
1. Puddle Jumping. Child Bereavement UK. o. March 21, 2022. https://www.youtube.com/watch?v=bmkbTnWSZ_U&t=34s
2. Karen Petty, *Developmental Milestones of Young Children* (Minneapolis, Minnesota: Redleaf Press, 2015), 18.
3. Alan Wolfelt, https://www.centerforloss.com/2016/12/helping-children-cope-grief/.
4. Jennifer Lansford, https://www.firstthingsfirst.org/first-things/babies-sense-parents-emotions-help-understand-world/
5. Karen Petty, *Developmental Milestones of Young Children* (Minneapolis, Minnesota: Redleaf Press, 2015), 1.
6. Ibid., 18.
7. Alan Wolfelt, *Healing a Child's Grieving Heart*, (Fort Collins, CO: Companion Press, 2001): 7.
8. Fogel, Alan. *Infancy: Infant, Family, and Society* (Belmont, CA: Wadsworth/Thomson Learning 2001): 218.
9. John Bowlby, (1988). Attachment, communication, and the therapeutic process. A secure base: Parent-child attachment and healthy human development, 137-157.
10. Fogel, Alan. *Infancy: Infant, Family, and Society* (Belmont, CA: Wadsworth/Thomson Learning 2001): 379.
11. Fogel, Alan. *Infancy: Infant, Family, and Society* (Belmont, CA: Wadsworth/Thomson Learning 2001): 381.

12. Stress.org, https://www.stress.org/take-a-deep-breath.
13. Marjorie Kostelnik, Anne Soderman, Alice Whirren, & Michelle Rupiper, *Guiding Children's Social Development and Learning* (US: Cengage Learning, 2017): 168.
14. Karen Petty, *Developmental Milestones of Young Children* (Minneapolis, Minnesota: Redleaf Press, 2015): 38.
15. Marjorie Kostelnik, Anne Soderman, Alice Whirren, & Michelle Rupiper, *Guiding Children's Social Development and Learning* (US: Cengage Learning, 2017).
16. Karen Petty, *Developmental Milestones of Young Children* (Minneapolis, Minnesota: Redleaf Press, 2015): 68.

33 *Growing Resilience in a Grieving Child*
1. Lucy Hone, *Resilient Grieving: How to Find Your Way Through a Devastating Loss* (New York: The Experiment, 2017).
2. Kenneth Ginsberg, *Building Resilience* (Itasca, IL: American Academy of Pediatrics. 2006): 239.
3. Lucy Hone, https://www.psychologytoday.com/us/blog/resilient-grieving/201710/dont-lose-what-you-have-what-you-have-lost.
4. Kenneth Doka, *Children Mourning. Mourning Children* (New York: Routledge, 1995).
5. Bob Deits, *Life After Loss* (New York: Hachette Books, 2017): 192.
6. Richard Carlson, *Don't Sweat the Small Stuff for Teens* (New York: Hyperion, 2000). 116.

34 *Staying Upright During Loss*
1. Kenneth Ginsberg, *Building Resilience* (Itasca, IL: American Academy of Pediatrics. 2006): 237.
2. Ibid.
3. Ernest Hemingway, *Across the River and Into the Trees*. (New York: Scribner. 2002).

35 *Risk and Protective Factors*
1. Robert Brooks and Sam Goldstein, *Nurturing Resilience in our Children* (New York: McGraw-Hill, 2002), 210.
2. Christie Eppler, "Exploring Themes of Resiliency in children after the death of a parent". *Journal of Professional School Counseling. v11 n3 Sage Publications 2008.*

36 *Bouncing Back, Moving Forward from Loss*
1. Karen Petty, "Ten Ways to Foster Resilience in Young Children—Teaching Kids to Bounce Back". *Dimensions of Early Childhood.* v42 n3 2014 35-39. (You can access the full article online: https://files.eric.ed.gov/fulltext/

EJ1045929.pdf)
2. Lao-tzu, *Tao Te Ching (The Way)* (Semi Valley, CA: NMD Books, 2011).
3. Alessandra Olanow, *Hello Grief, I'll Be Right With You* (Harper, 2022).

37 Bridging Home and School
1. Sue Bredekamp, "Play and School Readiness". In E. F. Zigler, D. G. Singer, and S. J. Bishop-Josef (Eds.), *Children's Play: The Roots of Reading* (Washington, DC: ZERO TO THREE, 2004): 159–174. www.zerotothree.org.
2. ADA-https://www.ada.gov/resources/service-animals-2010-requirements/.
3. Jean M. Twenge and W. Keith Campbell, "Associations Between Screen Time and Lower Psychological Wellbeing Among Children and Adolescents." *Preventive Medicine Reports.* Vol 12, 271-283.
4. American Academy of Pediatrics, https://publications.aap.org/pediatrics/article/138/5/e20162591/60503/Media-and-Young-Minds?_ga=2.230643804.1130601325.1687539491-1449998450.1687539491?autologincheck=redirected.

38 Grief Play
1. Karen Petty, "Using Guided Participation to Support Young Children's Social Development". *Young Children*, v64 n4 p80-85 Jul 2009.
2. Garry L. Landreth, *Play Therapy: The Art of the Relationship* 3rd Ed. (New York: Routledge, 2012): 378-379.
3. Joel Muro, Karen Petty, and Mavis DakoGyeke. "Facilitating the Transition Between Play in the Classroom and Play Therapy". http://www.jsc.montana.edu/articles/v4n17.pdf.

39 Using Art to Heal a Broken Heart
1. Joe Frost, "Lessons From Disasters: Play, Work, and the Creative Arts." *Childhood Education;* Olney Vol. 82, Iss. 1, (Fall 2005): 2-8.
2. Joan Bouza Koster, *Growing Artists: Teaching the Arts to Young Children.* (Belmont, CA: Wadsworth Cengage Learning, 2012): 178.
3. Robert Schirrmacher and Jill Fox, *Art and Creative Development for the Young Child* (New York: Thomson Delmar, 1998): 79.
4. Peggy Dunn-Snow, and Georgette D'Amelio, "How Art Teachers Can Enhance Artmaking as a Therapeutic Experience: Art Therapy and Art Education." *Art Education.* v53 n3 46-53 May 2000).
5. Sarah Ban Breathnach, *Simple Abundance.* (NY: Warner Books, 1995): 29.
6. Carolyn Joe Daniel/Dallas, Texas Artist. https://www.carolynjoe.com. https://youtu.be/tr6c1pzP5vw. (Used with permission/Personal communication).
7. MaryAnn Kohl and Kim Solga, Adapted from *Discovering Great Artists*

(Bellingham, WA: Bright Ring Publishing, Inc.): 85.

40 Journaling Their Way Through Grief
1. Albert French, Famous for the phrase "There is power in the pen." Author of *Billy* and *I Can't Wait on God*.
2. Mia Roldan, *How I Feel Grief Journal for Kids* (Rockridge Press, 2022).

41 Music as Therapy During Grief and Loss
1. Avery Hart and Paul Mantell, *Kids Make Music*. (Charlotte, VT: Williamson Publishing, 1993): 23.
2. Lev. S. Vygotsky, "Play and Its Role in the Mental Development of the Child." *Soviet Psychology* 5:6–18, 1967.

42 Books to Help Grieving Children
1. Jo Witek. *In My Heart: A Book of Feelings*. (Abrams Appleseed, 2014).
2. Lee Galda, Lauren Liang, and Bernice Cullinan. *Literature and the Child* (US: Cengage Learning, 2017): 48.

43 When Kids Say Final Goodbyes
1. Brene Brown Podcast Part 1; Dare to Lead; Nov. 15, 2021 with James Clear. Author of *Atomic Habits: An Easy & Proven Way to Build Good Habits and Break Bad Ones*. (New York: Penguin Books, 2018).

44 Funerals, Burial and Cremation
1. Alan D. Wolfelt, *Helping Children Understand Cremation*. (centerforloss.com. 2016.)
2. Home burials in Texas. *Facts About Funerals*. Texas Funeral Service Commission (2019).
3. Environmental Protection Agency. epa.gov.
4. Lerner, Harriet, *Why is My Child In Charge?* (Lanham, MD: Rowman & Littlefield, 2021).
5. Dr. JoLynne Reynolds, Regis University Professor of Counseling. Personal communication.
6. Kenneth Doka and Terry Martin, *Grieving Beyond Gender* (New York: Routledge. 2010): 150.

45 Don't Feel Bad, We'll Buy You a Puppy
1. "Time Is" poem was a sundial inscription crafted by the U.S. author, educator, and clergyman Henry van Dyke around 1901. https://americanliterature.com/author/henry-van-dyke.

46 Grief—How Long Does It Last?
1. Holly Prigerson and Paul Maciejewski, *Grief and acceptance as opposite sides of the same coin: setting a research agenda to study peaceful acceptance of loss.* Br J Psychiatry. 2008 Dec;193(6):435-7. doi: 10.1192/bjp.bp.108.053157. PMID:

    19043142.
2. Ibid.
3. John Bowlby, (1980). *Loss: Sadness & Depression. Attachment and Loss* (vol. 3); (International psycho-analytical library no.109). London: Hogarth Press.
4. John Bowlby, (1988). "Attachment, communication, and the therapeutic process. A secure base: Parent-child attachment and healthy human development," 137-157.
5. Elisabeth Kübler-Ross and David Kessler, *On Grief & Grieving: Finding the Meaning of Grief Through the Five Stages of Loss* (New York: Scribner, 2005).
6. Sheryl Sandberg and Adam Grant, *Option B. Facing Adversity, Building Resilience, and Finding Joy* (New York: Knopf, 2017).
7. SaraCormell.https://www.mayoclinichealthsystem.org/hometown-health/speaking-of-health/do-children-grieveCormell.
8. Kimberly Geswein, Instagram: @kimberlygesweinfonts (Jan. 19, 2023). Personal communication.

47 Seeking Help for Your Child
1. The Whispers, Season 1, Episode 1: X Marks the Spot, https://www.imdb.com/title/tt3487410/.
2. Brook Noel and Pamela Blair, *I Wasn't Ready to Say Goodbye* (New York: Sourcebooks, 2018).
3. Ruth Arent, *Helping Children Grieve (Grief Steps Guides)* (Naperville, IL: Sourcebooks, 2005): 37.
4. Patricia McDonald, "Observing, Planning, Guiding: How an Intentional Teacher Meets Standards Through Play, " *Young Children, 73, no. 1. (2018).*
5. Molly Blake, personal communication.
6. Kenneth Ginsberg, MD. *Building Resilience* (Itasca, IL: American Academy of Pediatrics. 2006): 70-72.
7. Emma Lee, personal communication.

48 Left Behind
1. John Pavlovitz, *The Mourning After: Grieving Someone We Love.* https://johnpavlovitz.com/.
2. Ibid.
3. Meghan O'Rourke, *The Long Goodbye: A Memoire.* (New York: Riverhead Books, 2012).
4. John Pavlovitz, *The Mourning After: Grieving Someone We Love.* https://johnpavlovitz.com/.

49 It's Not Over Yet! Signs Down the Road
1. Eleanor Haley, *Grief Triggers and Positive Memory: a Continuum'* https://whatsyourgrief.com/grief-triggers-positive-memories-continuum/.
2. Petrea King, Blog Post: *The Empty Chair at Christmas.* https://yogatherapy-

institute.com.au/articles/the-empty-chair-at-christmas-by-petrea-king/.
3. Ruth Davis Konigsberg, https://www.elle.com/author/5420/ruth-davis-konigsberg/.
4. M. J. Ryan, *Attitudes of Gratitude* (Conari Press, 2009): 180.

50 Continuing Bonds

1. Dennis Klass, Phyllis Silverman, and Steven Nickman, *Continuing Bonds: New Understandings of Grief*. (Washington, DC: Taylor & Francis, 1996).
2. Terrah L. Foster, and Gilmer, Mary Jo. *Comparison of Continuing Bonds Reported by Parents and Siblings After a Child's Death from Cancer Death Studies* 201135(5) 420-440. doi: 10.1080/07481187.2011.553308.
3. Dennis Klass, Phyllis Silverman, and Steven Nickman, *Continuing Bonds: New Understandings of Grief*. (Washington, DC: Taylor & Francis, 1996): 211.
4. Natashia Robbins, PhD. Instagram: @rootedgriefrising (Personal communication).

Bibliotherapy Books for Children

AFTER DEATH
- *The Mountains of Tibet* by Mordicai Gerstein (4-8)
- *Where Do People Go When They Die?* by Mindy Avra Portnoy (3-8)

DEATH OF PARENT
- *A Quilt For Elizabeth* (Father) by Bennett Tiffault (6-10)
- *A Hui Hou Until We Meet Again* (Father) by Ashley Bugge (6-9)
- *Daddy's Promise* by John. T. Heiney (4-8)
- *Daddy, Up and Down: Sisters Grieve the Loss of Their Daddy* (4-8)
- *Everett Anderson's Goodbye* (Father) by Lucille Clifton (5-8)
- *Geranium Morning* (Father) by E. Sandy Powell (6-9)
- *Grief is Like a Snowflake* by Julia Cook (5-14)
- *Her Mother's Face* by Roddy Doyle and Freya Blackwood (4-8)
- *Missing Mommy: A Book About Bereavement* by Rebecca Cobb (3-8)
- *One Wave at a Time: A Story About Grief and Healing* (Father) by Holly Thompson (5-7)
- *Remembering Mama* by Angela L. Choster (4-10)
- *Samantha Jane's Missing Smile: A Story About Coping with the Loss of a Parent* (Father) by Julie Kaplow and Donna Pincus (5+)
- *Saying Goodbye to Daddy* by Judith Vigna (4-8)
- *The Day My Dad Turned Invisible* by Sean Simmons (5-9)
- *The Heart and the Bottle* (Father) by Oliver Jeffers (3-6)
- *The Memory String* by Eve Bunting (4-8)
- *The Scar* (Mother) by Charlotte Moundlic (5-9)
- *You Shouldn't Have to Say Good-bye* by Patricia Hermes (9-12)

DEATH OF A SIBLING
- *Can You Hear Me Smiling?" A Child Grieves A Sister* by Aariane R.

Jackson and Leigh Lawhon (8-10)
- *Dancing on the Moon* by Janice Roper (2-4)
- *Lost and Found: Remembering a Sister* by Ellen Yeomans (2-6)
- *The Angel with the Golden Glow: A Family's Journey Through Loss and Healing* by Elissa Al-Chokhachy (4+)
- *The Empty Place: A Child's Guide Through Grief (Let's Talk)* by Roberta Temes (5-10)
- *Stacy Had a Little Sister* by Wendi C. Old (4-8)
- *Where's Jess* (Baby Brother or Sister) by Joy & Marv Johnson (3-6)

Death of Grandparent

- *Finding Grandpa Everywhere: A Young Child Discovers Memories of a Grandparent* by John Hodge (7+)
- *Grandad's Island* by Benji Davies (4-8)
- *Grandma's Scrapbook* by Josephine Nobisso (7+)
- *Grandpa's Slide Show* by Deborah Gould (4-8)
- *I Miss You: A First Look at Death* by Pat Thomas (3-7)
- *Ladder to the Moon* by Maya Soetoro-Ng (4-8)
- *My Grandpa Died Today* by Joan Fassler (4-8)
- *My Grandson Lew* by Charlotte Zolotow (4-6)
- *Nana Upstairs and Nana Downstairs* by Tomie dePaola (4-8)
- *Old Pig* by Margaret Wild (3-8)
- *Sending Balloons to Heaven* by Lindsey Coker Luckey 4-8)
- *Pearl's Marigolds for Grandpa* Jane Breskin Zalben (3-7)
- *What Happened When Grandma Died (Christian Perspective)* by P. Barker (4+)
- *The Grandpa Tree* by Mike Donahue (3+)
- *When Your Grandparent Dies: A Child's Guide to Good Grief* by Victoria Ryan (5+)
- *Ghost Wings* by Barbara Joosse (5+)

Death of Friend

- *Always and Forever* by Alan Durant (4+)

- *Always Remember* by Cece Meng (3-7)
- *Ida, Always* by Caron Lewis (4-9)
- *If Nathan Were Here* by Mary Bahr (5-9)
- *Chester Raccoon and the Acorn Full of Memories* by A. Penn (3-8)
- *The Goodbye Book* by Todd Parr (2-4)
- *Water Bugs and Dragonflies: Explaining Death to Young Children* 3-8)
- *A Taste of Blackberries* by Doris Buchanan Smith (8-12)
- *Ragtail Remembers: A Story That Helps Children Understand Feelings of Grief* by Liz Duckworth (6-8)
- *Rudi's Pond* by Eve Bunting (4-7)

Death of Pet

- *A Stone for Sascha* by Aaron Becker (5-9)
- *Dribbles* by Connie Heckert (7-9)
- *Everybody Feels Sad* by Jane Bingham and Clare Weaver (5-6)
- *Harry and Hopper* by Margaret Wild and Freya Blackwood (4-6)
- *I'll Always Love You* by Hans Wilhelm (3-7)
- *I Wish I Could Hold Your Hand...A Child's Guide to Grief and Loss* by Pat Palmer (6-12)
- *Jasper's Day* by Marjorie Blain Parker (5-8)
- *Jim's Dog Muffins* by Miriam Cohen (4-7)
- *Sammy in the Sky* by Barbara Walsh (4-8)
- *Saying Goodbye to Lulu* by Corinne Demas (3-6)
- *The Josefina Story Quilt* by Eleanor Coerr (4-8)
- *The Tenth Good Thing About Barney* by Judith Viorst (6-9)
- *The Elephant in the Room: A Children's Book for Grief and Loss* by Amanda Edwards (7-9)
- *Until We Meet Again: From Grief to Hope after Losing a Pet* by Melissa Lyons (6-8)

Death by Suicide

- *Bart Speaks Out: Breaking the Silence on Suicide* by Jonathan P. Goldman (6-10)

REMEMBERING A LOVED ONE
- *The Invisible String* by Patrice Karst (3+)
- *Grandpa's Slide Show* by D. Gould (4-8)
- *Rudi's Pond* by Eve Bunting (5-8)
- *Where Are You? A Child's Book About Loss* by Laura Olivieri (4-8)
- *The Copper Tree* by Hilary Robinson (Teacher) (2-6)

WITNESSING VIOLENCE OR TRAUMA
- *A Terrible Thing Happened* by Margaret Holmes (4+)

UNDERSTANDING DEATH
- *Gentle Willow: A Story for Children About Dying* by Joyce Mills (4+)
- *I Miss You: A First Look at Death* by Pat Thomas (3-7)
- *Lifetimes: The Beautiful Way to Explain Death to Children* by Brian Mellonie (5+)
- *The Saddest Time* by Norma Simon (6-9)
- *The Fall of Freddie the Leaf* by Leo Buscaglia (4+)
- *Remembering Crystal* by Sebastian Loth (3+)
- *Saying Goodbye* by Jim Boulden (6-11)
- *What is Death?* by Etan Boritzer (6-11)
- *When Dinosaurs Die: A Guide to Understanding Death* by Laurie Krasny Brown (4-8)
- *What Does Dead Mean?* by Caroline Jay (4-7)
- *When Someone Dies* by Sharon Greenlee (4-10)
- *When Someone Very Special Dies* by Marge Heegaard (3-10)
- *Where Are You? A Child's Book About Loss* by Laura Olivieri (4-8)

BOOKS ABOUT LOSS & GRIEF
- *Aarvy Aardvark Finds Hope: A Read Aloud Story for People of All Ages*

Kids and Grief

- *A Bunch of Balloons: A Workbook for Grieving Children* by Dorothy Ferguson (3-7)
- *Always and Forever* by Alan Durant (4+)
- *Badger's Parting Gifts* by Susan Farley (4-8)
- *Bear's Last Journey* by Udo Weingelt (4-8)
- *Everett Anderson's Goodbye* by Lucille Clifton (5-8)
- *Goodbye Mousie* by Robie Harris (4-8)
- *I Miss You: A First Look at Death* by Pat Thomas (4+)
- *I Wish I Could Hold Your Hand...A Child's Guide to Grief and Loss* by Pat Palmer (6-12)
- *Rabbityness* by Jo Empson (3-7)
- *Sad Isn't Bad: A Good Grief Guidebook for Kids Dealing with Loss* by
- Michaelene Mundy (6+)
- Someone I Love Died by Christine Harder Tangvald (4-8)
- *Tear Soup: A Recipe for Healing After Loss* by Pat Schwiebert & Chuck DeKlyen (8+)
- *The Elephant in the Room: A Children's Book for Grief and Loss* (4+)

SADNESS
- *The Boy Who Didn't Want to Be Sad* by Robert Goldblatt (4+)

FUNERALS
- *The Dead Bird* by Margaret Wise Brown (4-7)
- *About Loving and Losing, Friendship and Hope* by Donna O'Toole (All Ages) (6-8)

Index

Symbols

@carolynjoeart 251
@forwardtojoy 126
@kimberlygesweinfonts 288
@msmelissaradke 144
@rootedgriefrising 308

A

ADA National Network 243
Amanda C., mother of Hannah 2, 47-50
American Academy of Pediatrics 111, 243
anger 174-175, 181-189
Arent, Rose Helping Children Grieve 290
art 244-250
Art and Creative Development for Young Child 249
art therapy 248-252
Assess Your Pet: Is It Time to Say Goodbye? 78
atheists 152-154, 162
Austin, Sandy 112

B

bad grief 55, 56
Ban Breathnach, Sarah
  Attitudes of Gratitude 12, 251, 304
Bang, Molly 265
Banks, Dr. Tamara 100
Barbara "Bob", sister of Sarah 46
bargaining 172, 174, 190-192
Barrett, Justin 8, 136, 137, 151, 153, 164
Beck, Martha 13
bed wetting 208, 210, 295
Biancolli, Amy 127
Bibliotherapy x, 28, 242, 262, 265, 328
Blair, Pamela I Wasn't Ready to Say Goodbye 168, 289
Blanco, Pedro (P. J.) 111-112
Blue Zones 14, 15
born believers x, 136, 137, 154, 156
Bowlby, John 66, 206, 286
Boyatzis, Chris 138-139
Bredekamp, Sue 239
Brooks, Robert Nurturing Resilience in our Children 229
Brown, Brené The Gifts of Imperfection 104
Bryson, Tina 163
Buettner, Dan 14, 15
burial x, 75, 77, 97, 99, 100, 271, 274-276

C

Cacciatore, Joanne 11
Cameron, Julia
  The Artist's Way 6
  morning pages 12
Canty, Allana 44

Carlson, Richard Don't Sweat the Small Stuff 223
cemetery 200, 276, 309
Center for Disease Control 196
Cheryl Mixon, Dr. 98-99
Child Bereavement UK 202
Child Mind Institute 103
Chris, son of Maribeth Ditmars 39, 62
Chodron, Pema 297
Clear, James 272
coffin 210, 276, 281
Coles, Robert The Spiritual Life of Children 136
Cormell, Sara invisible grievers 288
continuing bonds 306-309
cremains 75, 77, 277
cremation 215, 274-280
culture 29, 36, 45, 66, 80, 95-101

D

DakoGyeke, Maavis PhD 246
D'Amelio, Georgette 250
Daniel, Carolyn Joe (Dallas artist) 251
Darryl, brother of Karen Petty 199
Day of the Dead 96, 97
Debbie, sister of Sarah 47
Deits, Bob Life After Loss 40, 70, 78, 89, 91, 145, 193, 223
Demaria, Thomas 106
Denney, Molly Blake (Dr.) 294-295
denial 172-180
Deployment: Strategies for Working with Kids in Military Families 50 (Karen Petty)
depression 5, 193-195, 242-243
De Roos, Simone 149
Developmental Milestones of Young Children (Karen Petty) 169, 203, 204
developmental selfishness 103, 107, 179
Devine, Megan 4
Dia de Los Muertos 96
Diane, sister of Karen Petty 199
Diederich, Remy 145
dissonant grief 86
Ditmars, Maribeth 39
Doka, Kenneth 86, 221 Grieving Beyond Gender 86
Dostoevsky, Fyodor 202
Dunn-Snow, Peggy 249

E

egocentricity 209
Elkind, David 148
Ella (Sissie), beloved aunt 276
Elmore, Tim 34
Emerson, Ralph Waldo 156, 189
Emily, prekindergarten teacher 34
Emma Lee, friend 51-52, 296
emotional milestones x, 202
Emswiler, James & Mary Ann Guiding Your Child Through Grief 168
Environmental Protection Agency 275
Eppler, Christie 22
Erikah and Daylen 2, 26, 27, 279
euthanasia 74, 75
Evie, paternal grandmother of Karen Petty 1

F

faith development 150
Ferrini, Paul Love Without Condtions 82
field of love 163
Fine, Carla 127

Index

first responders 20-21
Fogel, Alan 205-207
Foster, Terrah L. and Mary Jo Gilmer Comparison of Continuing Bonds Reported by Parents and Siblings After a Child's Death from Cancer Death Studies 306
Fox, James Alan 110
Fox, Jill 249
fringe survivors 106
Frost, Joe Lessons From Disasters: Play, Work, and the Creative Art 248
funerals 274-281

G

Galda, Lee 265
Garvey, Marcus 99-100
Gaultiere, Bill & Kristi 55
Geswein, Kimberly @kimberlygesweinfonts 288
Gibran, Kahlil iv, 27
    The Prophet iv
Ginott, Haim Between Parent and Teenager 67
Ginsberg, Kenneth 220, 224, 225, 310
Gire, James 95, 100
God vi, x, 3, 4, 7, 8-10, 36, 39, 48, 73, 135-164, 190-191, 213, 222, 269
God representation 141
Goldman, Linda Breaking the Silence 128, 131
Goldstein, Sam Nurturing Resilience in our Children 229
Goleman, Daniel 56 **Emotional Intelligence Theory**
good death 47
good grief 55-58

grace x, 3-10, 13, 18, 21, 82, 103, 121, 251
Gracie Bell, maternal grandmother of Karen Petty 199
Grant, Adam 286
gratitude
Grief play 244-247
grief recovery 5
grief triggers 9, 93, 170, 184-186, 189, 214, 232, 301-306
grieving style 85, 87, 88, 91
Growing Artists: Teaching the Arts to Young Children 249
guided participation 245
Guiding Children's Social Development and Learning 209
Guditis, Dr. Leslie 153

H

Haley, Eleanor 301
Hart, Avery & Paul Mantell Kids Make Music 259
Hamer, Dean 159, 161, The God Gene 159
happy accidents 249-250
Hawk Feinberg, Heather 84
heaven 73, 99, 135, 142-143, 147, 151, 177, 259
Hemingway, Ernest 225
Heraclitus 167
Hone, Lucy Resilient Grieving 219, 221
Howard, Jamie 103

I

Ikigai: The Japanese Secret to a Long and Happy Life 14-15
infants and toddlers x, 204-208
instrumental griever 87-88
intuitive griever 86

It's Okay That You're Not Okay 4

J

Jacob, Juanita 96
Jennings, Glen Family Therapist 181
Jones, Dustin 116
journaling 176, 246, 256-258

K

Karla, grandmother 36, 39
Kassidy Blake (Kassi), daughter of Karen Petty 27, 56, 71, 190, 226, 299
Keeley, Robert Bridging Theory and Practice in Children's Spirituality 161
Kefalas, Maria 10
Kellogg, Chamisa 84
Kessler, David 25, 173, 175, 190, 198-199, 224, 286 On Grief & Grieving 173
King, Petrea The Empty Chair at Christmas 300-301
Klass, Silverman, and Nickman Continuing Bonds: New Understandings of Grief 306
Kleon, Austin 17-18
Konigsberg, Ruth Davis 303
Kostelnik, Marjorie 209-210
Koster, Joan 244, 249
Kübler-Ross, Elizabeth 10, 25, 59, 172-173, 175-176, 183, 186, 198-200, 286, 293

L

Landreth, Garry Play Therapy: The Art of the Relationship 200, 245
Lansford, Jennifer 204

Lao-tzu 234
Laps of Love 76
Lerner, Harriet 278
Levine, Laura 150, 178
liminality 60
Linda and Laura's Story 8-9
Liz W, friend 74
losing a pet 70-78
Lyndsay, daughter of Karen Petty 9, 32, 35, 77, 299

M

Maciejewski, Paul 285
maker space 254, 261
"Mamaw Dorothy" Mother to Karen Petty 235
Maori parents 96
Martin, Terry Grieving Beyond Gender 86
Mata-Rubio, Kimberly 109
Mayo Clinic 159
McDonald, Patricia Observing, Planning, Guiding: How an Intentional Teacher Meets Standards Through Play 295
Military Child Education Coalition 224
Miller, Lisa 137, 140, 156, 158-159, 163 The Spiritual Child 140
mourning sickness 61
Munsch, Joyce 150, 178
Muro, Joel PhD 246
Murube, Juan 83
music as therapy 259-261
music and the brain 260
Myers, Michael 127

N

NAEYC 245
Newberg, Andrew 158

Index

Newport, Cal Deep Work 19
Noel, Brooke I Wasn't Ready to Say Goodbye 168, 289
North Star 13-16, 233
Nye, Rebecca 162

O

Olanow, Alexa 235
Oliver, Mary 31
On Grief & Grieving 173
optimistic mindset 221
O'Rourke, Meghan The Long Goodbye: A Memoire 298
Osher, David 111

P

Palomares-Fernandez, Ronald S., PhD 224
Pavlovitz, John 297-298, The Mourning After: Grieving Someone We Love
Pet Compassion Careline 78
pets x, 50, 58, 70-78, 140, 211, 253
Piaget, Jean 147-148, 167, 178, 199
Picasso 247, 248, 251
Plato 95
play 5-6, 51, 53, 58, 84, 91, 94, 110,
play therapy 198, 199, 239, 244
Pomodoro techinique 19
Preskin Zalban, 264
Prigerson, Holly 285
protective factors 10, 227-232
psycho-emotional tears 83
puddle jumping 202-203

R

Radke, Melissa 8, 144
    @msmelissaradke
resilience x, xi, 41, 49, 51, 105, 160, 178, 219-235, 232-233

Reynolds, JoLynne PhD 279
Rick W, grandfather 2, 9
risk and protective factors 10, 225-227
rituals 96-100, 140, 149, 151, 162, 222, 234, 270, 272
Rizzuto, Ana-Maria 141
Robb Elementary 109
Robbins, Natashia 308
Rockwell, Norman 255
Roe, Gary 125
Roldan, Mia 51, How I Feel Grief Journal for Kids 258
Ross, Winter The Sanctuary Garden 164
Ruttenberg, Danya Rabbi Nurture the Wow 162
Ryan, M. J. 12, 304, 340

S

Sandberg, Sheryl Option B. Facing Adversity, Building Resilience, and Finding Joy 286-287
Schirrmacher, Robert 249
Schonfeld, David 106, 116
school age children ix, x, 21, 22, 50, 107, 112, 177, 196, 213-214
school counselor 64, 111-114, 119, 130
school shootings 10, 102, 114; safety, prevention, & warning signs 115-124
Scott, Stuart Counseling the Hard Cases 3
secure base 65-66, 68, 206
seeking professional help 11, 42, 93, 180, 191, 289, 290, 295
Seigel, Daniel 163
Seligman, Martin 160
Serani, Deborah 5

Seton, Elizabeth Ann 4
sheltering tree 65-69
"Shine", father to Karen Petty 287
Shriver, Maria 25
signs your child is grieving 41-43
Sleeman, Katherine 47
sleeplessness 42, 292, 295
Smidt, Sandra The Developing Child in the 21st Century 97
Smith, Keith mourning sickness 61
Spielberg, Steven 289
spirituality 136, 138, 140, 148, 150, 154, 156-164
Steinberg, Laurence 157
Stella Polaris 13-16, 104
Stress.org 207
suicide (death by) 10, 25, 37, 125-131
superpower of grief 10-11
Swindoll, Charles 65

T

taboo topic (death) 44-49, 81-82, 125, 129, 215
Tammie and Elizabeth's Story 30, 45
Taylor Coleridge, Samuel 65
sacred tears 79-84, 86, 269, 297
Texas Woman's University xi, xii, 139, 181, 205, 246, 339
The Warm Place 58
Tously, Marty 74, 85
Travis, brother of Sarah 47, 276
Twenge, Jean and Keith Campbell Associations Between Screen Time and Lower Psychological Wellbeing Among Children and Adolescents 243

U

US Department of Education 120
Using Guided Participation to Support Young Children's Social Development (Karen Petty) 324

V

vade mecum 5
VanDerKamp, Tim 27
Van Dyke, Henry 284
Villalobos, Alice 78
Vygotsky, Lev 167, 261

W

Weaver, Gary 163
Westbrook, Granger 178
Whitehouse, Elaine There's a Volcano in My Tummy 182, 187
Why is My Child in Charge (Harriet Lerner) 278
Wigger, J. Bradley 139
Witek, Jo 262
Wolfelt, Alan 195, 204-205, 274
Wyman, Alexandra 126 @forwardtojoy; The Suicide Club 126

Y

"yes brain" 163

About the Author

Dr. Karen Petty is Professor Emerita from Texas Woman's University. With a doctorate in early child development and education, she is a longtime professor, researcher, former member of the graduate research faculty and department chair.

In addition to this book, Dr. Petty is the author of *Deployment: Strategies for Working with Kids in Military Families* (Redleaf Press, 2009) based upon her travels to numerous military installations stateside as well as internationally where she developed curriculum and trained staff who work with military connected kids.

A research and teaching focus on kids and resilience led to the writing of this book. She is also the author of *Developmental Milestones of Young Children* (Redleaf Press, 2015). Dr. Petty has over 20 published articles in journals such as NAEYC's *Young Children* and SECA's *Dimensions*. One of her most prized accomplishments is founding editor of Texas AEYC's journal, *Early Years*.

Karen grew up in East Texas but lived in the Dallas area for many years. She now lives in Tyler, Texas where she spends time with family, writes, quilts, paints, and travels.

Appreciation

I knew from an early age that I had this "one thing" guiding me. I would become a teacher and spend my adult life working with or on behalf of children. I give thanks to all the mentors, friends, family, and teachers who led me to this work. Most importantly, I give thanks to the children who encounter grief everyday and show strength and courage beyond comprehension. There is nothing more important than this "one thing", this foundation on which all else is built. M. J. Ryan described hers as gratitude and says it was "cooking in her soul" long before she wrote about it. I think that my "one thing" is the art of talking with children. I appreciate having been given the opportunity to do just that.

Thank You!

Thank you for purchasing *Kids & Grief: Talking With Children About Death and Dying*.

These pages are designed as tools to help with talking with children during times of grief but do not replace any need for counseling or therapy if needed for children.

Please return to this book again and again for information and share it with others who are on this same
grief journey with children.

Karen Petty, PhD

drkarenpetty.com
Instagram @kids_and_grief & @drkarenpetty
Facebook @Karen Petty

www.ingramcontent.com/pod-product-compliance
Lightning Source LLC
Chambersburg PA
CBHW050123170426
43197CB00011B/1687